WEEPING
in the
PLAYTIME
of
OTHERS

WEEPING
in the
PLAYTIME
of
OTHERS

America's
Incarcerated
Children

by
KENNETH WOODEN

McGRAW-HILL
BOOK COMPANY
New York/St. Louis
San Francisco/Dusseldorf
London/Mexico
Sydney/Toronto

Book design by Judith Michael.

56789BPBP798

Library of Congress Cataloging in Publication Data
Wooden, Kenneth
    Weeping in the playtime of others.
    Includes index.
    1. Juvenile detention homes—United States.
2. Juvenile justice, Administration of—United
States. 3. Imprisonment—United States   I. Title.
HV9104.W67   365'.42'0973   76–30838
ISBN 0–07–071642–0
ISBN 0–07–071643–9 (pbk.)

Do ye hear the children weeping,
Oh my brothers. . . . The young children
Oh my brothers, they are weeping bitterly,
They are weeping in the playtime of the others.

ELIZABETH BARRETT BROWNING

To Martha Braun Wooden

Acknowledgments

This book has had many midwives. Without them, the message between these covers would still be buried in the crowded wards and solitary confinement cells where children are being kept and destroyed. Major funding came from the following foundations, corporations and individuals: Ford, Grant, Quaker Oats, the LARAS Fund, the Louis Robinowitz Foundation, the G. Carrington Foundation, the New Jersey Bell Telephone Company, Volkswagen of America, Inc., IBM, the Morgan Guaranty Trust Company of New York, the late J. Edward Meyer, Jr., and Takehiko Kamo. These contributors all gave me a totally free hand to interpret the facts as I saw them.

Many whose names I would like to include cannot be acknowledged because they still work within the system they have helped expose. They are the people whose consciences took them to the Xerox machines and provided me with hard-to-obtain documentation. Their contribution has been immeasurable.

Dr. Hunter Durning at the United States Justice Department Law Enforcement Assistance Administration (LEAA) brought to this book a sense of perspective in its early stages of development. Hunter's untimely death, at age thirty, was a great loss to me personally as well as to the incarcerated children to whom we were both committed.

Though I had no research assistance as such, two universities provided limited research facilities

—Yale Law School, on the status offense laws, and Professor H. H. Wilson's class at Princeton University, on the effects of institutional drugs on children. It was also Dr. Wilson who first read the entire manuscript and offered suggestions and encouragement. My admiration exceeds only my deep appreciation for his help. The same is true of George Gallup, Jr., of the Gallup Poll. His office was always open, and at his urging, his many friends on major newspapers across the country sent me their stories and exposés on the subject of youth incarceration. The Honorable J. Edward Meyer III of New York State provided me contacts in every legislature in the fifty states for information concerning reading and IQ levels and the number of suicides.

In the state of Louisiana a federal court of law will soon hear a case dealing with banishment of children to distant states. A smile of satisfaction to Mimi Crossley, Edith Bach and William Rittenberg.

Senator Birch Bayh, Barbara Bode, Ed Budelmann, Dr. Larry Dye, Wayne and Ann Horvitz, Dr. Ruth Love, Ken Mason, Ed Meade, Pat Murphy, Tom Roeser, Jim Toner, Donna Van Horn, Carol White and Tom Wicker deserve special thanks, as well as do the many people who took this traveling stranger into their homes and listened to his anguish and sad tales.

Special appreciation to Joseph H. Rodriguez, chairman of the New Jersey Crime Commission, who took time from his important work to review the manuscript for possible libel, to F. Gilman Spencer, Pulitzer Prize-winning editor of the New Jersey *Trentonian*, and to Representative Lane Denton of Texas and his able assistant Bill Aleshire.

To Frederic W. Hills, editor in chief, and Kathy Matthews, editor, at McGraw-Hill, I thank you, not only for your expert help but your tolerance and patience in working with me. Because of you two gifted people, this book is more than just a collection of horror stories.

My deepest appreciation to all the incarcerated children, especially those who, risking institutional punishment, took the chance, gave me their trust and their poetry—some of which introduces chapters in this book. This poetry speaks for itself. To these children, I give my solemn promise: I will not forget.

Kenneth Wooden

Author's Note

When I began researching this book in the summer of 1972, it was with a firm determination that my only concern would be the children who suffer the pains of incarceration. I vowed I would not be influenced by anyone's personal ambitions, careers or professional fortunes. I kept that promise. No one was spared, from the humblest parole officer to a powerful United States senator currently running for the Presidential nomination of his party. In some instances it was difficult because there are those firmly entrenched within the system who rely on a penal career to support their families. Still, I've kept the promise.

It was a grueling three years filled with aggressive seeking, probing, investigating. At times I found horror; at times I found hope. Some institutions responded candidly to my inquiries; others disguised overt mistreatment and corruption with a cloak of religion, clever public relations or outright secrecy. There was even an attempted bribe by a California state official—a $500 "interview fee" to talk with Charles Manson.

It was a time during which I came to admire the press greatly. While for many Americans 1973–75 highlighted the role of the press to the Watergate exposé, for me it brought the realization that the American press has always played the leading crusading role for the rights of children.

Lastly, this work has given me greater insight into, and a deeper appreciation of, my own family and the basic family structure at large. Both my grandfathers perished in work-related accidents—Edward F. Wooden on a painting scaffold and Patrick Ward in the anthracite coal mines of northern Pennsylvania. My respective grandmothers, Iantha and Bridgit, withstood pressures to break up their families and institutionalize their children in times of great personal crisis. However, this meant that my mother, Grace T. Ward, had to start working in the textile mills of eastern Pennsylvania at age eleven, where she remained until her marriage ten years later. She was so small that the owner of the mill gave her a box to stand on while she worked twelve hours a day, six days a week.

So both my parents had a strong sense of family. My father, Edward F. Wooden, Jr., who worked as a common laborer in the mills, foundries and chemical plants of New Jersey and Pennsylvania, also thwarted well-meaning attempts to break up his rowhouse family of four sons during the depression years.

My immediate family has made the greatest sacrifice, yet always gave me their love and support from near and far as I traveled in thirty states. Three daughters, Grace Theresa, Rosemary Eileen, and Jennifer Lynn, little girls when I embarked on this journey, somehow crossed the bridge to young womanhood while I was rarely home. My son, John Allen, is now a very old four years, and I, sadly, missed his joyous, rapid development. My darling wife, Martha, held the family together while assuming the further responsibility of critically editing and collaborating in the writing of this book. It is to her, the heart of our family, that I dedicate this book. To Martha Wooden, who, during the early years of our marriage, with a mixture of anguish and patience, taught me, a semi-illiterate, to read and write. She gave me a new life—a life filled with hope and dignity and one that would have been impossible without her rare gifts of courage, endurance and love.

Contents

PART ONE / The Microcosm and the National Dilemma

I live in a house called torture and pain.
It's made of materials called sorrow and shame.
It's a lonely place in which to dwell,
There's a horrid room there and they call it Hell.

From the faucets run tears that I've cried all
    these years;
And it's hated by my heart made of stone.
But the worst part to face is
    I'll die in this place
And when I die I'll die all alone.

—Author unknown*

1/A Lawyer and the FBI v. the State of Texas

In Texas, during the summer of 1973, Steve Bercu, a brilliant, gutsy young attorney, ignoring threats, intimidation, financial crises and finally a physical beating, formalized a twin legal blitz in both state and federal courts. His battle in the state courts would culminate in the historic release of more than eight hundred youngsters incarcerated throughout that state, and, in the federal courts, massive litigation against the Texas Youth Council (TYC), a state governmental agency serving children held within all its penal facilities. At issue was the very purpose of the entire American juvenile corrections system. Is the function of state training schools to punish children who are in violation of the laws or are these facilities to rehabilitate them into society

* Gisela Konopka, *The Adolescent Girl in Conflict*, p. 107. Reprinted by permission of Prentice-Hall, Inc., Englewood Cliffs, New Jersey. Copyright © 1966.

useful to themselves and their communities? Bercu's federal court case (*Morales v. Turman*) was a major test that pitted a minor, Alicia Morales, whose father had her incarcerated because she refused to get another job after his erratic behavior caused her to lose her first one, against Dr. James Turman, executive director of the Texas Youth Council, to see if, in fact, children have a constitutional right to treatment.

For Bercu, the road to the United States District Court for the Eastern District of Texas was long and tedious. It all started in 1970 when a fifteen-year-old Chicano girl, Guadalupe Torres, walked into the young attorney's El Paso office and told him she had run away but feared being locked up at a detention center.

Bercu learned from an award-winning series by Bill Payne of the El Paso *Times* that El Paso County, with only 3.5 percent of the total scholastic population within the state of Texas, provided 14.8 percent of total new commitments to Gainesville State School. Old court records revealed that the county court had been sending an average of seventy-five children per year over the last five years to Gatesville and Gainesville State training schools. Fifty of the children had no benefit of a lawyer, and twenty-five never even had a legal hearing before County Judge Edwin Berliner. Few of the children had committed serious crimes. Most were status offenders—that is, guilty of minor infractions such as running away from unfavorable family situations (with girls the problem is often a forced incestuous relationship with an alcoholic stepfather or father or uncle), truancy or incorrigibility. Their data opened Pandora's Box.

From August through November 1970, Bercu labored to secure writs of habeas corpus for the release of El Paso children. In January of 1971 he won a "discovery order," which permitted him to examine resident records at Gainesville and Gatesville. He then interviewed the El Paso children incarcerated without benefit of lawyer or legal hearing. Alicia Morales was one of the twelve minors who asked Bercu to represent them. He agreed.

At this time, however, officials at both Gainesville and Gatesville, as well as Dr. Turman, refused to allow Bercu to talk in private with his twelve clients. All children were ordered not to discuss conditions at the seven state facilities, especially the major ones of Gatesville, Mountain View, Gainesville, Brownwood and

Crockett. Texas Penal Code Article 1176 states that guards cannot interfere with the rights of an inmate and his lawyer. This notwithstanding, on April 6, 1971, Richard T. Springstun of the Gatesville complex wrote the following memo to all supervisors and instructors: "Do not let any letters out addressed to the Legal Assistance Society, 109 North Oregon Street, Room 919, El Paso, Texas 79901."

In July a questionnaire issued by Federal District Judge Wayne Justice, to be completed on each child within the Texas corrections system, revealed that 60 percent of the subjects had had no legal representation at the time of their confinement.

That September, testimony of ten children attesting to cruel and unusual punishment at Gatesville and Gainesville prompted Judge Justice to have every child within all Texas Youth Council facilities interviewed. This was carried out during the first two months of 1972 by one hundred law students. Then, in a historic decision, he ordered a "Participant Observation Team," composed of psychiatrists, two masters of social work and a doctor of psychology, to study both Gatesville and Gainesville while living at those institutions for a period of time.

Findings from these interviews by the observation team gave Justice cause to request assistance from the Civil Rights Division of the United States Justice Department, which in turn mobilized the Federal Bureau of Investigation to examine the increasingly mushrooming complaints of brutal and sadistic treatment in the state's juvenile centers.

In May of 1972 two bright young lawyers out of the United States Justice Department's Office of Institutions and Facilities flew to Texas to aid Judge Justice and the embattled Bercu. Within a year attorneys Daniel Maeso and Malcolm Logan, with the aid of the Federal Bureau of Investigation and after perhaps one of the most thorough investigations of a statewide juvenile penal facility in American history, reported that the TYC neglected to provide rehabilitative treatment and that there was gross violation of basic civil rights of inmates. The United States, as *amicus curiae* (friend of the court), documented its evidence in a federal court of law.

In the state courts, moving quietly and efficiently, Bercu filed a writ of habeas corpus to release 565 children whom he believed had been denied their constitutional rights. Although State District Court Judge Charles Matthew agreed that the children were illegally incarcerated, he denied the writ and advised the disappointed lawyer to seek their release via the ninety-seven courts from which they originated.

Undaunted, Bercu quickly approached the state court of appeals. A few days before Christmas 1972 he scored. The court of appeals not only reversed but sharply criticized Judge Matthew's decision. Five hundred children were released on one writ of habeas corpus—an unprecedented first in the history of American jurisprudence! Shortly thereafter the other 65 children were released, including Alicia Morales. In March of 1973 the El Paso attorney moved again and 300 more children were released because the state lacked proof against them of wrongdoing.

Though Steve Bercu's victory in the state courts was impressive, the Morales case was to be of greater importance to the more than 2,000 youngsters still confined in the Texas youth facilities as well as the 100,000 other children imprisoned across the United States, for it would rule that all involuntarily confined juveniles have a statutory and constitutional right to treatment.

Sitting through a large segment of the federal trial in Tyler, Texas, in June of 1973, I heard some of the most astonishing testimony of my life. Bercu's opening statement to the court— "... The Texas Youth Council is a poorly directed operation that is vile, that is brutal, that is oppressive and that destroys any vestiges of individuality"—proved after weeks of direct and cross-examination to be a mild indictment of the horror of daily physical beatings, solitary confinement for weeks at a time and even the tear-gassing of young boys in small isolation cells. I watched the dark-haired attorney fight for kids who in the past had had no one to defend them. I witnessed the trust and understanding that existed between him and his clients. I began to appreciate the sacrifices these courageous children were making as day after day they sat in the witness chair and told it all to a strangely silent courtroom, knowing full well that when they left the proceedings, they would return to their keepers, who, in fact, were standing trial.

The Texas Youth Council is the umbrella organization under which all the state's juvenile penal facilities are administered. Dr.

Howard Ohmart, expert witness for the U.S. Justice Department and consultant to the American Justice Institute, compiled a damaging assessment of the TYC. Of 2,442 youngsters incarcerated in 1972, 587 (24 percent) had been committed for disobedience. A breakdown of this figure shows that 293 were locked up for running away, 164 for truancy and the balance of 130 for being "ungovernable children." Of the total intake of 2,442, 184 boys and girls were thirteen years or younger. Six hundred and twenty-six had no previous court history. Less than 10 percent had committed acts of crime against a person, 5 percent were institutionalized for acts of violence and 4.7 percent for robbery.

In his pretrial deposition Dr. Turman contended that "the only justification for the Texas Youth Council is to provide rehabilitation." But Justice Department attorneys later moved in with charts, graphs and expert witnesses to prove that rehabilitation was a farce with the TYC and that its real function was to punish the children delivered to its institutional doorstep.

Rational and/or legal sanction for the cruel and unusual discipline described in the Texas courtroom is supplied by the "Corporal Punishment Laws of Texas," which states:

> Corporal punishment in any form shall not be inflicted upon any boy except as a last resort and then only after evidence has been gathered and presented to the Superintendent and the Chaplain. After an examination by a physician and found to be in good health, the Superintendent and Chaplain shall sign a whipping order ... the boy shall not receive over ten licks with a light strap ... at no time ever have the skin broken or be struck except as herein provided nor abused or threatened by any guard or employee. If any employee does not follow this procedure, he shall be filed on for aggravated assault.

The law, as stated, is vague and open to a wide range of interpretation. And as far as can be determined, never once has any criminal charge of aggravated assault been filed against any person within the TYC who went beyond even the broadest allowances of the law.

Gatesville School for Boys is the Texas Youth Council's oldest and largest facility. It was established in 1889 and is the major industry for Gatesville, Texas, providing jobs for employees and other business opportunities for rural farmers and cattle ranchers. Located in the central part of the state, it is forbidding and prisonlike. Security is paramount. Guard uniforms resemble the Texas Rangers', and trained dogs are kept to track down boys who "run." Seven subschools, ranging from very old to new, form the network of institutional life for its 1,048 youths. Each dormitory houses twenty or more children. There is no privacy. Windows are covered by steel mesh screens or bars and the buildings have no rear doors. In the event of fire all occupants must leave through the only entrance at the front or perish. Those who break "major" regulations are further isolated in tiny cells within the solitary confinement section. Gatesville and Mountain View Maximum Security Facility (for hard-core delinquents) house more than 60 percent of all children incarcerated by the state of Texas.

According to a fourteen-year-old inmate, Oscar Jackson, "the peel" is a favorite punishment at Gatesville. Here the guard administers blows to the child's bare back with the palm of his hand while the boy kneels with his head between the guard's legs. "Running in place" puts the youngster in the same position except the guard runs in place. The friction to the sides of the head causes burning and severe headaches. Another punishment, "the tight," forces the child to bend over and hold his toes while the guard beats him with a broom handle. "Crumb" or "sitting on lost privileges" is usually reserved for weekends. The student is forced to sit facing a wall or fence all day, forbidden to speak or fall asleep. Many inmates at Gatesville receive large dosages of Thorazine, a tranquilizer that induces drowsiness. However, no allowances are made. A Chicano youth testified that when he fell asleep, he was slapped to the floor and kicked.

Nor does sex offer any boundaries for harsh and inhuman treatment with the TYC. At the Crockett School, female offenders are often placed in handcuffs and beaten. Testimony revealed that Mr. Venters, the supervisor, liberally struck the girls with open hands or fists. Houseparents Mr. and Mrs. Watson also gave severe beatings. Although 24 percent of the TYC inmate population are Mexican-American, the Spanish language is forbidden and those caught speaking it at either Crockett or the Gainesville School for Girls are punished.

One witness told how Mr. Johnson, principal at Gainesville, pulled a girl threatening suicide off a tower, put her arms behind her back, "kneed" her to the ground, applied handcuffs, threw her in the back of a truck and drove her to solitary confinement.

Another girl, four months pregnant, enrolled in a pregnancy class. Here, under threat of spending time in the Special Treatment Cottage (STC) (solitary confinement), she was given ten small pills and told to exercise. Four days afterward she aborted. She was not seen by a doctor until a month later.

For the boys the most fearsome threat is the constant reminder of Mountain View, the maximum security facility down the road from Gatesville. With its high double fence topped with massive rolls of barbed wire and patrolled by armed guards in jeeps, the facility is imposing and menacing. The reputation is deadly. The following excerpts from a "Personal Injury Report" were uncovered by the Federal Bureau of Investigation. They give testimony to the lengths to which frightened Texan youngsters went to escape transfer to Mountain View.

"Fredie was attempting to cut his wrists.... Fredie used a broken light bulb. Fredie had one 3" long shallow cut on his left wrist, scratches on both arms and all over his chest." Fredie's description was somewhat different:

> I was really feeling low, and thinking about when my brothers and me used to play catch and they always wanted a ride on my bicycle. I'm scared to death I'm going to Mountain View State School and I have been crying most of the day. I cut my wrist, arms and chest, but I still don't really know why and I'm sorry I done it, but I guess its too late now, but I'm going crazy in this small room and I'm real nervous, and I feel like banging my head against the wall and I can't sleep.

Twenty-four hours later, guards took suicide precautions and removed all light fixtures from Fred Thompson's room after he attempted his life again by the same means. The boy wrote:

> I was sitting around all day trying to find something to kill myself with, because I don't want to go to Mountain View State School, and I know that's probably where I'll go. I'm still willing to take my punishment for running and also for cursing inside the school's

office, but this little room is driving me wild and I can't hardly sleep anymore. When I do, I dream about when my family and I used to have fun or sometimes I dream of how miserable I'll be when they send me to Mountain View State School. I realize my mistakes now and whenever I get out of this little room, I'm going to correct them, but I cut a gash in my left wrist because I'm going wild.

His caseworker wrote: "We were again notified by phone that the above named student sliced his wrist. . . . This student committed this act again for the purpose of gaining attention. He has a past history of manipulation." Two days later Fred Thompson was sent to Mountain View.

Mountain View was built in 1962 for hard-core delinquents. However, the FBI found in May of 1972 that 68 percent of Mountain View's total population of 385 were incarcerated for the first time at a state school. Reading like statistics in a basic psychology text dealing with crime and its causes, the report showed that 48 percent were black, 33 percent Anglo-Saxon and 19 percent Latin. Two thirds were minority children and all but a few were poverty level. Sixty-eight percent had parents who were divorced and the vast majority were six to seven years behind on their scholastic achievement levels.

The average IQ was 86, with Anglos, blacks and Latins testing 89, 79 and 83 respectively. Clarence Stephens, a caseworker supervisor, said that 30 to 40 students had IQ's of less than 70 and some as low as 54. By most accepted standards this is considered mild retardation. The Texas Youth Council's own pre-entrance diagnostic testing classified 293 boys as "emotionally disturbed," 158 of which made up 25 percent of Mountain View's entire population.

And so in actuality, Mountain View is primarily a punitive instrument used at each guard's individual discretion. Charles Derrick, who the court later appointed ombudsman for the children, substantiated this fact when he told of the following incidents:

Otis was a three-timer, always for runaway. His Mama and Daddy were separated, but he was still very involved with them both. His Mama lived in Louisiana and his Daddy in Texas and whenever he ran away, he ran from one to the other. But that's not legal. So they put him in Gatesville. His dorm parent was very control oriented. He carried a big stick wrapped with tape to beat the kids with. When he saw a kid misbehaving, he'd hold up his hand with a certain number of fingers up. However many fingers showed, that was how many licks they'd get later with the stick. One night Otis's dorm was marching to mess hall. They had to walk in unison in straight rows and were not allowed to talk. That kind of thing depends on the dorm parent. Some permit talking, some don't. The inconsistency is not good. Anyway, some kid messed up and the dorm parent looked at Otis and flashed five fingers three times. Otis told me later, he thought, "Jezz, I don't think I can stand that many." On the way back some other kid messed up and again the dorm parent looked at Otis and flashed another fifteen.

Otis knew he couldn't take thirty, so he bolted. He hid in the hog wallow. They got the dog man and sent the dogs and horsemen after him. They scared him, so when they got close, he stood up and hollered, "Here I am, Mister." So after that they sent him to Mountain View. Otis stayed there two whole years.

Derrick also told of a ninety-pound, hopelessly retarded, epileptic Chicano boy at Mountain View who had a seizure. Mack O. Morris, who had been promoted from a cook at Gatesville to assistant superintendent of Mountain View, gave orders to lock the sick boy in a solitary confinement cell. Tear gas canisters were then thrown through a slot in the bottom of the steel door and as the gas enveloped the terrified youth, he turned and dug his nails into the wall. According to Derrick, "He clawed marks into that wall all the way down to the floor where they found him subdued."

There is an uncanny intercommunications system within the penal community and almost every boy in the state of Texas knows about solitary confinement—or lockup or the "special treatment center" at Mountain View. Here the primary goal of Morris and his staff is to "maintain secure custody—rehabilitation is of secondary importance." The cells in this brick dormitory are approximately eight by ten feet in size and furnished solely with a mattress and a bucket for body waste. Iron bars cover the quarter-moon windows. Each door has a slit at the bottom through which food trays are served on the floor. Like other juvenile solitary cells throughout the United States, they are dirty and insect-infested and smell like outhouses. Mattresses are stained with the urine of hundreds of previous children. There is little or no light. And there is nothing to do.

A breakdown of records by FBI agents revealed that children were indiscriminately placed in solitary for a wide range of reasons: wishing a man would die, throwing soap at a boy, smoking in class, pretending to be ill, tearing a tag out of jeans and chewing corners off books. Eighteen boys totaled close to one year in lockup for the following: writing illegal letters and getting another boy to mail them, trying to make a long-distance phone call, writing a "Black Power" letter, attempting to slip letters out illegally, trying to mail film for development, giving film to parents to develop, and stealing stamps.

With an average age of 17.3 years, the boys are men physically and sexually frustrated. Given the circumstances of confinement for an average of 18 months, nothing could be more normal than for a seventeen-year-old boy to masturbate. Notwithstanding, fifteen students totaled 357 days in solitary for masturbating. Five boys served 131 days for writing vulgar letters and drawing dirty pictures. One letter was to a boy's girlfriend. He got 15 days. Three boys got 63 days for dancing together; another got 22 days for talking about kissing another boy; two lads received 16 each for kissing. Another boy got 10 days for watching a woman teacher from the ceiling of a restroom. Still another was hit with 14 days for feeling the leg of a woman teacher. Four youngsters were given 86 days for exposure. Seventeen sodomy attempts served over one year, and eighty-seven that were successful were confined for a total of 6 years.

These monster prisons of steel, concrete and silence consumed 12 years of life from almost two hundred children. Perhaps the saddest case was of the young man who was given 32 days for writing "I love you" to a teacher at the school. James Turman indicated in his pretrial deposition that he approved of putting a boy in lockup for writing "I love you" to a teacher.

Dr. Ohmart best assessed Mountain View's solitary confinement for the United States Justice Department:

As we approached the work squad, the nine coverall-clad figures [with the security emblem emblazoned on the back] were seated on the ground taking the carefully timed break. Elbows on knees, head between hands, they sat staring at the ground, fourbidden to either talk or look at each other. Shortly after our arrival, one of the two supervising officers gave the work signal and without a word, the group arose, still in line and started swinging their hoes. The hoe comes high overhead and chops into the earth, in a pointless and completely unproductive exercise.

Three or four swings and the line moves forward in unison, wordless, and with faces in a fixed, blank, expressionless mask. Except for the occasional furtive and fearful glance, they were like so many automatons. The depressed and depressing atmosphere was continued as we visited the group during the noon hour. They waited silently in the cells as two youths, equally silent, slid the trays on the floor and under the door. The youths, forbidden to sit on the bed until after being showered, sat on the floors, trays on lap and ate their lunch. Upon the completion of their lunch, the youths are showered and then may lie upon their beds. However, they are forbidden to sleep prior to ten o'clock at night and will be further penalized if they should fall asleep. . . . The silence rule prevails throughout their incarceration unless they are addressed by a staff member. In our visitation at correctional institutions and programs in some twenty-two of the states we have never seen anything quite as depressing, or anything that seemed so deliberately designed to humiliate, to degrade and debase. . . .

Over the years most of the abuse has been effectively concealed by the falsification of some of the official records of the TYC. The children are forced to aid and abet in the deception under fear of more beatings and further isolation.

FBI investigators Robert Nixon and Thomas Tarla found that the practice of gassing is not uncommon. Although Mack O. Morris claimed that only ten such incidents had occurrred over a period of eleven years, Nixon and Tarla found twenty-four gassing incidents recorded in the security gate log alone in the last nine and one-half years. Nixon reported the following to the United States Justice Department:

On February 23, 1972, Wilbur Watts broke a fluorescent light bulb and ate glass. The next day while in the Coryell Hospital he attempted to eat excrement, and lick up his urine from the floor.

On August 23, 1972, Wilbur Watts refused to work on garden detail. Forcibly placed in pickup by Hill and Freeman and taken to security. Pulled end rail off bed and started breaking windows, then was gassed for the second time in one morning. Morris' statement includes comments that there is nothing mentally or physically wrong with Watts.

Agent Nixon was astounded that an air-activated tear-gas canister was used in a closed eight-by-ten room. He shook his head in disbelief, knowing that this type of gas, when released inside a small room, is activated in dust form. The dust adheres to wet skin and creates serious chemical burns. This was precisely what happened. It was Wilbur Watts who, a young boy testified, "[came] out the next day with skin peeling and hanging off his face."

Section 18 of the Texas Youth Council Act of 1957, Article 5143d, states:

> Type of Treatment Permitted—As a means of correcting the socially harmful tendencies of a delinquent child committed, the Youth Council may:
> b. Require such modes of life and conduct as may seem best adapted to fit him for return to full liberty without danger to the public.

Wilbur Watts's mode of life and conduct was, apparently, well adapted to returning him to full liberty: today, Wilbur is hopelessly insane. His once black skin is covered with large blotches of pink scars from the chemical burns of gassing—a lifelong remembrance from his keepers at the Mountain View School for Boys. Wilbur Watts was mentally disturbed when he arrived, and rather than provide helpful professional services for which they are responsible by law, the Texas officials in Austin and at Mountain View must now share the guilt for the destruction of this human being.

The Texas Youth Council employs what the penal trade refers to as the "three empire system." Made up of (1) guards and other custodial workers, (2) teachers or (3) caseworkers, each group is different in scope and totally separated from the others.

Of the three, guards and other custodial staff spend the most time with inmates but are the least educated and the lowest paid.

As many as 90 percent of them are full-time farmers and cattle ranchers, with guard work supplementing their income. Training consists of "floating" to learn by observation how an experienced guard keeps control. Job interviews last about ten minutes and although psychologists at Gatesville are equipped with testing techniques to screen out potentially abusive applicants, such screening is not done.

The second group, the educators, are basically townspeople with a rural background and trained for normal classroom teaching. Unfortunately the background and training ill prepare them to relate to youngsters from an urban setting with a history of failure in schoolwork.

In a 1973 study of the TYC's 2,200 children, 212 were diagnosed as very retarded with IQ's of 69 or lower. At Gatesville, only 72 out of 1,048 students were at proper grade levels. Ninety-four were a year behind and 882 were two or more grades below proper level. More than half were reading at third-grade level or lower. Remedial reading teachers were untrained and the principal at Gatesville felt that "special education was not their business."

Teachers cannot visit or tutor anyone in lockup. Interest in the child seems to stop at the classroom door. There is no teacher effort to work or communicate with the child's caseworker or security personnel at the dorm.

Caseworkers, seeing the students on a one-to-one basis, are usually better educated and generally more concerned than the guards or teachers about the needs of their charges. But frustrations, such as thwarted attempts to visit and advise students in lock-up, the futility of counseling children after they have been beaten by guards, and the actual physical abuse carried out in the institutions make the turnover rate among caseworkers the highest of the three groups.

However, caseworkers have been known to abuse the confidentiality of their relationship and become instruments of further control over the child. Like some penal chaplains, they discover secrets and personal feelings of a child and pass them on to the security force, which in turn uses them against the student. This type of destructive relationship seems to be the only real communication between caseworkers and guards or between teachers and guards.

So while the empire system grinds away, each group concerned with its own special interest, the children must adapt to the system of oppression or perish. If they obey the security personnel and stay out of trouble, in due time they'll go home. During 1972, however, there were twenty-two Texan children who could not adjust and attempted suicide.

Either way, adjust or perish, the problems that lead to incarceration are left untouched and untreated. This massive $22 million complex employs no full-time medical doctor or psychiatrist—not even a nurse for after hours. Many of the part-time psychiatrists live some distance from the facility and visit only once a week.

The need for psychotherapy for many young girls is most pressing; yet Dr. Herbert G. Quay, consultant of the U.S. Bureau of Prisons, testified that the TYC staff in the three female schools is inadequately trained to deal with the emotionally disturbed. For example, many of the girls are runaways because of an incestual relationship imposed by alcoholic stepfathers or real fathers or uncles. They are confused, distraught and disturbed. Adding to their personal problems is the emotional experience of incarceration, where they find the only concern is that they conform and structure their goals toward the rules and expected behavior of the facility. The deep problem, with the stepfather or father or uncle, is left unattended, untouched.

This total apathy toward the causes of child crime, minor or serious, though subtle, is more destructive to the young disturbed person than the beatings. Cases in point are two youths from Mountain View. One boy had committed sodomy on an infant girl. He had no previous history of delinquent behavior. At Mountain View he presented no problems, got good marks on his behavior and was released. Not once during his entire stay did he have a psychiatric work-up or treatment to deal with his very serious problem.

The second boy, on extra work duty, went berserk and hit himself on the head with a pick handle. The guards subdued him and placed him in solitary confinement, where he was tear-gassed for hollering and hitting the wall with his fists. Mr. Morris wrote about the event:

He started pulling a temper tantrum, attempting to destroy state property. . . . Afer administering the tear gas, and bringing Eddie under control, we moved him back to the work crew, and have observed him very closely since that time . . . thus far he has been a model student since that time. He has appeared to have had a complete change of attitude and behavior, and has worked well.

The "state property," the pick handle, was given priority and saved from destruction. No records show that Eddie ever received any form of counseling or psychiatric work-up to deal with his behavior.

Morales V. Turman took six weeks to try. On August 31, 1973, Federal District Judge Wayne Justice handed down a temporary restraining order entitled "Emergency Interim Relief." After two long years Steve Bercu was able, through an honest and courageous federal judge, to bring relief to children still within the penal system of Texas.

Judge Justice's interim ruling said that the widespread practice of beatings and other forms of corporal punishment throughout the TYC system, particularly at Mountain View and Gatesville, "violates the eighth amendment because it is inflicted in a wholly arbitrary fashion, is so severe as to degrade human dignity and is unacceptable to contemporary society." He also ruled that "juveniles committed to the custody of the Texas Youth Council enjoy both a state statutory and a federal constitutional right to treatment."

In mid-September 1973, two weeks after Judge Justice issued his restraining order, all hell let loose. Riots and fires broke out in Mountain View. At Gatesville, 138 boys performed a "Geronimo." A mass break and a riot ensued shortly thereafter at the facility. But this time, when the students who were caught running away and placed in isolation cells started to riot, correctional officers did nothing. Contending that their hands were tied by the recent court order, they withdrew and let the kids rampage through the isolation wing. Dr. Turman came up from Austin and told the press, "I'm not going to risk human life by sending anybody in there to quell those boys."

The riots at Mountain View destroyed half the industrial shops— a cost of $500,000. At Gatesville the destruction was concentrated mainly in solitary confinement. The kids did what the courts could not and the state would not do. With their own hands they ripped out and destroyed the contents of those cells where countless numbers of them lived in daily fear of being beaten into submission. Twenty-six children were rounded up after the riot and transferred to nearby county jails, some booked as felons.

There is a distinct parallel between Texas youth facilities and the nation at large. Ever present, but rarely mentioned, is the basic national structure that not only prevents treatment of the troubled child but actually perpetuates the penal industry. That structure is politics—the politics of jobs, of corruption, of professional power and, most damning, of secrecy, which allows the destruction of young children generation after generation.

The Texas Youth Council has never been free of controversy except concerning its annual budget. As its operating allocations grew from $2 million in 1960 to $22 million in 1973, political clout grew proportionately. When reform state legislators Frances (Cissy) Farenthold and Lane Denton sought to visit Gatesville, they were refused admission. In May of 1971 Representative Curtis Graves of Houston told NBC-TV that nearly two hundred parents and juveniles had complained to him of brutal treatment at Gatesville and Mountain View. His attempt to make it an issue was callously ignored by the powerful leaders of the Texas Legislature.

Former Representative Vernon Stuart of Wichita Falls claimed it was no accident that each new facility constructed by the Texas Youth Council was built for urban children in a rural county that just happened to be in the political district of the current Speaker of the House or of the chairman of the Appropriations Committee.

All Texan youth facilities are located in small rural areas and supply the main industry of their community. At Gatesville, where the town population is roughly five thousand, approximately three thousand persons either work at the youth facilities or are related to someone who does.

In December 1971, Gatesville School for Boys and Mountain View (also located in Gatesville) had a combined annual operational budget of $18,118,000, of which $5,900,000 went for payroll of their nine hundred employees. Before the *Morales v. Turman* trial, the youth population of these two facilities was 2,279. On

December 6, 1973, it had shrunk to 545 at Gatesville, 66 at Mountain View—a total of 611 youths. Employment level remained at nine hundred.

The basic commodity needed for this industry to flourish is children; without them there would be no jobs, no income, no plant, no town. Therefore, any threat of or actual running away from the facility takes on serious economic ramifications, serious enough to warrant severe punishment. Many children are transferred from Gatesville to Mountain View for this very reason.

The Morales trial revealed that because children had been injured by dogs, the bloodhounds used to track down runaways at Gatesville were banned. However, within three weeks the Texas Youth Council had not only donated their dogs free but had agreed to pay Coryell County $1,500 per month for the operation of a bloodhound service. Deputy sheriffs Jack Fry and Gerald Kitchens, the same two men who supervised the same twelve dogs at Gatesville School for Boys, were sworn into office to operate the service. Now located in the northern part of Gatesville, they stand ready to seek and search the area for those boys who would disturb the "inventory" at the school.

Because of a family code recently passed in Texas, children can no longer be committed to the Texas Youth Council for truancy, incorrigibility or running away. This new law, coming on top of the Morales case, threatens the economy of Gatesville. In early December of 1973, when General Superintendent Swain Place was forced to close Hilltop, one of seven units at the Gatesville School, there were 696 staff people to care for 545 boys. However, no one lost his job; as Mr. Place reassured the town, "I don't feel we are overstaffed in any way, with the possible exception of a few extra dormitory matrons."

There have been murmurings against the gratuitous operations at Gatesville. Psychologist Albert Burnstein of the University of Texas Medical School in San Antonio testified that "only twenty percent of the youths in the state correctional schools need to be there." A unit superintendent at the school told the local press that "most townspeople who are connected with the school are in it just for the money. They don't give a damn about the kids." And the new acting director of the TYC, Ron Jackson, said he didn't believe in large institutions as necessary or good: "Personally, I'm against large institutions. They depersonalize the kids."

Rumors from Austin that the Gatesville facility was going to close down caused the concerned community to respond. The economic foundation of the town was threatened. Mayor Bob Miller said, "It would be a big blow to the community if the Gatesville State schools went away." Dr. Joseph M. Kenworthy of the local Chamber of Commerce told the local newspaper, the Gatesville *Messenger*, that most of the citizens need Gatesville because a "significant number are farmers and ranchers and consider the state school a secondary source of income."

The Chamber of Commerce organized an eleven-member team who attended TYC meetings regularly. A massive lobbying assault went into effect to save the school and jobs—the children weren't even considered. The Chamber of Commerce Industrial Team also organized a publicity committee to espouse the positive aspects of the training school. The editorial comment in the town's newspaper called this a "most worthy goal" and wished that every person in Texas could come see the nice facility at Gatesville with its "picnic areas, ball fields, gymnasiums, swimming pools, and well-tended, tree-dotted lawns."

The political pressure to keep the school open was intense. Within a short period of time the TYC backed down and issued a statement saying they would not close Gatesville.

While Judge Justice was in the process of handing down his final decision about the TYC, political pressures from the governor's office and business leaders were constantly brought to bear on him. The same types of public relations campaign and political connections awarded the two schools the following citation from the acting governor of Texas on September 20, 1969:

> WHEREAS, The Gatesville State School for Boys, in operation since 1889, and the Mountain View School for Boys, in operation since 1962, are charged with the task of rehabilitating youthful offenders and providing these young boys with the skills and knowledge they need to live useful lives as contributing members of our society; and
>
> WHEREAS, These two schools have commendably carried out this task under the wise direction of the Texas Youth Council; and
>
> WHEREAS, The success of the Gatesville and Mountain View

Schools is, in large part, due to the outstanding job done by the employees of the schools, employees who are dedicated to helping these young boys get back on the right track,

Now, THEREFORE, I, J. P. WORD, GOVERNOR OF TEXAS, do hereby recognize the excellent service of the employees of the Gatesville and Mountain View Schools and urge the people of Texas to give their support to these individuals.

J. P. Word was also the local politician representing Gatesville in the Texas House of Representatives.

Political influence and connections notwithstanding, the Morales case shed light on some indisputable facts. Children are incarcerated for noncriminal behavior. Children who are mentally retarded or have serious emotional or mental disorders are used for the express purpose of swelling the institutional population to create jobs and money.

When Jimmy King ran away from Gatesville back in 1971, he was shot in the leg by a farmer. Many of the children wrote home about the incident, but not one parent received that particular piece of correspondence. When NBC News did its White Paper on Juvenile Justice, "This Child Is Rated X," its request to film the facilities and interview children incarcerated with the Texas Youth Council was denied. This deliberate "politics of secrecy" in Texas, indeed throughout the United States, keeps the American public ignorant of what is happening to their 100,000 children imprisoned at this very moment.

The FBI investigation of Mountain View was nearly completed. Walking to the car with Justice Department Attorney Malcom Logan, Agent Bob Nixon reflected on the horrible effect the treatment in that institution would subsequently have on the children. Peering into the gathering dusk through the car window, he said almost as if he were thinking aloud, "These are the kids who someday will kill a cop for giving them a traffic ticket just because of attitudes developed toward authority while in Mountain View."

One year after handing down his emergency interim order, Judge Justice made a final ruling that children have a constitutional right to treatment and ordered the TYC to close down Gatesville and Mountain View. His decision was appealed by the attorney general of Texas. Never before in the history of United States juvenile justice has one state been so comprehensively investigated by the federal courts, the U.S. Justice Department and the Federal Bureau of Investigation. Never before have the abuse and destruction of children been so substantiated and documented. The state of Texas has been exposed and disgraced.

But Texas is not alone; few states would fare much better under similar examination. Day after day, year in and year out, across the landscape of America, local, state and federal justice systems continue to incarcerate our children, to abuse them and qualify treatment while the mechanics of juvenile justice increasingly become enmeshed in abuse and corruption.

The right of the State, as parens patriae, *to deny to the child procedural rights available to his elders was elaborated by the assertions that a child, unlike an adult, has a right not to liberty but to custody. He can be made to attorn to his parents, go to school, etc. If his parents default in effectively performing their custodial functions—that is, if the child is "delinquent"—the state may intervene. In doing so, it does not deprive the child of any rights, because he has none.*

—In re Gault
Supreme Court of the United States, 1967

2/The Bastard Stepchild of *Parens Patriae:* The American Juvenile Incarceration Structure

The practice of incarcerating children and the conditions existing therein have legal roots dating back to England during the late fourteenth and early fifteenth centuries. There, under the doctrine of *parens patriae*, the King's Court of Chancery held power of guardianship over children who were abandoned or willfully neglected by their parents.

In 1636, *parens patriae* was introduced in America when young Benjamen Eaton of Plymouth Colony, indentured by the state, was given to Bridget Fuller, a widow, and ordered by the governor "to kelp him at schoole two years and to imploy him after in shuch service as she saw good and that he should be fit for; but not to turne him over to any other, without ye gov'n consente."

Still another legal concept that derived from the Common Law of England was that of *mens rea*—guilty mind. A child of seven or younger could not be found guilty of a crime because he had not reached the age of reason. From age eight on, however, the law forced the child to stand trial and endure the severity of full criminal prosecution. For example, in the early 1800's a child of eight who was accused of "malice revenge and cunning" for setting fire to some barns was convicted and hanged. In 1828 a New Jersey boy of thirteen was hanged for a crime he committed when he was twelve.

In 1727 the city of New Orleans built the first institution in America for neglected or homeless children. Up to that time and well into the nineteenth century, neglected and delinquent youths were placed in jails, prisons and almshouses with adults. Even today the same practice persists in many areas of the United States: the laws of forty-six states still approve placing juveniles in county jails, and thirty-four of these states don't even require a special court order.

It wasn't until 1825 that New York City set up the House of Refuge, the first separate institution whose sole purpose was to aid juvenile offenders. Within a few years other cities—Philadelphia and Boston, for example—followed suit and established similar accommodations. Although these facilities were set up to deal with juvenile offenders, unfortunately they were eventually obliged to admit neglected children because there was no place else for them to go once they became wards of the state. This practice is still common in all but three states.

These "houses of refuge" proved to be a historical milestone in the American family culture. For the first time family-centered discipline was replaced by institutional discipline administered by city, county or state governments. Parents, grandparents, older sisters and brothers were replaced by guards and superintendents.

Progressive in its philosophy, the New York House of Refuge early initiated the practice of "binding out" or placing delinquent children in foster homes. In his daily journal the superintendent of the Manhattan House of Refuge recorded the following entry on May 10, 1828:

We saw the eight boys for Ohio start in good spirits. . . . It excited considerable warm good feeling to see so many little fellows bound for such a good and suitable place from the House of Refuge, among the passengers on board the steamboat.

Sixty-five years later, in 1893, foster home advocate Homer Folks vigorously promoted the practice of binding out delinquent children. Folks believed that of all the children incarcerated within institutions, "only a very small number show lack of moral sense and are dangerous to the community." The genuine human concern of this nineteenth-century progressive has been echoed by each new generation of reformers for the last eight decades. As children's justice becomes an increasingly popular issue in the 1970's, more and more groups are quoting the National Council for Crime and Delinquency, which has said that only 10 percent of all juvenile offenders require incarceration.

However, the rhetoric of reformers and progressive organizations did little to prevent the powerful growth of the state-supported and state-operated training school complex. Massachusetts created the first such penal facility for children in 1847. Called the Lyman School for Boys, it became one of the worst institutions in America and one of the first training schools to be closed down in 1972 for massive failure and child brutality. By 1960 there were two hundred training schools in fifty states, the District of Columbia, Puerto Rico and the Virgin Islands. The daily population numbered 40,000, with close to 100,000 children a year being processed through their gates. By 1974 the national network of these schools had a combined operating budget of close to $300 million and a recidivism* rate of eight out of ten children.

The early juvenile penal facilities were located on the outskirts of urban areas, but as the cities grew in size and encompassed the old "reform schools" and "houses of refuge," there was a movement to relocate on large acreages in rural areas. Thus began what is known in youth corrections as "the colony system." Whole institutions became self-sufficient entities. The economics of the small towns where they located have become tightly interwoven

---

* Recidivism rate is really a failure rate; it refers to the number of children who return to the institution.

with the institutions because a majority of the local townspeople have become dependent on them for their livelihood.

World War I imposed its military mentality on the youth correctional system, when, according to one historian, "Living units became barracks; cottage groups, companies; housefathers, captains; superintendents, majors or more often colonels; and the kids wore uniforms." That influence is still alive in Texas and Arizona State training schools; I personally witnessed boys in the atmosphere of a military stockade, forced to march and take orders in a military fashion from guards in military-style uniforms.

One of the most distressing social phenomena in juvenile justice is that earlier liberal reforms designed to help children ended up hurting them. In 1890 the first juvenile courts were organized and they quickly spread throughout the country after the turn of the century. Compulsory educational laws were also passed, making it mandatory for children to attend school. Yet another reform was the progressive Social Security Act of 1935, a section of which permitted governmental agencies, using tax monies, to provide for the neglected child. What has happened, though, is that the well-meaning intent of reform has turned into the tyranny of reform: the state now has gained greater social control over the dependent youngster. Children who fail to attend school for any of an assortment of reasons are hauled into juvenile court and incarcerated in state training schools for years. State welfare agencies, with vast sums of money, arbitrarily take children from blood relatives and ship them to institutions in and out of state.

In 1967 the United States Supreme Court concluded that "the Latin phrase (*parens patriae*) proved to be great help to those who sought to rationalize the exclusion of juveniles from the constitutional scheme; but its meaning is murky and its historical credentials are of dubious relevance." Regardless of such legal rhetoric, America's youth are still being incarcerated in every state of the union. Because of old legal procedures and laws, because of our national tradition of juvenile institutionalization and because of numerous "social reforms," neglected and delinquent juveniles find themselves caught in the destructive net of incarceration behind locked doors in one of four different institutions: juvenile detention center, county or municipal jail, state training school or private facility approved by the presiding juvenile court judge.

First offenders are usually sent to one of the 300 detention centers, where approximately 13,000 kids* sit for an average of twelve days with nothing to do, awaiting the court's decision on their fate. Because the police and most juvenile workers fear they'll run away, they are detained behind locked doors. Most detention centers I have visited throughout the country are situated in or near the same building that houses the juvenile court. To the casual observer or group on tour given by the personnel, these facilities look rather harmless and almost like college dorms. But behind the public relations veneer, a penitentiary atmosphere prevails; guards, heavy iron doors, countless keys and closed circuit TV give paramount security and control. Solitary confinement is readily employed for the slightest infraction.

According to the National Council on Crime and Delinquency, 50 percent of the youngsters in detention centers have committed no crime and 40 percent will be released from custody after court appearance. Still in increasing numbers, children are filling up our detention centers, and the politicians are calling for new multimillion-dollar facilities that will be operated by county governments. The politics of jobs are very real.

Where no juvenile detention center exists, the child is held in a county or municipal jail until he appears before a juvenile judge. United States Senator Birch Bayh, chairman of the Senate Subcommittee on Delinquency, commented during hearings on the subject in September of 1973: "On any given day, there are close to 8,000 juveniles held in jails in the United States. It is estimated that more than 100,000 youths spend one or more days each year in adult jails or police lockups."

These local penal accommodations, the oldest facilities in the United States for both youthful and adult offenders, are, in the words of Daniel P. Starnes, a leading expert in the field of cor-

---

* A shocking report entitled "Hidden Closets" by George Saleebey, former Deputy Director of the California Youth Authority, reveals that in January, 1975, California was locking away noncriminal youngsters at such a rate that, based on national figures, the Golden State would account for one third of all children so incarcerated throughout the country. Prior to this controversial report, California was listed as having a moderate amount of children in detention. If the report is accurate, the ramifications are ominous as to how little we really know concerning the actual numbers of children locked away.

rections, "notorious as a constant source of verified filth, perversion, sadism and corruption." More than a million town drunks and men and women of violence, most with criminal records, enjoy the company of nearly 100,000 youngsters annually, 75 percent of whom are locked in the same rooms with adults. In 1970, 66.1 percent of these were later released, free of any charges.

In 1970, a statewide breakdown of a national survey by the University of Chicago showed that in Illinois ten thousand children made up 6 percent of the total city-, county-jail population for that year. Out of 160 jails in the state, 142 detained juveniles and only 9 of them segregated the children from adults. A mere 15 percent of the 142 jails had supervisory personnel to keep the children from the harm of molestation and rape.

Training schools, which operate in every state except Massachusetts, represent the nadir in a class filter system for juvenile malefactors who are picked up by police, arrested, detained in a juvenile hall and eventually sentenced by a judge for rehabilitation. Almost all are state-operated and -controlled. The laws that govern their legal functions specify that training schools are to provide custody and to rehabilitate the child so that his confinement will build toward a more useful life for himself and his community.

I found basically two types of training schools. The first is a miniature penitentiary with high walls surrounding the grounds. All the buildings and cell block wings therein are interlocked by long corridors. Not only are individual cell doors secured, but each wing is also locked at all times. There is almost always a self-sufficient industrial complex on the grounds—laundry, hospital, maintenance shop and any other facility needed to keep strangers out and the children in. Dubious educational and religious services are available to the children, along with the standbys of solitary confinement and of bloodhounds to locate any who run away.

The second and more common type of training school is the cottage system. Its concept was introduced in 1856 to give children the closest thing to some form of home life. Those in charge are "house parents" rather than "guards." The outside area is usually quiet and pleasant and bears little semblance to a penal facility. The cottages are usually small, esthetically pleasing, dormlike structures. Unfortunately, those I have seen have no back or side doors, or if they do, the doors are always chained and locked. The windows are also secured with heavy wire and in the event of emergencies such as fire, escape would be impossible except through the front door.

Such a situation occurred in Arizona sometime during the 1960's according to several state employees I interviewed. After a fire the charred remains of seventeen youngsters were found piled in front of a chained exit door, but the full circumstances of their needless deaths have been kept from the general public to this day.

The cottage system always reserves one building for secure treatment, solitary confinement. Any child who acts up in a solitary cottage is further isolated in a special single room for indefinite periods of time.

Still another facility for the incarceration of wayward youths is the private institution. Few people know much about these private institutions and very little has been written about them. Generally these facilities are for children of well-to-do parents or parents who have special benefits because of their job or station in life. They are usually located in isolated, wooded, rural areas. Their geographic setting and private nature adds greatly to the public's lack of information about their performance. These private "hospitals," "ranches," "homes," etc., run the gamut— from exceedingly good to exceedingly poor; from state-approved and -licensed to unsupervised and unevaluated. Some have established excellent reputations; others have recently sprung up in response to newly available state and federal monies. Some, like the Menninger Foundation in Topeka, Kansas, have the noble purpose of truly helping to relieve and direct the troubled; others are designed to help themselves by warehousing and administratively exploiting both disturbed and normal children while the owners amass sizable fortunes.

In many cases the only difference between the private institution and public state training schools is the cost. The control philosophy is the same. The children are usually there by court order. They are locked in the buildings during the day and in their rooms at night. The view from the windows is obscured by steel and thick wire mesh. Solitary confinement is used consistently as punishment for breaking minor rules. Most frightening of all is the unsupervised environment that allows for a new agent of control—chemical restraints—to be used with little thought to their ultimate effects on the child's body or mind. And all the while the American taxpayer is paying, directly or indirectly, financially and socially.

What we have today, then, is a juvenile justice system that originated as a small community concern, by people of good will but whose reform programs and laws created a national industry. Without public awareness a system that was designed to help children in trouble has become a tyrannical monster, destroying the very children it was mandated to save.

*I started doing time when I was 11 years old and
have been doing practically nothing else since
then. . . . What you have done and are doing to me,
you are also doing to others. . . . I have done as I
was taught to do. I am no different from any other.
You taught me how to live my life, and I have lived
as you taught me. . . . In my lifetime I have
murdered 21 human beings, I have committed
thousands of burglaries, robberies, larcenies, arsons
and last but not least I have committed sodomy on
more than 1,000 male human beings. . . .*

—Excerpts from "The Killer," published diary
of a federal prisoner

3/Initiation into Criminal Life: Status Offense Laws

Ten-year-old Emmett Player had no mother or
father when the state of Alabama locked him in
its Industrial School for Negro Children at Mount
Meigs on June 14, 1968. Like thousands of other
youngsters, Emmett was neither a criminal nor a
juvenile delinquent. He was a neglected child
who served four and a half years without as much
as a judicial commitment order.* Although dependent and neglected children are usually placed
at the Alabama Baptist Children's Home, the
Alabama Sheriff's Boys Ranch, the Presbyterian
Home for Children or the United Methodist

* Denny Abbott, a chief probation officer in Montgomery,
was fired by Judge William Thetford when Denny brought
his second major federal law suit against the state of
Alabama on behalf of Emmett Player and all status offenders incarcerated within its penal facilities.

Children's Home, poor black children like Emmett Player went, in the words of Alabama Juvenile Court Judge R. Bell, to the "poor boys military academy"—the state training schools. The normal stay at Mount Meigs is eight months.

Emmett Player's case typifies the solution most states now apply to this modern social problem. Neglected orphans are processed through the courts, detention centers and jails and finally, for lack of proper facilities, are incarcerated in state training schools along with serious offenders. The same arbitrary treatment is given school truants, runaways and children who fall under the legal fog of "incorrigible," "ungovernable," "wayward" or even "stubborn." Though there are no precise figures, most experts in the field agree that these children make up half of the young inmates in America today. These are the children who run afoul of ill-conceived and outdated state laws; these are the children whose parents find the easy way out by dumping them in our juvenile junkyards; these are the children whose major problem, by and large, is how to grow up and experience normal adolescent development without benefit of proper guidance. These children are called "status offenders"; their crime is their social situation.

From the very beginning this country's laws and courts have been stringent with regard to minors. As far back as 1646 a Massachusetts Bay Colony statute decreed: "If a man has a stubborn or rebellious son of at least 16 years of age, the father may bring the lad to the magistrates' courtroom where such a son shall be put to death." In Washington State, after the turn of the century, a girl named Lulu Roller filed a rape suit against her father. The state supreme court threw the case out on the ground that "the rule of law prohibiting suits between parent and child is based on the interest that society has in preserving harmony in the domestic relations." Today the attitude, if not the decree of the law, remains basically the same. Almost all state judges have the power to incarcerate status offenders. In 1971 a Massachusetts court (*Commonwealth v. Dianne Brasher*) held that a punishment statute, including imprisonment, for "stubborn children" is legal and constitutional. I have actually seen these so-called stubborn children locked in county detention centers as criminals.

In Arkansas, county judges have the power to commit children from three to fifteen "who live in notorious records of bad character" to "reform schools or find a suitable home." Kansas refers to troubled children as "the miscreant child." Other states refer to them as "vicious." Even the laws specifically written to protect children called them "depraved," "wicked" and "evil." In Vermont, parents can apply to have their children incarcerated at the Weeks School if they pay half the cost. Most states are similar to Oregon, where the statutes are extremely vague and all-encompassing when they deal with the incarceration of children ". . . whose behavior is found to endanger his own welfare or that of others." Under the guise of legal protection, a juvenile judge can give a status offender an indeterminate sentence.

One such case was Barbara Oles, a mentally retarded Elizabeth, New Jersey, girl who served a seven-year term for truancy. Hunterdon County Judge Thomas J. Beetel, who discovered four similar cases, called Miss Oles's case "a travesty" and observed: "As the statute is interpreted, you can get 10 years for manslaughter, and you can also get 10 years for truancy."

Generally speaking, there are three classifications of juveniles who come before the courts for adjudication. First are the "dependent or neglected children" whose parents or guardians fail to take proper care of them. Second are those declared incorrigible or ungovernable by their parents, school officials or the courts. And lastly is the group most Americans believe make up the total population of our youth penal facilities—those who violate criminal laws. All too often children in the first group quickly slide down into the second group, are incarcerated and then graduate to serious crimes.

It must be made clear again that the second group, whom legal experts call status offenders, have violated no criminal laws but are imprisoned just the same and take up considerable police and court time. In 1971, of 28,740 juvenile court cases in Cook County, Chicago, 9,200 were status offenders and only 3,500 committed serious crimes. During the same year 56.4 percent of all juvenile arrests in California were for "delinquent tendencies" (status offenses) and only 38 percent of all detained children in Florida were accused of criminal acts. In Seattle, Washington, referrals for ungovernable behavior had the greatest likelihood to become formal petitions, and ungovernable children were detained longer than any other referral category, including homicide.

Paul Lerman, in a well-documented article called "Child Convicts," examined the complex range of injustice to which the noncriminal child is vulnerable. Checking dispositions of juvenile cases in nineteen of the thirty largest cities in the country (1965), he discovered that although 57 percent of the young offenders were petitioned by the court for serious adult crimes (homicide, forcible rape, armed robbery, aggravated assault and theft) and 42 percent were petitioned for status offenses, the latter had a higher conviction rate—94 percent compared with 92 percent for the former.

More amazing was that 26 percent of the noncriminal children were committed, while only 23 percent of the serious offenders were incarcerated. Status offenders also serve longer terms than delinquents. In New York State the child who committed a crime stayed an average 10.7 months as compared with the non-criminal, who stayed an average 16.3 months. In other areas of the country, status offenders are held from nine to twelve months longer than those convicted of major violations.

The cost of processing juveniles through our courts is also staggering. Sacramento County, California, pays an estimated $173,000 per month ($2,076,000 per year) to process "incorrigible children" legally. Calculated on a national scale, the drain on the taxpayer is enormous.

Who are these children? In the 1830's they were mostly off-spring of Irish immigrants who crowded into House of Refuge, the first juvenile correctional institution in the country. Today they are young blacks and Puerto Ricans, with problems that reflect their station in life—alcoholic parents, home units destroyed by unemployment, lack of money, poor education, deficient diets, no future and no hope. Here they dwell in the social prison of the poor until snared by our archaic juvenile system, which will then throw them into actual prisons of concrete and steel.

Perhaps most disheartening is the sheer stupidity of the juvenile courts, the law enforcers and those citadels of malfeasance, the state legislatures.

Case in point: Back in 1962, New York's state legislature enacted a Family Court Act which forbade training school placement for status offenders. However, the Albany body shortly thereafter recanted and called for a three-year stopgap measure until alternative programs could be developed. The allotted time passed. No new programs were forthcoming, so in 1968 the legislature, with calloused wisdom and political expediency, voted to make incarceration of status offenders with pure delinquents a permanent arrangement.

If politicians won't or can't act to save children from the plight of imprisonment, our higher courts may be the only answer. By 1971 the New York State Supreme Court had authorized a study to determine the usefulness of state training schools for juvenile offenders. The Committee on Mental Health, headed up by Manhattan Family Court Judge Justine Wise Polier, wrote: "The fragmented, fractionalized and inadequate psychiatric, psychological and casework services made available by the state for the training schools cannot possibly provide even a modicum of the treatment services that the children require." In 1973 the New York Court of Appeals handed down a decision that stopped the practice of placing status offense children (PINS)—Persons in Need of Supervision—with delinquents.

Thanks to a budget-cutting governor and legislature, however, a whole generation of children were forced to live with and learn from convicted criminals, while officeholders enjoyed the best of both political worlds: not only could they boast to their constituents how they kept the budget down, but they could also exploit the issue of law and order on a new crop of future criminals cultivated by their own malfeasance.

Another New York state law, the Wayward Minor Statute, was struck down by Federal Circuit Court Judge Irving Kaufman when he heard cases of young girls being incarcerated for willful disobedience and moral depravation. One such girl was Marion Johnson, who had been in and out of foster homes since she was five years old. When she was seventeen, she had an illegitimate child, which her social worker wanted her to give up. She refused and was adjudged wayward. Another girl, Dominica Morelli, also seventeen, was the victim of a sexual assault by one of her mother's four husbands. She ran away and was put on probation. She ran off again without her mother's permission and was charged with violating probation. Judge Kaufman, and subsequently a three-man federal court, denounced the Wayward Minor Statute as "unconstitutionally vague," with Kaufman stating: "The law permitted punishment as if they were criminals. But they are punishing a condition, not a crime.... The state will simply have to find different ways to treat these youths. Foster homes, halfway houses—but not penal institutions."

The question of removing status offenders from the jurisdiction of juvenile courts is curently much debated. A young boy sitting in a Boston family courtroom was approached by a friend who asked what he was doing in court. The boy bitterly spat back, "This ain't no court, it's a railroad station!" Though many well-meaning judges would take issue with the boy on his remark, it is a fact that the President's Commission on Crime and Delinquency described the legal process as "the five-minute children's hour." The same commission recommended, along with the Second United Nations Congress on the Prevention of Crime, that the whole question of noncriminal behavior on the part of children should be taken out of legal courtroom jurisdiction. Chief Judge David L. Bazelon of the U.S. Court of Appeals for the District of Columbia advised a conference of juvenile court judges in 1970: "... We ought to stop fooling ourselves and the community. You ought to tell the community that you are failures—yes, failures at preventing delinquency and crime. As long as the community views you as a prevention agency and refers its social and behaviorial problems to you, the root problems will not be attacked." Former Juvenile Judge Ted Rubin agrees with Judge Bazelon. He feels that the amount of time and funds devoted by the courts to status offenders is counterproductive and a waste of the courts' resources needed to help the delinquent with serious offenses.

Still others strongly disagree. Many good, progressive judges like Lindsay Arthur of Minneapolis feel they belong in the court, where there is power to decree treatment if the family refuses. Judge Lindsay has stated: "I simply and strongly suggest, let's not phase out the courts [for status offenders] until we have phased in the new alternatives, and let's have the court as a backstop for those who refuse the new alternatives." Other judges, agreeing with Lindsay, feel that current status offense laws give the judges power to keep a child's record somewhat clean. For example, if a boy runs away from home and steals a car, the judge can, if he sees fit, charge him only as a runaway.

In the early 1960's California took the lead in separating delinquents from status offenders. The law was divided into three sections: Section 601 dealt with noncriminal conduct; Section 600 dealt with dependency/neglect statutes; Section 602 with criminal conduct, commonly known as delinquency. Other states followed suit. In 1963, New York created a new juvenile code and the legal "baby" PINS. Illinois was next in line with MINS (Minors in Need of Supervision). As of this writing, about half the states have similar classifications. In the other half, the child is still legally known as a delinquent, his status offense category making no difference to his keepers.

During the last few years Pennsylvania, Maryland, Massachusetts, Texas and New Jersey have moved beyond simple classification and made it mandatory that status offenders not be incarcerated in penal facilities. Unfortunately however, a closer look at those states reveals, for example, that juvenile court judges in Pennsylvania still have the option to incarcerate as a last resort. And they do. Chip Ashwell, head of the Westfield Detention Center in Massachusetts, told me that the new law "is a mere change of labels and the formalization of a judicial process which locks children into the system."

Others, agreeing with Chip Ashwell, call the new labels and legal separation a "cruel hoax," because courts, communities and states have not provided commitments necessary for alternative models. New York State, as mentioned earlier, is the classic example of weaving an elaborate veil of deception for over a decade.

Former Juvenile Judge Ted Rubin would like to see the courts get out of the status offense business. But he is a realist; he knows the vested interest involved. Of one million youths who came before juvenile courts in 1972, well over one third were status offenders. They also constitute 30 to 50 percent of the population in detention centers, county jails and training schools. We are talking about many jobs, professional careers and millions of dollars cut from budgets and earmarked for new, alternative programs. In 1970 alone the cost of operating and maintaining public institutions (state training schools) for delinquent children reached an estimated $291.9 million. Imagine the electrifying economic ramifications if all those youngsters who have committed no crimes were suddenly eliminated.

I was not, therefore, surprised when a young assistant attorney general told me how political forces in Washington State were organized to kill legislation that would have benefited status offenders. New Hampshire's lower house also passed legislation that was killed by vested self-interest groups in the senate. The same story again and again throughout the country—the penal industry perpetuated by hapless children and supported by the taxpaying public.

In California, Sacramento County's probation department teamed up with the Center on the Administration of Criminal Justice at the Davis Campus of the University of California for an interesting experiment. The university provided staff specially trained as "crisis intervention teams" to work with status offenders for four days and nights of the week. Their purpose was to help the child avoid penal detention and formal court petition if possible—in short, to provide community help to troubled youth. The remaining three days and nights of the week, regular Sacramento County probation officers performed normal court procedures for the same type of child.

Up to this time about 30.4 percent of referred youths received formal petitions. During the experimentation, only 2.2 percent of the status offenders under care and supervision of the university received court petitions as compared with 21 percent by the other group. In the first month, only 9 percent of the project youths were detained in Juvenile Hall as compared with 61.2 percent handled the usual way. Seven months after the project was terminated, 35 percent of the project youths had been rebooked for either status offenses or delinquency. The regular group had a 45.5 percent failure rate. Cost studies done at the conclusion showed "significant probation department savings"; yet there are few counties in the country currently offering anything that resembles the University of California's program.

"The path from dependency-neglect to delinquency to crime is well worn," Joe Rowen, Florida's new state director of youth services, told the Miami *Herald* on February 26, 1973. The fact that 75 percent of all adult prisoners now serving time started on that path in the juvenile court system would bear out Rowen's statement. One such person wrote in a letter to the editor of a Baltimore newspaper in the spring of 1973:

> I am currently serving a 25 year sentence for armed robbery and burglary. My criminal career began at the Maryland Training School for Boys, where I was committed for the henious crime of truancy. ...At the training school, I soon learned to steal a car...how to mug someone so they could not make an outcry, how to use celluloid to open a house door, how to make checks to see whether people were at home before a burglary, how to make up and use a burglar's kit and various other little things necessary to a successful criminal career.

Ralph Johnson, head of the educational department at Southern Ohio Correctional Facility, wrote the following letter to me in March of 1973:

> Many of the residents whom we come in contact with at Lucasville, have been in and out of state institutions since early childhood. For instance, one of our students who is in his early twenties was committed to a juvenile home when he was nine years old for disobedience. While confined, he tried to run away several times. Subsequent additions to his original sentence were tacked on and it wasn't until he was 16 or 17 that he was released for his original offense. From there he was educated in petty crime and unsuccessfully tried to practice it, which in turn led to his present 10–25 year sentence for armed robbery.

Three men with whom I talked at the Adult State Correctional Institution in Camp Hill, Pennsylvania, traced their criminal lives back to school problems, incorrigibility and truancy. The same was true with Richard Dye of Portland, Maine. First incarcerated for truancy, he was released fourteen years later. He hit a guard when he was fifteen, so personnel transferred him to the adult prison without even touching base with the courts.

In Philadelphia three sociologists did a mammoth study for the University of Pennsylvania—"Delinquency in a Birth Cohort"— which examined the criminalization of youngsters who reach the courts. Their subjects were boys, all born in Philadelphia. Their histories were traced from the eighth to eighteenth birthdays, and their contacts with the police, the juvenile courts and juvenile institutions were determined. In conclusion the research indicted the juvenile justice system, especially where the noncriminal child is concerned:

> Not only do a greater number of those who receive punitive treatment [institutionalization, fine or probation] continue to violate the law, but they also commit more serious crimes wih greater rapidity than those who experience a less constraining contact with judicial and correctional systems. Thus, we must conclude that the juvenile justice system, at its best, has no effect on the subsequent behavior of adolescent boys and, at its worst, has a deleterious effect on future behavior.

A recent California legislative report also questioned many assumptions concerning the disposition of status offenders:

> ... no one can prove that truants who became wards of the court end up better educated than those who do not. No one can show that promiscuous teenagers who are institutionalized have fewer illegitimate children than those who are not. Nor can anyone show that runaways who become wards of the court end up leading better adjusted lives than those who do not. Finally, no one can prove that unruly, disobedient minors who come under court supervision end up in prison less often than those who do not.

The state of Connecticut is a classic example of how we create criminals. In 1971, state correctional officials agreed that 30 percent of the children (roughly half of whom were classified status offenders) did not belong in their penal institutions. Bill Cockerham of the Hartford *Courant* did two stories, one in 1971, another in 1973. In the first, he disclosed that more than half the inmates from Meriden's training school ended up as adults in the hands of the police. Statistics from the Connecticut Department of Corrections showed that 23.9 percent of the youths at Cheshire Reformatory, and more than 10 percent of the adult population at Somers Prison, had spent time at Meriden. In 1973, Cockerham reported that 75 percent of the Connecticut adult prison population were rearrested after release.

Red O'Heal, a parolee from the Connecticut prison system, told me this story concerning a man in his forties, one of the most vicious, violent inmates now serving time in Somers, an adult maximum prison. The man was about seven years old, from a broken home and charged with truancy, when he came to Meriden School. As time passed he became a chronic runaway and car thief. Each escape added to his term and escalated his anger and rebelliousness, so he was transferred to Cheshire Reformatory for hardened, dangerous juveniles. There he beat up a guard and was given twenty-five years. But he escaped again and stole another car, which he wrecked. He was transferred to the adult prison at Somers with a notorious reputation for violence. Recently he knifed an inmate to death and threw him off a tier. And so the training schools of this country "rehabilitated" a hooky player into a violent aggressor and murderer.

Stanley Eldridge was eight years old when he ran away to his aunt's house, hid in her closet and, "trying to be cool," lit a cigarette and caught the clothes on fire. Stanley was institutionalized. Thirteen years later he was released from Rikers Island. Eldridge, now working with the Fortune Society in New York and author of a recently published book of poetry, reminisced about those early years: "... it didn't make sense to commit a petty crime. The judge usually gave you the maximum sentence out of contempt. No one bailed you out and fellow cons either ignored you or tolerated you. So what one did was listen to tales of bank jobs and felonious assaults and shootouts and write yourself a script and find out where to cop a piece when you hit the streets."

One of Eldridge's published poems would have had special meaning for an Irish boy from South Boston named Walter Elliott. The poem is entitled "Return Me to My Mind."

At age twelve, Walter Elliott was taken into custody for stealing a few candy bars and living alone in an abandoned factory. His mother was dead, his father was a disturbed alcoholic. A sympathetic caseworker recommended that because of his family situation, Walter needed someone to act as a "big brother," that he needed a tutor because he could not read or write and that someone should counsel the boy's father. The judge ignored the recom-

mendations and committed Walter Elliott to the Lyman School
for Boys.

> Return me to my mind
> let me snuggle up and rest . . .

In the early 1950's, Lyman was an extremely brutal place and
Walter reacted in a normal fashion: He ran away. He was caught
and confined to the discipline cottage, where harsh treatment inflicted humiliation and physical pain. He was beaten and forced
to "pull down his pants, spread his cheeks and show his brains."
He ran several more times; the disciplinary procedure was repeated. Finally he was placed on parole but shortly thereafter was
back at Lyman for being present at a gang fight. More runs and
lockups ensued.

He was paroled a second time but again incarcerated, this time
for being a passenger in a stolen car. Another escape from Lyman
prompted a transfer to the Shirley Industrial School, where yet
again he ran. Now he was placed in their discipline cottage for
nine months. In solitary confinement, there was no program, no
movement, no sound; he could speak only when spoken to.

> Return me to my mind
> let me snuggle up and rest
> among the darkness
> like the cell I know so well . . .

He ran again from Shirley so was transferred to the Institute for
Juvenile Guidance at Bridgewater, Massachusetts. He was kept in
the high-walled segregation unit for one year.

Free again, he went with several boys to Connecticut, where
Walter Elliott got into serious trouble. One of the group (not
Elliott) held a knife to a driver's throat and stole his car. The
charges this time were major—kidnapping and assault. Walter
was sent to Concord adult prison, where he unsuccessfully attempted to escape. He was placed in solitary confinement, where
he led a small revolt and punched a guard in the mouth with his
fist. Authorities transferred the boy. When he arrived at Walpole's
maximum adult prison, he went to cell block ten—solitary confinement for another year. He was seventeen years old at the time.

> Return me to my mind
> let me snuggle up and rest
> among the darkness
> like the cell I know so well
>
> When past was nothing frustrating
> where nothing is better . . .

They kept him in prison till his mid-twenties. He was dangerous and mentally disturbed when he re-entered society. However, he fell in love and married. The bride's name was Katherine King. His happiness was short-lived. Found at the scene of two murders in the public housing project where he lived, he was quickly convicted of murder. Within months Elliott was back in Walpole prison on two consecutive life sentences.

The night before he murdered two prison guards, Walter Elliott gathered some Irish records and a record player from other inmates. He placed them in a room. The next day when Katherine came to visit, he pulled a gun and shot the two officers he told fellow inmates he would kill. Though armed, the Elliotts made no attempt to leave the prison but went to the room he had prepared the night before and barricaded themselves. There Walter Elliott and his wife made love, and while Irish music filled the room, they ended their lives.

> Return me to my mind
> let me snuggle up and rest
> among the darkness
> like the cell I know so well
>
> When past was nothing frustrating
> where nothing is better
> where no rush decided nothing
> where no age perceived.

PART TWO/Pathways to Oblivion

My home town is jail house city,
Police took me from my mama's titty.
I got no thought and got no pity.
Your society treated me mighty shitty.

—Charles M. Manson

4 / No Name Maddox: Case History of Charles Manson

Charles Manson was thirty-five years old when he stood trial for the Sharon Tate–LaBianca murders. The macabre multimurders and the trial that convicted Manson commanded national media attention. So absorbing was the story that even Richard Nixon, President of the United States, found time in August of 1970 to say, "Here is a man who was guilty, directly or indirectly, of eight murders. Yet here is a man who, as far as the coverage is concerned, appeared to be a glamorous figure."

Today, Manson sits in a maximum security cell at San Quentin Prison in northern California. What was called one of the most baffling and horrifying murder cases of this century is now well-known history. What is not well known is the early childhood of Charles Manson and the effect of some twenty-two years spent in more than a dozen penal institutions.

Manson was born to sixteen-year-old Kathleen Maddox on November 12, 1934, in Cincinnati. His mother was allegedly violated by a Colonel Scott, so Charlie's birth certificate read: "No Name Maddox." Two years later Kathleen Maddox filed a bastard suit in Boyd County, Kentucky, and the father agreed to a judgment of twenty-five dollars and a five-dollar-a-month support for the child. She later married a William Manson, and gave his name to the illegitimate boy—Charles Milles Manson.

During the first few years of his life, Charlie was bounced between the care of his grandmother and maternal aunt because his mother, leaving the baby with neighbors "for an hour," would disappear for days and weeks at a time. In 1939, Kathleen and her brother were arrested for armed robbery when they knocked a service station attendant unconscious with a Coke bottle. She was sentenced to five years in the West Virginia State Penitentiary. Manson also went to West Virginia, to live with an aunt and uncle, who, he later told prison authorities, had a "difficult marriage until they found religion... and became very extreme." During this time, he started school.

Charlie was eight years old when his mother was released from prison. The youngster then began to live with a long line of "uncles," who, like his mother, drank heavily. Home was an assortment of run-down hotel rooms, where many times Charlie was forced to stay alone all day. He ran away, but returned.

Manson was next placed with foster parents for about a year—perhaps the best situation of his young life. But it was short-lived. His mother moved to Indianapolis with a salesman and sent for her son. A later report would state: "Manson received little attention from his mother and from the many men who were reputed to have lived with her."

In 1947 his mother tried to place him in another foster home, but there was none available. So Charlie became a ward of the county, who sent the unwanted boy to his first of many institutions, the Gibault Home for Boys in Terre Haute, Indiana. His record* there revealed: "Poor institutional adjustment... his attitude toward schooling was at best only fair... during the short lapses when Charles was pleasant and feeling happy, he presented a likable boy... a tendency towards moodiness and a persecution complex." (Mrs. Angles McMoney, a volunteer at his second institution in Plainfield who tried to help Manson, told me:

---

* Limited information obtained by District Attorney and by author Vincent Bugliosi of *Helter-Skelter*, W. W. Norton, New York, 1974.

"He was very quiet, very shy, didn't want anything to do with anyone else." Teachers said, "He professed no trust in anyone.")

After ten months at Gibault, Manson ran away to his mother, who again rejected him. (This "return-rejection" pattern was to persist right up to the time of the Tate–LaBianca murders.)

Manson now drifted toward a life of crime. From the take of burglarizing a grocery store, he was able to rent a room. Later, however, he was caught stealing a bike and sent to the Juvenile Center in Indianapolis. He escaped but was apprehended and sent to Father Flanagan's Boys Town. Four days into that institution, he and another boy stole an old Plymouth and made it to a ditch in Johnsonville, Iowa. Along the way, they committed two armed robberies—a gambling casino and a grocery store. They hitched the rest of the way to the other boy's uncle—a World War II disabled veteran, who tutored them in "slipping through skylights." Their first take was $1,500; the second time they were arrested. Manson was still only thirteen.

He was incarcerated at the Indiana Boys School at Plainfield. He stayed three years and attempted to run away eighteen times. On his nineteenth try, with two other youths, Charles Manson finally made good his escape from the thousand-acre youth jail with its own cemetery of over 135 graves. Stealing cars and burglarizing gas stations for transportation and support, they headed for California but were stopped near Beaver, Utah, at a roadblock set up for another robbery suspect. Crossing state lines with a stolen car is a federal offense (Dyer Act). Sixteen-year-old Manson was now under federal jurisdiction and was sent to the National Training School for Boys in Washington, D.C., to which he was sentenced to stay until he reached twenty-one.

In the late fall of 1974 I visited the Gibault Home in Terre Haute. The Catholic brothers there declined to discuss Manson and were embarrassed that he had ever been under their care. They told me it would take approval by the board of trustees for me to review his record. I was, however, given the opportunity to tour the facilities and see some of the buildings and grounds where Manson, the neglected child of thirteen, had been forced to live. I was struck by the old dormitories where the boys slept. Eight beds lined the walls and in the middle of one end of the room was a toilet within a windowed structure resembling a telephone booth. I also learned that discipline was meted out via the rod. I don't know how severe the beatings were. No one was talking.

When the Manson murder story broke, the Indiana Boys School at Plainfield refused anyone in the media permission to see his file in its entirety. So again, very little is known about Manson's treatment during a critical time of his young life. An enterprising New Yorker offered superintendent Al Bennett a good price if he would review and reveal the records, but Bennett declined. However, when I visited the Indiana school, Bennett did tell me that when Manson or any inmates ran, they were beaten, then thrown into solitary. He showed me the leather straps that were used. They were 26 inches long, 3 inches wide and ½ inch thick. The handles were stained from sweat, the ends worn thin by those who administered the beatings. The youngsters who were to be disciplined were placed on wooden racks at an appointed time (4 P.M.) "with their ass up in the air." The big debate was "should they beat the boys with their trousers on or off." When the leather strap had no effect, the guards would "take them out in the cornfield and beat the piss out of them."

According to the superintendent, records hidden from press and public reveal that on several occasions Manson was beaten so severely that he received treatment at a local hospital. Many years too late, in January of 1974, the United States Court of Appeals for the Seventh Circuit ruled on the Indiana Boys School:

> In beating the juveniles, a "fraternity paddle" between ½" to 2" thick, 12" long, with a narrow handle was used. There is testimony that juveniles weighing about 160 lbs. were struck five blows on the clothed buttocks, often by a staff member weighing 285 lbs. . . . It is . . . constitutionally cruel and unusual punishment.

It was also at Plainfield that Charles Manson was first homosexually attacked and raped. Thereafter he too engaged in homosexuality.

From Manson's records at the National Training School for Boys, Washington, D.C., a profile emerged: Though he had had four years of schooling, he was illiterate, with an IQ of 109. His first caseworker found him a "sixteen year old boy who has had an unfavorable family life, if it can be called a family life at all" and "aggressively antisocial." Three months later: "It appears that this boy is a very emotionally upset youth who is definitely in need of some psychiatric orientation."

Still, during the early years in the training school, a psychiatrist noted that though Charles Manson had a number of strikes against him, he hadn't quite given up on the world: "Because of a marked degree of rejection, instability, and psychic trauma—because his sense of inferiority in relationship to his mother was so pronounced, he constantly felt it necessary to suppress any thoughts about her. However, because of his diminutive stature, his illegitimacy, and the lack of parental love, he is constantly striving for status with the other boys . . . has developed certain facile techniques for dealing with people, those for the most part consist of a good sense of humor and an ability to ingratiate himself. . . . This could add up to a fairly slick institutionalized youth, but one is left with the feeling that behind all this lies an extremely sensitive boy who has not yet given up in terms of securing some kind of love and affection from the world."

In a special progress report during Charlie's stay at the National Training School, the following entry was made in his file:

He got along fairly satisfactory at the school although it was felt that he might be a custody risk unless something could be done to work out his feelings of depression and moodiness. He had a fairly good attitude and was cooperative when not in a depressed mood.

Shortly thereafter, officials at the National Training School decided that the Natural Bridge Honor Camp, a minimum security institution, would be the best possible place for the youth. Three weeks later he turned seventeen and was visited by his aunt, Mrs. W. L. Thomas of McMechen, West Virginia, who promised him a home and employment if he was released to her supervision. Manson was due for a parole hearing three months later, and with his aunt's offer his chances for release were very good. However, one month before the hearing, he pressed a razor blade against a fellow inmate's throat and sodomized him.

For that offense Manson was transferred to the federal reformatory at Petersburg, Virginia, and classified as dangerous. He became more and more involved in homosexual acts and inceasingly entered into institutional mayhem. He served time in solitary confinement for "stealing food from the kitchen, shirking his assigned duties in the kitchen, fighting with another inmate, etc." During this time he had no visits from anyone and received only a few letters from his aunt and mother.

Finally officials felt that for the protection of Manson as well as others, it would be best to transfer him to a more secure prison, the federal reformatory at Chillicothe, Ohio. He arrived on September 23, 1952, and by now it was written: "in spite of his age, he is criminally sophisticated." And later: he "... has no foresight for the future, is thoroughly institutionalized and doesn't appear to be the type that will take advantage of the opportunities afforded him." The report concluded: "He has been a neglected child all his life."

Manson's conduct improved at Chillcothe, however, and he was granted parole on May 8, 1954. He was nineteen. He went to live with his aunt in McMechen, where he married seventeen-year-old Rosalie Jean Willis in early 1955. He worked at a number of odd jobs, from busboy to parking-lot attendant. During this time he saw his mother briefly.

He began to hustle cars, two of which he took across state lines, and was arrested again for violation of the Dyer Act. He pleaded guilty in a federal court and requested medical assistance by telling a judge: "I was released from the Federal Penitentiary in Chillicothe, Ohio, in 1954 and having been confined for nine years, I was badly in need of psychiatric treatment. I was mentally confused and stole a car as a means of mental release from the confused state of mind that I was in."

The judge had Dr. Edwin McNeil examine Manson on October 26, 1955, in the Los Angeles county jail. The psychiatrist commented on both Manson's early family life and his years of incarceration: "It is evident that he has an unstable personality and that his environmental influences throughout most of his life have not been good. . . . This boy is a poor risk for probation; on the other hand, he has spent nine years in institutions with apparently little benefit except to take him out of circulation."

Manson told the psychiatrist he had spent so much time in institutions that he never really learned much of what real life on the outside was all about. Commenting on his wife, Charlie said: "She is the best wife a guy could want. I didn't realize how good she was until I got in here. I beat her at times. She writes to me all the time. She is going to have a baby." He opined that since he was about to become a father, it was important for him to be with his wife on the outside. "She is the only one I have ever cared about in my life." Perhaps it was Rosalie Jean Willis who touched Manson when he wrote the following lines to the presiding judge:

> Only walls of your prisons
> Is all I've ever seen
> I run away from your cities
> My brothers who are so mean.
>
> Once I did see the sun
> Where the eagle flies
> I look at the agony of my world
> And all the love that dies.

The judge placed Manson on probation for five years.

But Manson still had another charge to face—auto theft in Florida. A hearing was set, but he skipped town. A warrant was issued; he was arrested and sentenced to three years at Terminal Island, San Pedro, California. The new father held his baby son in the courtroom just before he left for prison.

At Terminal Island, a caseworker observed: "We have here a young man who comes from a very unfavorable background, has no worthwhile family ties and has been subjected to institutional treatment since early childhood. He is an almost classic textbook case of the correctional institution inmate.... His is a very difficult case and it is impossible to predict his future adjustment with any degree of accuracy."

In April of 1957, "the only one I have ever cared about in my life" ceased to visit Manson. His mother brought the news that his wife was living with another man. Charlie attempted to escape from the minimal custody unit to which he had been transferred. A parole committee commented: "This episode, however, is in keeping with the pattern he has exhibited from early childhood of attempting to evade his responsibilities by running away" and refused parole. Rosalie then filed for divorce, which was granted in

1958. She was given custody of their child. Manson has never seen either of them again.

Now, because his institutional conduct and behavior became intolerable to prison officials—he would not dress properly and "contraband[ed] food"—the man was placed in "punitive segregation on a restricted diet for indefinite periods of time." His medical and psychiatric record revealed that he had now become totally dependent on institutional life and had anxiety over leaving the security of confinement. Bill Casey, an official at Terminal Island, told me during an interview that he felt Manson was a "real introvert, a loner and a quiet type—like a cat... strictly an institutionalized person who didn't want to leave prison." Casey said he was a little surprised at the violent behavior of Charlie Manson, but "when they grow up in institutions, they have a tendency toward violence. It gives them an identity and makes them somewhat of a hero, a leader, something they never were."

When released from prison, Manson quickly returned to the routine of stealing cars. He then started to pimp and he was arrested for trying to cash a stolen government check for $37.50. After a series of such episodes, Manson, at twenty-six, was back in jail, this time the United States penitentiary on McNeil Island, Washington. Staff evaluation summarized a neglected childhood and years of incarceration:

> The product of an emotionally disruptive formative period, Manson has never really reconciled the overt rejecting aspects of his maternal relationship and has functioned primarily in a dependent manner, hiding his loneliness, resentment, and hostility behind a facade of superficial ingratiation. In many respects, he has a childish need for acceptance without knowing how to go about securing such acceptance in an adult manner. He has commented that institutions have become his way of life and that he receives security in institutions which is not available to him in the outside world.

During his last five years of imprisonment before the Tate–La-Bianca murders, total institutionalization was effected. A second marriage, just prior to incarceration, to Leona Musser (1959) failed and terminated in divorce. It was now that Manson struck up a friendship with the last survivor of Ma Barker's gang, Alvin Karpis, who taught him to play the guitar, opening a whole new world to Charlie. He also developed a keen interest in scientology and, according to the annual progress report of the penitentiary, that interest "has led him to make a semi-professional evaluation of his personality which strangely enough, is quite consistent with the evaluations made by previous social studies." Another year, the report read: "Even these attempts and his cries for help represent a desire for attention, with only superficial meaning.... In view of his deep-seated personality problems ... continuation of institutional treatment is recommended."

Finally, in June of 1966, Charles Manson was transferred back to Terminal Island Prison in California for release. His last report read: "Manson is about to complete his ten-year term. He has a pattern of criminal behavior and confinement that dates to his teen years. This pattern is one of instability whether in free society or a structured institution community. Little can be expected in the way of change in his attitude, behavior or mode of conduct.... He has come to worship his guitar and music ... has no plans for release as he says he has nowhere to go."

On the morning of his release from prison, Charles Manson begged his jailers to allow him to remain: "Prison has become my home"; he doubted he could "adjust to the world outside." His request was denied. On March 21, 1967, Manson hit the free world and drifted into the Haight-Ashbury section of San Francisco. There the Manson family, which was to terrorize and take the lives of forty-odd people, was born.

Manson did not choose his own pathway to oblivion and crime. It was charted for him, first by parental abandonment, and then, in a far greater sense, by the massive failure of the correctional system, particularly those in charge of juvenile offenders. Manson was the product of too many impersonal institutions, too many endless days in solitary confinement, too many sexual assaults by older boys and far too many beatings by guardians and institutional personnel. The U.S. Court of Appeals, which ruled the use of wooden paddles cruel and unusual punishment, also documented the destructiveness of beating: "... the practice does not serve as useful punishment or as treatment, and it actually breeds counter-hostility, resulting in a greater aggression by a child."

A review of all Manson's prison records reveal some interesting facts: Of twenty-two years in prison, seventeen were spent in federal facilities for crimes that, under state jurisdiction, would carry sentences totaling less than five years. There was never once a serious treatment program for young Manson. At the federal reformatory at Petersburg, Virginia, his rehabilitation program consisted of helping in the kitchen; he bitterly opposed being enrolled in elementary school, so he never showed up after the first class. Also he was always physically "fit for regular duty," and reports consistently recommended that he "continue on the same program." But what was the program?

The Chillicothe federal reformatory listed his treatment as follows:

Medical:	Fit for regular duty
Athletics:	No restrictions
Psychiatric:	Not indicated at this time
Employment:	Foundry
Education:	Voluntary enrollment
Religion:	Routine contact
REMARKS:	"Because of this man's history of vicious homosexual assaults, he was given Close Custody and assigned to Cell House #1."

Although Manson had held a razor blade against the throat of an inmate and sodomized him, no psychiatric help was "indicated." Treatment for Charles was "Close Custody" and "continue on same program."

Manson and the countless thousands of children locked away from society during the late forties and fifties became part of the bitter harvest of crime this country reaped in the late sixties and early seventies. What of future children? According to the FBI's annual report, more than 80,000 children under ten were arrested in 1972. Charges were placed against 585,000 children between eleven and fourteen years of age. Without proper treatment, without proper care and education, how many future Charles Mansons will emerge from these statistics? How many, in a new harvest of failure, will echo the words Charles Manson spoke just before being convicted of murder?

... I haven't decided yet what I am or who I am. I was given a name and a number and I was put in a cell and I have lived in a cell with a name and a number.... I never went to school, so I never growed up in the respect to learn, to read and write too good. So I stayed in that jail and I have stayed stupid, and I have stayed a child while I have watched your world grow up.... I have ate out of your garbage cans to stay out of jail. I have wore your second-hand clothes. I have done my best to get along in your world and now you want to kill me.... Ha! I'm already dead, have been dead all my life. I've lived in your tomb that you built. I did seven years for a $37.50 check. I did 12 years because I didn't have any parents.... When you were out riding your bicycle, I was sitting in your cell looking out the window and looking at pictures in magazines and wishing I could go to high school and go to the proms, wishing I could go to the things you could do, but oh so glad, oh so glad, brothers and sisters, that I am what I am.

School I no like. Cannot understand. Teacher say,
"I too busy," I no like go. I think, forget school,
man. So I no go. Social worker find me, take me
back school. Vice Principal say, "You punk kid. You
nothing but trouble, you no go school, we no want
you. You expel." Crazy, man. I no go school, go
back because man say best, then school kick out.
Crazy.

—Incarcerated youth, Hawaii

5/Life Imprisonment for Delinquents: Walls of Illiteracy and IQ Testing

The typical educational profile of incarcerated
children is definitely one of underachiever in the
public school system. Victims of outdated laws,
they, like preceding generations, fall prey to a
merciless class structure that almost insures learning failure, antisocial conduct and, finally, life
behind the walls of our juvenile and adult penal
institutions. Here more than 80 percent of them
are locked within yet another prison whose walls
are more formidable, whose confinement is more
restrictive and whose sentence is harsh and un-
just. The walls are the printed word, the confinement is the inability to read and the life sentence
is that imposed by an arbitrary judge—American
Education. The records of these children are
marked for life—mild to borderline retardation.

After assessing the reading levels of juvenile
inmates in twenty-four states, I found that clearly

these youngsters are crippled in the most basic skill—reading. Their average age is fourteen, but their reading ability is approximately fourth-grade level, which sets their IQ at around 80–85.* A devastating fact, if based on the IQ scale compiled by the American Association on Mental Deficiency, which regards 80 as borderline retardation. Nor has there been any change in the average IQ score of incarcerated youths for the last fifty years. Findings by Slawson in 1926, Durea in 1935 and Durea and Taylor in 1948 revealed findings identical to mine in 1974!

The IQ test itself discriminates against every segment of America but middle-class white children. The WISC (Wechsler Intelligence Scale for Children) test was standardized in 1940 on 2,200 urban-rural white children. The same was true with Stanford-Binet and Peabody Picture Vocabulary Test. Not one black, Puerto Rican, Mexican-American or American Indian was included on the original test, which serves as the basis for measuring IQ in many of our juvenile institutions.

For instance, in state facilities that broke down their IQ scores for me by both sex and race, the difference between blacks and whites ranged from 7 to 18 points.

State	*Race-Sex-IQ Score*	
Tennessee	Black Male:	76
	White Male:	84
	Black Female:	76
	White Female:	83
Arkansas	Black Male:	76
	White Male:	94
Nebraska	Black Male:	83.1
	White Male:	100.5
Michigan	Black Male:	80
	White Male:	95
Louisiana	Black Male:	74
	White Male:	90
Texas	Black Male:	80
	White Male:	95.3

* My own state-by-state information on IQ's is supported by two separate studies. It was established in one survey that 78 percent of New Orleans' jailed youths had an IQ below 83. In Boonville, Missouri, an academic profile of inmates at the training school for boys showed their IQ norm as 80, while 61 percent of the students scored below 79.

Within the academic world the validity of current IQ testing is argued in two schools of thought. The first is represented by Nobel Prize-winner (for his invention of the transistor) Dr. William B. Shockley and by Dr. Arthur Jensen of Harvard University, who hold that low IQ among blacks is an inherited weakness. At variance with Shockley's and Jensen's view are educational leaders like Dr. Jerome Kagan of Harvard, Dr. Leon Kamin of Princeton and Dr. Jay Samuels of the University of Minnesota, who feel the problem is caused not by generic inheritance but rather by the destructive environment into which many blacks and other poor people in general are born.

Dr. Samuels has done massive research on the subject and reasons: "Most teachers in ghetto schools in this country do not have high expectations for their students and the students generally fail to succeed. In a real sense, a self-fulfilling prophecy seems to be working." Dr. Samuels found an exception to this in a black ghetto school in the heart of Kansas City, Missouri, most of whose students read at national norm. Their IQ's are comparable to those of middle-class white Americans.

Complementing Samuels' findings are those of anthropologist Peggy Sanday of the University of Pennsylvania and psychologist Dr. Ruth Rice. Peggy Sanday plotted the IQ scores of 2,000 children in the Pittsburgh public schools from 1962 to 1970. The intelligence quotient of black students in largely segregated schools worsened year after year, from kindergarten to eighth grade, while blacks attending middle-class white schools projected improved IQ's during the same period. Sanday concluded: "IQ's are simply a measure of what you need to do well in the mainstream culture of White middle-class America...."

Dr. Rice lived and worked for three months at the Tennessee State Training School for delinquent girls. She tested inmates who read poorly and found they had learning disabilities. A reading program was designed that took into consideration the girls' learning problems, and as their reading levels improved, so did their IQ's. Dr. Rice summarized her findings: "The positive relationship of reading score increases to IQ increases in some of the cases could be anticipated in view of results found in other similar studies. Still, considerable speculation could be made about the fact that the greater rises in reading (double or more than expected) were accompanied by the greatest rises in IQ."

Unfortunately, many teachers use IQ simply to prejudge a student's ability and give up immediately on those registered as slow or retarded, expecting nothing but difficulty from them. But IQ measurement is derived from the ability to read, and studies have shown that children of the poor are not taught to read properly. For example, disadvantaged adjudicated teen-agers in Georgia paralleled poor reading averages of 3.7 with IQ scores of 75. The same was true in Nevada, where poor readers and nonreaders were tested as "educationally deprived or mentally retarded." Youthful inmates from Philadelphia averaging fifteen years of age tested out at reading levels between first and second grade and IQ's of around 80.

What becomes obvious is the vicious circle of virtual mental genocide committed against certain segments of the population by those who devise IQ testing or promote its use. This tyranny of testing was recognized by the District of Columbia Circuit Court in 1967 when it held testing to be "in violation of plaintiffs' constitutional rights":

> The aptitude tests used to assign children to the various tracks are standardized primarily on White middle class children. Since these tests do not relate to the Negro and disadvantaged child, track assignment based on such tests relegates Negro and disadvantaged children to the lower tracks from which . . . escape is remote.

If one is to make a case of the causal relationship between poor reading/low IQ and the running afoul of the law, it is important to first touch upon the state of American Education. For it is within the educational system that the child experiences his first definable failures and consequently begins the journey down the antisocial path to penalization.

In December of 1969 the late Dr. James Allen, former United States Commissioner of Education, encouraged the President of the United States to announce a National Right to Read Effort because, he confessed, "one out of every four school children suffers from serious reading deficiencies." In 1974 the Washington, D.C., Right to Read Effort out of the U.S. Office of Education gave a major reason for the reading crisis in our schools: "Most teachers have never been taught how to teach reading!" Sixteen states do not require future elementary teachers to take any reading courses; another eighteen states require only a single course to qualify them for teaching reading.

Many experts have long felt that prevention is the best way to end juvenile delinquency. The institution that could best serve as an effective deterrent for delinquency—because there is no other with so many available resources—is the public school system. What a cruel disappointment then to find that detention facilities, county jails, state training schools and private institutions are the dumping grounds for many American schools today. In the words of Superior Court Judge Alfred O. Holte, from Everett, Washington: "Angry failures ... non-learners provide an excellent source of raw material for our system of justice.... The frustrations these children face cause them to drop out, to turn to drugs, to act out, to reinforce and continue their delinquency patterns until they are institutionalized.... A child forced by law to attend school but who cannot read and write well enough to accomplish his work is being warped and destroyed by the system designed to benefit him."

It is a fact that youth correctional facilities enjoy their lowest inmate population when the children are in the streets during the summer months. Most delinquency occurs during regular school time. This point is supported in a study compiled by sociologist Eloise Snyder while working in the family court of Richland County, South Carolina. Ms. Snyder found that the lowest cases of delinquency occurred between May and September. From October to April the cases doubled. The same is true in Maryland and in the city of San Francisco.

Is there a correlation between the inability to read and future delinquency? I am convinced that there is and my conviction is based on a complex of attitudes and platitudes ingrained in our educational system. For the child who falls behind, who experiences the humiliation of homogeneous or track or special placement and hears such words as "dumb," "retarded," "nonreader" and "failure" follow him from kindergarten to high school or whatever grade at which he drops out (the U.S. Office of Education states about one million such children drop out of school yearly), the damage to his self-esteem is almost certainly irreversible. These years of educational failure shatter the self-confidence of the child. Failure leads to frustration and hopelessness, which in turn can lead to aggressiveness. Acts of aggression, mild or violent, if detected by the schools, police, parents or an associated agency, could well mean incarceration for the child.

In 1973, at the Lansing Boys Training School in Michigan and the Red Wing Boys Training School in Minnesota, Dr. Dennis L. Hogenson researched each boy's reading skills, IQ scores, his complete family history and police court records. Hogenson made confidential reports on each boy. His findings revealed "that in both training school populations, reading failure was the only variable found to be related to aggression in delinquent boys.... The kid that was No. 1 in meanness also was No. 1 in reading failure." The meanness to which Dr. Hogenson referred, now circles most of our large cities with fear—assault, arson, major vandalism and sadistic acts directed against peers. Those children who do not take out their aggressions on others turn inward and the end result, according to Hogenson, is mental illness.

I attempted in five different states to obtain the reading levels of each criminal offender at one adult prison and one juvenile training school, but the information was not available for many and various reasons. In Ohio and Arizona, even with the assistance of the governor's office, my efforts were futile. I feel strongly, however, that if the data were forthcoming, a definite relationship between low verbal skills and serious violent crimes would be apparent.

At the Tennessee State Training School for girls, where reading skills were improved, Dr. Rice made the following comment:

> The staff noted less hostile and aversive behavior and a more positive cohesiveness among the ten subjects, demonstrated by their expressing more feelings of joy and a more calm and friendly attitude. There was less abusive language, destructive behavior and fighting.

Truancy is one form of mild aggression. The youngster fails in his schoolwork and, not wanting to face that failure and with no seeming alternative, reacts by playing hooky. Unfortunately for the child, truancy is a violation of state law and punishable by indefinite incarceration. The Honorable J. McNary Spigner, a family court judge in Columbia, South Carolina, wrote the following letter to concerned citizens when he got tired of sending school truants to state training schools:

> It is apparent, that the Compulsory School Law and the suggested changes are not going to cure the truancy problem. *The problem is not a legal nor judicial problem; it is a school problem.* From what I have seen in this court, truancy, on the most part, results from the inability of the school system to offer courses to children so that all of them can succeed and grow toward responsibility. For the most part, it is an academically oriented system geared to capacities of the middle class child from a relatively stable home, whereas the needs of the culturally inept child from a poorly structured home environment are not met. The latter are the children who cannot succeed in school. These are the children who are truant; these are the children who become delinquent; these are the children who graduate into crime rather than from school.

In Cook County, Chicago, at the Thursday-morning truancy trials in juvenile court, I saw the very kinds of children to which Judge Spigner referred—children who could not read and would not attend school—being handcuffed and taken away in a police van to be institutionalized.

Numerous teachers I interviewed feel that truancy is not a school problem and that parents and children are solely responsible for school attendance, or, like the state commissioner of education for South Carolina, they believe it is a legal problem for the courts to settle. It seems, however, that if a child experiences basic educational failure day after day, the schools have a moral and professional responsibility to develop alternative programs within their curriculum which could provide new and creative opportunities to ensure the child's success. Instead, a $43 billion industry called American Education stands far removed from its lost children. School programs to provide counseling for students resorting to truancy or other antisocial behavior, programs to provide counseling and teaching for those already lost in the penal net, or programs to establish reorientation for incarcerated children returning to school are almost nonexistent.

Chief Judge David L. Bazelon of the United States Court of Appeals for the District of Columbia elucidated the attitude of the public schools toward the troubled child:

> Almost every juvenile court client has a poor school record—truancy, poor grades, misbehavior with teachers and classmates. What is the school's response now? Usually to single him out very early for the wrong kind of attention; bad marks, reprimands, petty scoldings and humiliations. Later come the special adjustment classes and twilight schools and suspensions and expulsions, finally the referrals to juvenile court. In between may come some sporadic, hurried and usually unsuccessful counseling. The child's miserable record follows him from teacher to teacher and becomes its own self-fulfilling prophecy.

In recent years this potentially destructive record-keeping has been further enhanced with the help of science. An ominous and little publicized educational program is reaching out in the form of a big brother police computer. The city of Baltimore, using federal and state monies, tested 4,500 children to detect potential or future delinquents—without the understanding or knowledge of their parents. This $72,000 pilot project, funded largely by LEAA (U.S. Justice Department's Law Enforcement Assistance Administration) was defended by school officials who feel that the data from the predelinquency testing can be used "to develop comprehensive programs to deal with children with either maladaptive behavioral or learning problems."

In California the project is more ambitious. Three Southern California counties are involved in the $2 million program, also funded in large part by LEAA. Social planners within this program believe it possible to identify future criminals when they first enter school at age five or six. On his official records, this "early detection measuring device for the propensity of a person to riot or commit a criminal act" will follow the child through his entire schooling and can even later be fed into a national centralized computer record! In San Diego County's "Simplified Analytical Methods of Behavioral Systemization," any child over the age of seven who is accused of commiting a crime becomes part of this new electronic record. Teachers who feel that a student is a problem, out of control or incorrigible to authority can feed his or her name into the computer. Truancy, breaking curfew and drinking beer are additional crimes that will haunt San Diego children for life.

Psychologists agree that people's behavior is congruous to the way they're treated. Santa Paula, California, calls its project "A Community-Based Modification Program for Pre-Delinquents." Will not the child called "predelinquent," as well as educators who pore over his records, soon begin to believe the label? If a child's normal acting-out of records is interpreted by educators as criminal behavior, he may well be treated accordingly, and tragically end up in the mold designed for him by social planners.

Equally frightening as the computer are the behavior-modifying amphetamines being administered by educators and psychiatrists to those 3 to 6 percent of American classroom children "suffering hyperkinetic problems" (hyperactivity). Two drugs being used, dextroamphetamine and Methylphenidate (Ritalin), are said to have extreme, hazardous effects on the health of children. Doctors Daniel Safer and Richard Allen of the Division of Child Psychiatry at Johns Hopkins University reported after two years of research that the use of dextroamphetamine has caused a "drop of 38% in weight and 25% reduction in height. Ritalin has also produced a 17% drop in growth and some weight loss over the same period of time." Researcher Donald M. Thompson of the Georgetown University Medical Center has documented that both drugs impair the learning process of pigeons. Ritalin has been banned in Sweden and Japan because of its ill effects on children.

Chicago pediatrician Robert Mendelsohn, who has been involved in a major law suit to prohibit Ritalin in this country, reported in *Medical World News* (April 1971): "What the school child needs is not a pill but a good teacher. Drugs represent depersonalization.... As public schools continue to deteriorate, there will be a growing conspiracy by doctors, parents, and teachers to use drugs to deaden the natural liveliness of more and more pupils." Dr. Mark Stewart of Washington University School of Medicine in St. Louis observed that too many of our school children are identified as hyperactive and that "it's ludicrous to believe they are all sick and need to be drugged." Dr. Thomas Szasz, professor of psychiatry from the State University of New

York Medical Center, wrote the National Legal Program on
Health Problems for the Poor:

> I consider the characterization of hyperactivity, in children some-
> times labeled the hyperkinetic syndrome, in the absence of ob-
> jectively demonstrable evidence of neurological malfunctioning, so
> absurd as not to deserve to be taken seriously. The labeling of such
> children as ill is a social strategy to justify controlling them by
> means of drugs.

In November of 1972, New York State officials were debating the
virtues of building a gymnasium at Attica Prison. A prisoner there,
R. Anthony Schettini, wrote of his disapproval in a letter to *The
New York Times*. The letter ended: "Give me an education and
to hell with the gym!"* The American taxpayer would do well to
heed Mr. Schettini's message. Rather than lock up truants and
incorrigibles, rather than create a big brother state for kindergarten
innocents, rather than control our youngsters with drugs, we who
foot the bill should demand education for all our children. And
that education must include, if nothing else, the ability to read.

"Reading is one of the liberating experiences of life," Dr.
Edward Meade of the Ford Foundation told American educators.
Following is a short summary of how that educational skill did,
indeed, liberate a young man from a possible future of crime and
violence.

Ken started his thirteen years of public education in kindergarten, in the small river town of Burlington, New Jersey. His
teacher thought him a bright boy, but eventually his elementary
education eroded whatever self-esteem he brought with him.
Taunts and jokes from peers about a speech impediment, which
went untreated until late in junior high, caused Ken to withdraw
increasingly until he was placed with slow students, who, like
himself, could barely read.

---

* The severity of poor educational skills among adult prisoners prompted
Chief Justice of the United States Warren E. Burger to say: "The percentage
of inmates in all institutions who cannot read or write is staggering.... The
figures on illiteracy alone are enough to make one wish that every sentence
imposed could include a provision that would grant release only when the
prisoner had learned to read and write."

Teachers told the boy's mother how dumb and slow he was and report cards recorded their professional predictions: in fifth grade he had seventeen F's. Failing assignments or tests were marked with F's as large as the paper itself. Psychological assaults from peers, neighbors and teachers fed the fire of frustration and hostility. Soon he was constantly in trouble and had become the class clown. He spent more and more time in the principal's office and in after-school detention. He destroyed books and classroom equipment and broke school windows. One seventh-grade teacher predicted the kid would end up in prison because of his rowdy behavior and attitude. The secondary principal informed Ken's mother that he had a vile temper, and expulsion was threatened. Ken beat up one classmate so badly the victim had to be taken to a hospital.

Later his vandalism spread to the streets. A hotel, movie house, yacht club, machine shop—all were his targets for breaking and entering. Streetlights were broken and arson lit the riverfront more than once. He was arrested at gun point in a small alley, a block away from his home, for stealing a neighbor's car. It was only through the efforts of his parents that a juvenile judge spared him imprisonment.

He graduated from high school and was denied employment at a soap factory because he couldn't read well enough to fill out the firm's application blank. Finally he became a construction laborer for a year, then was drafted into the army. To while away empty hours, he became a library assistant and slowly, painfully read his first book, and another and another. After two years in the service, he went back to his high school and said he wanted to go to college. They laughed at him.

His new wife didn't laugh, however, and helped tutor the young man till he graduated with honors from Glassboro State College in 1962. Burlington High School gave him a contract to teach— the same school from which he graduated with a folder stating his IQ was 78.

That boy, who knew the humiliation and bitter frustration of a crippling education, who was judged marginally retarded and who constantly broke the law, believes very strongly that there is a close relationship between poor reading ability and crime.

That boy became the author of this book.

Oh! Why does the wind blow upon me so wild?
Is it because I'm nobody's child?

—Phila H. Case

6/Dumping Grounds for the Retarded: Human Abuse and Experimentation

Mental retardation is that condition in which a child is slow to develop and to learn emotionally and intellectually and therefore, academically. In the mid-1960's there were 5½ million retarded people in the United States. Recent findings of the American Association on Mental Deficiency indicate that 90 percent of all mentally retarded persons can be classified as borderline or mildly retarded, the IQ range of which is 70–84 and 55–69 respectively. Those with an IQ or 40–54 are considered moderately retarded. IQ's of 25–39 are considered severely retarded; below 25, profoundly retarded. The two latter groups represent a small 5 percent of all those classified retarded.

As sophisticated as modern American society is, many of us still believe that institutionalization is the only course for all mentally retarded persons because they are nonfunctional. This is an unfortunate misconception. Many retarded persons lead virtually normal lives. Most are literate and can hold jobs under supervision; some can take care of their personal needs and perform simple tasks and may partially or wholly support themselves. Only the severely and profoundly retarded actually may require long-term professional care.

Why then are the retarded incarcerated? For the same reasons the status offenders are kept under lock and key. First, incarceration is a convenient out for parents who want to avoid responsibility* or disconcertion. Second, these retarded provide state bureaucrats with the needed raw material for jobs, professional power and massive operational budgets.

It should be made clear that there are many good facilities in the United States, both public and private, dedicated to serving the needs of the mentally retarded. But a large segment of the industry is rife with abuse and corruption. The retarded child, even more so than the normal youngster, cannot fend for himself when bombarded with the arsenal of institutional abuse that ranges from inhuman neglect to highly professional experimentation for the twin goals of scientific research and pharmaceutical profits. There is also the widespread and shocking policy of educators, social workers and state administrators who dump normal children in mental hospitals and facilities for the mentally retarded "as a last resort."

Far too often we find a mixed bag of children within institutions designed to help in areas other than where help is needed. I have seen hundreds of retarded children in jails and many normal children in mental hospitals or mental retardation facilities because the states either don't screen them properly or lack the resources to fill a child's needs. In Texas, for instance, I saw mentally normal youngsters who were blind or paralyzed confined with the severely retarded. In 1973 it was disclosed that two apparently normal Illinois children had spent six years in a Texas facility for the mentally retarded because the "state had sent the children to the wrong sort of facility."

In South Carolina, I found two hopelessly retarded boys in a Richland County jail with adults and derelicts detained for felonies and misdemeanors. The boys were jailed for allegedly

---

* Beverly Rowen, an attorney and fellow to the Joseph P. Kennedy Foundation for the Mentally Retarded, told me she gets many threats from parents to "stay away from my son or daughter." Ms. Rowen, an outstanding litigant for the retarded in Florida, feels "they're afraid they will find out their child is normal."

raping another retarded child, but while they awaited their fate, they in turn were repeatedly raped by the adults. South Carolina, one of the states exposed several years ago by Howard James in his book *Children in Trouble*, has since written a new Juvenile Code and has built a commendable diagnostic center where all children are tested and counseled in order to determine their treatment needs. In the wake of these reforms, however, increasingly large numbers of retarded children fill the penal facilities because the state lacks separate quarters.

Through the combined diligence of private citizens, lawyers, state legislators and foundations, this national dumping network is being exposed. As normal children emerge and tell their tales of institutional atrocities and bureaucratic incompetence, major litigation dealing with the constitutional rights of the mentally retarded is hitting courts around the country.

One suit in Pennsylvania (*Bartley* et al. *v. Haverford State Hospital* et al.) involved two normal children and contested the procedure of incarcerating a person without a hearing, without any voice in his commitment or without any means of obtaining release from a state mental hospital.

Another case is now pending in the U.S. District Court for the District of Iowa, where state officials, without supported evidence, declared the children of Charles and Darlene Alsager retarded. They seized the children in their home and placed them in the care of foster parents and a children's shelter, where they could "be raised by persons who could afford them a greater degree of stimulation and discipline."

Yet another case involved a normal Jamaican girl who came to this country with her mother. She took employment in a fine home on the North Shore in Chicago as a domestic worker and made arrangements to attend the New Trier Township East High School. Even though she was working and doing well in school, because she was on her own, the educators at the high school referred her to the state. Children Services took over and she quickly passed into near oblivion—to the Audy Home, to Elgin State Hospital and finally to a home for retarded children called Laurel Haven at Baldwin, Missouri. The following is part of her court transcript:

I was not retarded.... Most of the people were so retarded they
could not use the toilet themselves or feed or clothe themselves. I
was paid only $6.00 a week to clean bathrooms and teach the re-
tarded children how to talk and play.... They gave me painful
birth control shots and said it was necessary to regulate my cycle.
... I told them there was no reason why I should have to take a
pill.... They would strap me to a bed as a form of punishment.

She told how she and eleven other normal children sought help
from a visiting social worker from the Illinois Department of
Family Services, but "she was very angry at us and said we wasted
valuable time.... This was only a visit to see the staff."

The effectiveness of legal suits is minimal when one appreciates
the tight and complicated web of procedures that fosters these
destructive placement procedures. In Cook County, Illinois, Pat
Murphy, an Irish attorney with both intelligence and courage,
clashed with bureaucats on this very issue. After a lengthy battle
with the State Department of Corrections, Murphy litigated, resulting in the closing of Sheridan, an infamous youth penitentiary.
But he soon discovered that the Illinois Department of Children
and Family Services simply started using Elgin State Hospital, the
Chicago-Read Mental Health Center, the Tinley Park Mental
Health Center and private institutions for the retarded and
mentally ill, as placements for neglected children. At one hospital,
Murphy found that at least 80 percent of the children needed no
psychiatric care. In others, he found the figure at about 65 percent.

I made arrangements to meet Attorney Murphy during a
recess in the Texas Morales trial. We visited several institutions
in Dallas and San Antonio, where children, sent by the Illinois
Department of Children and Family Services, were housed. We
visited private facilities for the mentally retarded and compared
notes on our Illinois and Texas investigations. In Texas we saw
some of the worst forms of mental retardation and left the state
with profound admiration for those who love and work with children thus affected.

Murphy and I also left Texas with a deep resentment toward
the child entrepreneurs who are in the business to make a fast
buck. Dixie Jones, owner of the Dallas Child's Haven, told us
that a friend of hers who wanted to get into the business of caring
for the mentally retarded sent her brother to the city zoo to

measure animal cages so they could construct exact duplicates for
her future clients. That was my first initiation into the hellish
world of the retarded. Until then, most of my time had been spent
evaluating conditions within juvenile penal facilities only. But
Pat Murphy's work, along with the scandal I was uncovering in
Texas, would change all this. More visits and investigative digging
would reveal that the worst horrors are realized in these rarely
visited facilities. The beatings, the sexual abuses by staff and inmates, the deaths of retarded children, span the country from
Austin, Texas, to Lynchburg, Virginia, and on to the wooden
cages at Polk State School in Pennsylvania; from broomstick
beatings at Willowbrook, New York, to the Chicago-Read Mental
Center, where children are tied spread-eagle on bare steel bed
springs.

As described by Dr. Gunnar Dybwad in his testimony before
Federal Judge Frank M. Johnson in Alabama (*Wyatt v. Stickney*),
there are also the more subtle dehumanizing effects of locking
away the mentally retarded:

> I think if you walk through Partlow,* you can see it; you can see
> the effect—the people who begin to become involved in eccentric
> mannerisms, the rocking back and forth, peculiar behavior mech-
> anisms, the people who sit in a semi-stupor, the people who slowly
> deteriorate and turn to the simple elements of human behavior. . . .
> In other words, it is a deterioration. I would further add from my
> own observations, but not at Partlow, that we have ample docu-
> mentation in this country that individuals who come to institutions
> and can walk, stop walking, who come to institutions and can talk,
> will stop talking, who come to institutions and can feed themselves,
> will stop feeding themselves; in other words, in many other ways, a
> steady process of deterioration.

In late 1973, a few months after the Morales trial, E. M. Scott,
assistant commissioner for the Texas Department of Mental
Health and Mental Retardation, informed his board that the
department was "vulnerable" if a similar case was brought against
it. Vulnerable areas included "using physical force, placing inmates in solitary confinement, censoring inmate mail, failing to

---

* Partlow State Hospital in Alabama.

screen prospective staff personnel and the whole question of right to treatment." During the same period of time, a state organization of parents of retarded children told the taxpayers that every state school for the retarded was far below minimum national standards. Their director, David Sloan, chided state representatives, saying children were "literally dying because of extremely overcrowded and understaffed child care facilities."

Shortly after Sloan's statement, three retarded children were dead within Texas facilities. Officials at the Austin State School failed to report two of the deaths and, when they did, listed them as natural causes. Richard Halpin, social worker, and Ben Standley, psychologist, both members of "Free the Slow, Inc.," revealed to me, however, that the causes were far from natural. One child was found with sand in his mouth; one was badly beaten and the third, a fourteen-year old girl at the Austin State School, died, according to Justice of the Peace James Dear, "at the hands of another person." Interviews with staff personnel showed that within a period of eighteen months, thirty-eight questionable deaths occurred at Austin and Travis State schools for the retarded. The villain, they felt, was the cold-bloodedness of institutionalization which permits overcrowding and inadequate, poorly supervised care from staff, themselves institutionalized, who slowly but surely become apathetic to their work and their wards.

This apathy also extends to daily medical treatment, as documented in records of Texas State mental facilities, which cost two children their sight. One girl was admitted to Austin State School and given a clean bill of health by the resident doctor. Two weeks later, she was admitted to the state hospital with a positive diagnosis of Shigella, an epidemic disease prevalent in institutions. In lieu of medication the state doctor removed her eyeballs—today she is totally blind.

Another inmate was prescribed eye drops for his glaucoma by a private physician. Reports show the staff was consistently negligent about giving the medication and at one point the state doctor stopped the eye drops. When they were resumed, it was too late. According to a statement by Alice B. Ruckman: "I no longer work at Sunrise [Texas] but have been informed that Joe is functionally totally blind . . . he is now in the building designated for those most emotionally disturbed. I am shocked. In my opinion, Joe is definitely one of the five or six most socially 'normal' kids at Sunrise."

At Austin State School a twenty-year-old nonambulatory died of acute pancreatitis. It was ruled a death of "natural causes." Dallas Representative Eddie Bernice Johnson said she was "dismayed at the apparent total lack of even minimal medical care afforded the residents of the Austin State School."

Though there is little documentation on just how widespread the practice is, evidence exists that mentally retarded children in institutions are providing science and medicine, particularly the pharmaceutical industry, with highly suitable and unsuspecting or at least intimidated subjects for research.

Nine hundred women in Texas state hospitals were given the controversial drug Depro-Provera, for birth control and menstrual regulation. The Texas Department of Mental Health and Mental Retardation claimed it was not used for experimental purposes. However, from large grants donated by pharmaceutical companies, the department has established a foundation from which supplemental salaries are paid to select officials of the department that is using Depro-Provera and other drugs. An employee of the Department of Mental Health and Mental Retardation commented: "I don't think Depro-Provera is the best contraceptive available ... but it is probably the best for the retarded.... You've got these things, these pieces of protoplasm with an IQ of 8 to 10 and a social age of less than one or two...." Conscientious veterinarians will not use Depro-Provera on dogs, because prolonged use will kill them.

Dr. Betty Alford, with the Nutrition Research Department of Texas Women's University in Denton, used institutionalized children—"because their situation gave better control"—to conduct a test that substituted one third of a child's animal protein intake with cottonseed flour. A control group continued their normal rate of animal protein intake. Dr. Alford wanted to see if one group would show changes in development. A second experiment was planned for the future, using a greater rate of cottonseed flour than previously used.

On February 6, 1973, a letter went out from Dr. Robert E. Weibel of the Department of Pediatrics at the University of Pennsylvania to the chairman of the Committee on Outside Research in State Institutions—Pennsylvania Department of Health. In the letter Dr. Weibel and Dr. Maurice R. Hilleman of the pharmaceutical firm of Merck & Company proposed to test a new gonorrhea vaccine on mentally retarded boys at the Glen Mills School. The vaccine had, up to that time, never been tried on human subjects in this country. However, it had tested satisfactorily on three rabbits, three guinea pigs and twenty mice.

Key parts of the letter read: "Under current policy to conduct research in Pennsylvania institutions, we are requesting approval for Clinical Study #334—Inactivated Neisseria Gonorrhea Vaccine. With the approval of the necessary review committees and with individual informed consent of the vaccinees, parents or guardians, we plan to immunize a small number of residents at Glen Mills School in Delaware County."

A *"Review Committee Concurrence Form"* enclosed with the basic proposal read: "In an effort to protect the residents of the Glen Mills School against gonococcal infection, the Institutional Review Committee has evaluated Clinical Protocol #334 ... the Committee feels it would be beneficial and therefore grants permission for the residents to receive inactivated Neisseria Gonorrheae Vaccine." Also included was the *"Informed Consent Form."* In part it read: "Despite effective antibiotic therapy, the incidence of gonorrhea continues to increase especially among the young. The development of an effective vaccine could resolve the clinical problems associated with gonorrhea. Through the cooperation of the University of Pennsylvania and the Merck Institute for Therapeutic Research, an inactivated Neisseria Gonorrheae Vaccine has been made available without cost to residents of Glen Mills School who may contact gonorrhea." *Clinical Protocol —Study #334* stated that its basic purpose was to "evaluate the safety and antigenicity of the vaccine." There were proposed two groups of ten students each. Group One was to be "free of gonorrhea or other venereal infection" and would be injected with the gonorrhea vaccine. Group Two would serve as the unvaccinated control group. Under *"Adverse Reactions,"* the protocol stated: "Any serious or alarming reaction, including death due to any cause during this investigation, whether related or not related to the test material, must be reported immediately to Merck and Co."

The proposal went to the Department of Public Welfare, the custodial guardians of the Glen Mills children. Fortunately, Michael Golding of the Justice Department and then Robert Sobolevitch, director of the Bureau of Youth Services, raised alarm against the test. But although the Department of Public Welfare hardened against granting approval, an interesting typed telephone conversation between the superintendent of Glen Mills, Mr. Harold Novick, and Robert Sobolevitch took place which clearly indicated political pressure to go ahead with the University of Pennsylvania–Merck test. Novick told Sobolevitch that he was, himself, somewhat opposed but felt some pressure from his board, specifically the chairman of the Medical Committee, to proceed in this matter: "Although the Chairman did not say so, I gathered that there was some sort of communication between medical members of his Board and the faculty at the University of Pennsylvania who are interested in pursuing the experiment."

Thanks to the negative reaction of state welfare and justice, the proposal was never carried out. However, when one considers that this sort of research is being carried out on unwitting mentally retarded and that reputable institutions such as the University of Pennsylvania's Medical School and Merck & Company would even make such a proposal, the ramifications assume chilling dimensions. In the words of one staff member at a school for the retarded, "We are wrestling with our own retardation to cope, ultimately, with the retardation of others."

As the horror stories emerge from institutions in every state of the Union, so do the fabrications, the threats, the payoffs, the cover-ups by the perpetrators. What did not lie, however, was the hidden camera in the belt of free-lance photographer Fred Kaplan, whose pictures, along with the text written by Dr. Burton Blatt, sociologist, served to indict former Governor Nelson Rockefeller and New York State in a book entitled *Christmas in Purgatory*.* The then governor's political denials, against a backdrop of Kaplan photographs depicting the rawness of the forgotten—naked

* Allyn & Bacon, Boston, 1966.

and partially clad patients sitting on hard wooden benches or concrete floors; human feces smeared on walls and furniture and the various postures of hopelessness and despair—could well serve as an indictment for what we failed to do for the retarded in the sixties and seventies.

What makes our contemporary treatment of the mentally retarded so wantonly cruel is the well-documented fact that the very human beings we have been hiding from the general public for generations because of the stigma of retardation, if provided proper education and training, could lead useful lives—both to themselves and to their communities. Regardless of the level of retardation, children are capable of gaining from education. Out of every thirty retarded persons, twenty-nine can become self-sufficient in varying degrees, with twenty-five of these capable of achieving sufficient skills to enter the labor market and secure employment in competitive jobs. Of the remaining five, four, with some training and education, could obtain employment in a "sheltered or supervised setting." The remaining one, with proper, intensified training, could also learn some degree of self-care.

Allowing the mentally retarded to languish in institutions is financial insanity. This was pointed out by Dr. Ronald W. Conley in his recent book, *The Economics of Mental Retardation*. The custodial cost of lifetime incarceration of a retarded person is $400,000. If, on the other hand, a mildly retarded male is trained to work and obtain employment, he could expect lifetime earnings of over $600,000. The total gain to society for each averted case of severe retardation among males is almost $1,000,000. Yet in 1970, of an estimated 690,000 retarded adults who were not working, 400,000 could have been employed if they had the proper education and training. It takes little calculating to realize how devastating this inhumaneness is to the taxpayer, much less to the immediate victim—the retarded.

Death has reared himself a throne
In a strange city lying alone
Far down within the dim West. . . .

—Edgar Allan Poe

7/The Runaway:
The American Family,
Congress and
Chicken Hawks

"How could at least twenty-three youths, many of them from the same neighborhood, be missing and the police not suspect that something was very, very wrong?" Verne Cobble of Houston, Texas, asked this anguished question after being notified that his son, Charles, seventeen, was one of twenty-seven young victims of homosexual mass slayings discovered during the summer of 1973.

Most major news stories break on the wire services first, are picked up by the major TV networks and are then carried on the evening news into the American home. This particular item, the grisly details of sexual abuse to the children before their untimely deaths, greatly disturbed many Americans. Some of the victims were believed to have been runaways; so, suddenly, the police were inundated with frantic inquiries. As one Hollywood police investigator commented, "Good Lord, you wouldn't believe it. I've got missing kids on file who've been gone months, even years. And suddenly their families are calling up, talking about Houston, demanding to know what we're doing to find the kid. They're coming out of the woodwork!"

79

As more details of the bizarre murders by Dean Allen Corll were uncovered, the latent fears and apprehensions of parents rose to such a point that they were felt in Washington, D.C. Congressional and Western Union phones were busy. Republican Congressman W. J. Keating of Ohio alone received more than two thousand calls and letters. So explosive became the issue of the old but growing problem of "runaways" that congressional leaders quietly demanded a meeting at the White House with Melvin Laird, former Secretary of Defense and Chief Domestic Advisor to the President.

Bureaucrats at the Justice Department and at HEW scratched frantically for data on the runaway problem. Six months earlier I had failed to interest the Justice Department in a proposal to study status offense laws, which applied to the runaway. When the tragedy was unveiled in Houston, however, I overnight became an indirect advisor to Mr. Laird through the Justice Department's National Institute of Law Enforcement and Criminal Justice.

Concrete national data do not exist, but conservative estimates are that annually 600,000 to well over one million youngsters run away in the United States. What little data are available show that, in fact, hundreds of thousands of children—average age fourteen—are hitting the streets and highways and flooding into our large cities. New York reported 20,000 runaways in 1972. Chicago police processed 9,461 cases in one year. Washington, D.C., has 10,000 runaways at any given time. The FBI reported in 1972 that arrests for running away jumped by 60 percent from 1967 and 1968.

I saw them as I traveled the country, researching this book. I saw them late in the evenings, hitching rides to nowhere; I saw them sleeping in bus and train terminals; I saw them in youth centers and shelters like Huckleberry House in San Francisco; Project Place in Boston; Roots, Inc., in Hartford, Connecticut; and Runaway House in Washington, D.C. I interviewed runaways in jails, detention centers and state training schools—catalogued, programmed, numbered and hating. They share a common bond: all are young, troubled, confused and incarcerated—either in institutions or by drugs, pimps or loneliness.

Who are these children who run? Where do they come from?

Congressional leaders were jolted to learn there are no economic or social boundaries. They are the sons and daughters, brothers and sisters, nieces and nephews of anyone reading this book. They are a cross section of American Youth. They are the rich (95 percent of the runaways who go to Greenwich Village, New York, are from white upper-income homes, and such a stable community as Evanston, Illinois, reported, for the first time, that its runaway rate rose 90 percent in one year); they are the middle-class and they are the poor. They are running from urban, suburban and rural homes. Their educations range from the very best to the poorest. The potential runaway is generally a problem within the family structure, who, in a charged emotional conflict, makes a decision to run and disappears into the busy, complex world of adults. Unnoticed, uncared for, he travels to an unknown fate with help from dubious newfound friends or, worse, strangers who prey on him while he is confused and uncertain.

A disturbing phenomenon about the runaway is the declining average. Ruth Martin, a former social worker and valunteer at The Listening Ear runaway shelter, told *U.S. News & World Report* in April of 1972: "They're getting younger every year. They used to drop out of college. Now they drop out of high school." In 1963–64 the average age was sixteen to seventeen years. In 1972 the age had dropped to fifteen. Of the 20,000 children flooding New York City's travel terminals, 43 percent of them are between the age of eleven and fourteen!

A second phenomenon is that more girls are running away from home than boys. In the early sixties, boys outnumbered girls. Now the trend has reversed. San Diego informed Congress that the average runaway is a 14½-year-old white Protestant female.

Why do these children run? For about one third of them it would be the healthy thing to do if they had a desirable place to go. But all too often their only alternative is the streets. Many young girls told me they were raped by alcoholic fathers, step-fathers, uncles, etc. One little 10½-year-old boy told a Senate investigation subcommittee in 1972 that he lived with grandparents and a father, all alcoholics, who constantly beat him when they were drunk. His older brother was incarcerated in a state institution for running away from the same situation, plus a related drug offense. In Georgia two boys, victims of a family problem, were locked up in a regional state youth detention center. The boys' parents divorced and swapped mates with another couple. The boys were ordered to stay with their mother but kept running away to join their father. So they were incarcerated.

San Diego's County Probation Department estimates that only one of every three runs are reported to the police. Most parents do not want to reveal to friends and neighbors the telltale signs of family problems. During 1963–64, Dr. Robert Shellow studied 731 youths who ran from suburban Prince George County, Virginia, and discovered that more than half were having problems at school and almost none had received any family counseling or therapy.

In 1969 a group of citizens studied the problem in Minneapolis, where 2,338 runaways came into contact with the police. After much deliberation on "who is guilty," the study concluded that cause or blame could not be isolated; there seemed to be too many factors beyond the control of the family. Anthropologist Margaret Mead also told the United States Senate Subcommittee on American Families: Trends and Pressures: "And families that are absolutely crucial to the health of the nation crumble under burdens too great to bear.... Three million doorstep children roam the country with no one responsible for them."

Frightening as it may be, it is important that we fully realize and understand the various factors beyond the family's control which give impetus to a child's decision to run away. The United States Bureau of the Census defines a family as a group of two or more related persons who live together in a house or apartment. Historical trends of the past thirty years have placed heavy odds against a close-knit family structure. In 1940 about 85 percent of all families included a husband and a wife. In 1973 it was less than 70 percent. Four out of ten marriages are failing. Divorce rate is currently reaching epidemic proportions; if the trend continues, it will soon reach 50 percent. In 1974, 970,000 marriages failed, directly affecting more than one million children. And a new and disturbing phenomenon is the unwillingness of either divorced parent to take custody of the children.

For other youngsters the root of family alienation is not loss of mother and father through divorce but through employment.

Shift work, compulsory overtime, corporative-forced moving, career opportunities—all contribute to the spending of less and less time with their children. The following quote is from "Report to the President—White House Conference on Children—1970":

> For families who can get along, the rats are gone but the rat race remains. The demands of a job or often two jobs, claiming mealtimes, evenings, and weekends as well as days; the trips and moves one must make to get ahead or simply hold one's own; the ever-increasing time spent in commuting; the parties, evenings out, and social and community obligations—all the things one has to do if one is to meet *one's primary responsibility*—produce a situation in which a child often spends more time with a passive babysitter than a participating parent.

One study done of fathers who claimed to spend an average of at least 15 to 20 minutes a day playing with their one-year-old infant, revealed that the actual average was only 37.7 seconds per day!

During March of 1975, women of husband-wife families accounted for nearly 44.6 percent of the labor force, compared with 27 percent in March of 1952. There were also more than 5.6 million mothers employed with children under six years of age, and of that number, 4.1 million were rearing children without a husband. It is not surprising then to learn from Dr. Edward Zigler, former director of the U.S. Office of Child Development, that there are currently "over a million latch-key children,* cared for by no one, with probably an equal number being cared for by siblings who are too young to assume such responsibility."

Because of the vacuum created by parental withdrawal, studies now show there is, at every age level, greater dependency of children on their peers. A similar investigation of the problem reveals that "peer-oriented youngsters portray their parents as less affectionate and less firm in discipline." Still another study (Siman, 1973) claims that "attachment to age-mates appears to be influenced more by a lack of attention and concern at home than by any positive attraction of the peer group itself. In fact, these children have a rather negative view of their friends and

---

* Children who are locked in their rooms and ignored.

of themselves as well ... they are more likely to engage in such antisocial behavior as lying, playing hooky or doing something illegal."

Child abuse is another cause of sibling alienation from parents. There are between two to four million American children annually who are subjected to bodily injury, the highest incidents occurring during adolescence, the runaway years.

High mobility—20 percent of all Americans move every year—removes the family from familiar neighborhood surroundings, friends and other members of the blood family. So during times of stress or crisis, the unit is left to contend alone.

Finally, as we have seen, poor school performance, which is uniformly found among children of long-term unemployed and marginally employed workers, often contributes to the decision to run away.

Collectively, all these conflicting demands that an evolving society makes upon the family cause many children to abandon that crumbling structure for an unknown world. The reason they run is, by and large, understandable; the punishment of imprisonment for such action is intolerable.

Throughout the entire country, there are only sixty facilities known as "shelter-care homes" which give runaways safe and professional help. Children fortunate enough to find a runaway shelter are given a warm bed and counseling and may make a phone call to their parents if they desire. Most do. Within a few days, after a cooling-off period, roughly 75 percent return home. Twenty-five percent either move on or become self-sufficient, breaking the apron strings at an early age. The shelter concept ideally serves as a bridge to the parents. It also gives the staff an opportunity to suggest and urge families to begin long-term counseling.

The average runaway has enough money for three days—an indication that he or she only wants to leave for a short time. However, because shelter and needed counseling are lacking, the youngster must eventually turn to the streets for survival. The Chicago Police Department, in researching the runaway in 1967, found that 70 percent of all delinquents have a case history of running away from home and 22 percent of all crimes committed on the city's South Side involved runaways. The thousands of children picked up by police spend time in juvenile detention facilities, county and city jails or, if they run too often, state training schools. For those who know nothing of the shelters but who slip through the institutional nets, the real world is out there facing them. It is called "survival!"

In many cases a child, in desperate need of basic human love, denied or misplaced at home, will leave the unit and "crash a pad." Jerry Cagiao of New York, who worked for Operation Eye Opener, a church-sponsored juvenile-help group, warns runaways: "At first they will be taken into the crash pad on a friendship basis; for like two or three days they will feed them, take care of them. But after that, they say, well, you have got to go out and sell drugs and prostitute yourself to support the crash pad. So they go out and sell drugs or a girl prostitutes herself. If the youngster refuses, the leader or lord of the crash pad will wait until a very cold or rainy day and tell the child to leave. Crashing a pad is usually crashing a new life style which ends in several ways—from drug addiction to a criminal record of a felon."

Rev. Fred Eckhardt, pastor of St. John's Lutheran Church in the East Village and director of Operation Eye Opener, gave the U.S. Senate Juvenile Delinquency Subcommittee an eye-opening account of one crash pad:

> I might cite one illustration of a 16-year old girl who was living in a pad on Bleecker Street, just east of Sullivan. Together with the officers of the 16th precinct, knowing she was there—our youth had cased the joint literally for two days . . . they broke down the door. There were some 30 people on this wall-to-wall mattress, with cockroaches running everywhere, pots and pans, filthy clothes, the stink of socks. . . . The mother and father were there with us; they wanted to bring their daughter out and she refused to go because of the "intolerable" home situation. The police and the pastor said, "You have to take her or we will arrest her." The mother said, "No, if I take her, she will just run away again." Five days later, this girl turned herself into Beth Israel Hospital with acute gonorrhea.

Others, like thirteen-year-old Frances L., never make it to the pad:

> When I got off the bus from Philadelphia, my feet hadn't even hit the ground before these two girls approached me. They said they knew a place where lots of kids from out of town crashed until

they could find work.... I thought they were do-gooders...I felt lucky. We took a taxi. Then we got to this big shiny car parked near the river and there was another black girl in the car. She looked very friendly. So I hopped in and said hi. She grabbed me and shoved something under my nose. The last thing I saw was a black dude who was also in the car handing all this money to the two girls.... I woke up tied down to a bed; a bunch of blacks were standing over me and one of them said, "Honey we gonna get you in good shape."...They did a train on me [gang rape]. I passed out from exhaustion, woke up and passed out again. They kept it up all night.... Later, there were other men there. I started crying and screaming. Somebody took my arm and worked on it until he got a vein to pop up. They shot me up with scag for a week. After that, nothing seemed real. I was hooked. Then they took me out on the street. At thirteen, I was a mainlining hooker, working for the street pimps.

The pimps know about Reverend Eckhardt's Operation and know that if they miss the runaways at the Port Authority Bus Terminal, many of these kids will end up at Operation Eye Opener. So they come and wait across the street in expensive cars, luring the girls with talk about the good life in the big city. Larry Zicht, director of Administrative Services for Contact, which is part of the runaway program at St. John's, reflected on the danger involved, as when one of his counselors attempted to prevent a young girl from taking off with a street pimp: "It was quick...a knife flashed. There was a scuffle, and our man was stabbed. They started open-heart surgery on him in the ambulance on the way across town to St. Vincent's Hospital. He was dead on arrival. We never caught the guy."

Boys are victimized in the same brutal, animal fashion as their sisters. Those who specialize in buying young boys for sexual purposes are called "chicken hawks" and they, too, wait at the Port Authority for "chickens" to get off the buses. It is very perverted and very big money. Captain Kenneth Gussman of the Manhattan Public Morals Division of the New York police said "the scene" was discovered by accident in June of 1972. "We frankly didn't even know the problem existed." Sixty-four arrests were made, thirteen of which were pimps and included the following indictments:

—Hollywood Al—promoting prostitution, endangering the welfare of children, sodomy, and sexual abuse. He gets his name from his sunglasses and is known by every chicken hawk in the city. He can be found in Times Square any night or afternoon.

—Ace the Space—selling a 12-year-old. A Black, whose specialty is White runaways.

—Cigar Murray—cigar-chewing manager of a call-boy operation out of the Village hotel he manages.

—Sideburn Eddie—sodomy, sexual abuse, endangering the welfare of a minor and unlawfully imprisoning a child. Until his indictment, this man was a psychologist at Kings Park Hospital where he worked with disturbed children. His arrest was for keeping two brothers, age 11 and 14, locked in his apartment.

In June of 1972, Captain Gussman got his first conviction of a pimp. Arthur Cohen, who was selling young boys for $50 to $150 a night, was sentenced to a year in jail. But he hired a good lawyer and was out in a few months. The captain talked about the children trapped in male prostitution: "There are the runaways, some from places like Jersey City, some from affluent homes. Some of the richer boys had become actively homosexual in the private boys schools; some of the working class kids had unwillingly been introduced to sodomy when they had been raped by older, stronger youths at one or another reform school." Gussman also said that most of the runaways are raped, beaten and locked up in cheap West Side hotels until the pimps can trust them to go out to make money for them. They are forced to take drugs and finally are no longer children but instruments of very sick adults, working the streets of the city which has aged them generations in just a few short weeks.

The chicken hawks have their own stories and perspectives. One talked to gifted newspaper reporter Howard Blum of *The Village Voice*:

I get a call from this scum and he tells me to meet him at his house. He says he has a nice chicken for me. When I get there, I find this kid tied to a bed. He's been tied to this bed for four days already. Steve tells me he's been raped 17 times. He says the kid resisted at first so he beat him and just to teach him a lesson, burned his initials on the kid's back with a hot cigarette. I spoke to the kid. He was some poor 13-year-old kid from Baltimore. You know why he ran away from home. Get this—he got a bad grade in mathematics and was afraid his father would beat him!

Another chicken hawk, Nevada, a well-educated accountant with a slight Boston accent who lives in an Upper West Side apartment, told both Blum and me his insights on the runaways:

> You know what these kids on the street are looking for? Love and affection.... You know why 42nd Street is full of kids? Do you know why the runaways are coming off the buses? I'll tell you why—it's because something went wrong at home and they're just looking for someone to take care of them.... You can buy any type of boy in this city, if you're willing to pay. It's no problem. On 53rd and Third, the scene is more expensive and older. Usually there's a row of expensive cars along the curb. The pimps make a deal and the boys disappear into the cars.... Super Sam keeps his flock at a restaurant on Christopher Street. He gets kids who are runaways and will do anything for a place to stay by the time he spots them. ...Once he gets them, he keeps them by turning them on to heroin.... Look, there's even a number where you can call up and get a boy delivered to you. They say it's a place in Connecticut, where they take kids and make them pose for pictures.... The only problem is that there just are not enough new kids. New York makes kids too tough too soon. A lot of us chicken hawks and the pimps, too, drive down to Philadelphia to a place on 17th and Walnut on weekends to look for new faces. Or we go to the meat market in Baltimore. Or we hang out in Jersey City.

Howard Blum observed two pimps he had talked with earlier make contact with a man. While a deal was being made, the chicken was kicking an empty paper cup. The man shook hands with the pimps and he and the boy walked off down the street, the child still kicking the paper cup as they moved toward the subway.

While investigating the runaway problem among American Indians, I found a curious inconsistency. As other segments of America's youth are leaving the family structure, Indian children are running *back* to their homes. The size of most Indian reservations and the lack of funds for roads and buses force tribes to ship their children many miles away to boarding schools operated by the Bureau of Indian Affairs (BIA). Many times the BIA staff is insensitive to Indian rituals and sacred rites and has little understanding of the cultural heritage of these children. This lack of staff sensitivity, the long periods of separation from their loved ones, and even, in the words of the Albuquerque *Journal*, "the racist policies employed at the schools," cause the youngsters to run. The runaway rate is very high, but the BIA refuses to release the numbers, even to HEW officials and members of Congress. However, the papers of New Mexico, Arizona and other western states frequently carry accounts of the children's determined efforts to return home. In early January of 1973, three Navajo boys ran from the Chuska Boarding School and were lost in the mountains of New Mexico. Four days later rescuers found John Marvin High, seven, his brother, Johnny Mike, eight, and Allison Bryant, ten, near the top of the 8,795-foot Chuska Peak. Allison was lying on the younger High boy, trying to keep him warm with his body. A few days later, the children's frozen feet were amputated. Another time, Eddie Pinto Sandoval, a seventh-grade student at the Dzilth-Na-O-Dithle Boarding School near Bloomfield, New Mexico, was found frozen to death.

The day after I visited the area where the frost-bitten High brothers and Allison Bryant were found, I met with some older militant tribal brothers. Hanging on the wall of their office was the following poem:

> Cover my earth Mother
> Four times with many flowers
> Cover the heavens
> With high piled clouds
> Cover the earth with fog
> Cover the earth with rains
> Cover the earth with lightning
>   Let the thunder drum all over the earth.
> Let the thunder be heard. . . .

On January 13 and 14, 1972, long before the Houston murders were revealed, Senator Birch Bayh, chairman of the Senate Subcommittee on Juvenile Delinquency, held legislative hearings on Senate bill 2829 called "The Runaway Youth Act." Bayh, way ahead of everybody else in Washington on the problem, was bitterly opposed by the Nixon Administration. Unfortunately, the opposition was not based on the substance of the bill but rather on Bayh's politics.

During the hearings the Nixon stand emerged in the testimony by Phillip J. Rutledge, a HEW official. He said:

"What is called for is not legislation establishing new categorical programs dealing with one aspect of this larger problem. Instead, efforts are needed at the State, Federal, and local level to integrate those services that are already available, and to fill gaps in the provision of services in each community. . . . New Legislative authority is not necessary for the Department [HEW] to support the development or continuation of homes to shelter runaway youths; authority already exists under the Juvenile Delinquency Prevention Control Act of 1968, as amended (Public law 90–445). . . . The Youth Development, Delinquency Prevention Administration, for example, is presently funding several of these homes."

The following dialogue then occurred between Rutledge and Senator Bayh:

> BAYH: "How many, Mr. Rutledge?"
> RUTLEDGE: "There are only four."
> BAYH: "In other words, you tell us that we need no new legislative authority to deal with the problem. That AN ACT WHICH WAS CREATED IN 1968 is sufficient to deal with the problem. Yet between 1968 and 1972, you have funded four projects and you tell us that you do not need any new authority?"
> RUTLEDGE: "These particular ones were only funded recently. I think, Mr. Chairman, the magnitude of this problem simply has not been adequately recognized and has not been adequately addressed . . ."

The Senator's bill is now law. When the Houston mass murders became public during the summer of 1973, the taxpayers responded, pressuring the White House and Congress to pass the Runaway Act, which provided $10 million a year for three years to initiate runaway shelter-care programs. It also provided complete medical and psychiatric counseling services and supplied the Department of HEW with the resources to collect data and devlecp a profile for future planning and new legislation.

Still, even with government-sponsored laws and programs, there is no assurance that the help that is embodied within the laws actually reaches the child in trouble and on the run. I found, in

Hartford, Connecticut, one such tragic example of government's total unresponsiveness. I went to Hartford to visit a runaway facility called ROOTS, Inc., organized by a group of young, dedicated people. Something I discovered in the records there sent me to a local newspaper, the Hartford *Courant*, then on to the Hartford police station and finally to place numerous calls to the coroner's office before the entire story emerged:

Gloria C. DuPont, sixteen, ran away from her home at 209 Zion Street in Hartford in May of 1973. She felt that no one cared about her or her problems. The disturbed girl sought help at ROOTS, Inc., which tried to assure her that even though she had problems at home, there were resources in the city to meet her needs. They first called the Department of Protective Services. They said no. Next they called the state's Department of Youth Services, who also refused Gloria help even though the department had $16,000 unused funds for emergency housing. The city welfare department couldn't do anything, nor could the Hartford High School guidance counselors. ROOTS even tried the Gray Lodge, a private home. That, too, was out, because no one was willing to assume the cost. The girl left the office very despondent. On the afternoon of June 2, two boys found the body of a young woman floating in the Connecticut River near Wethersfield Cove. When no identification had been made after several days, the police asked the paper to run the story and description again in the Sunday paper. The paper said she was wearing blue jeans, frayed at the cuffs, and a smocklike blouse with purple and orange stitching around the neck and down the front. Her hair was dark, shoulder-length with reddish tints. The staff at ROOTS knew then that the body was that of Gloria DuPont.

After the notice of her death, telephone calls to ROOTS, Inc., from those government agencies that had refused to help, even though they had the necessary funds, sealed the cover-up.*

> . . . Cover the earth with lightning
> Let the thunder drum all over the earth.
> Let the thunder be heard. . . .

* On February 4, 1974, Hartford County Coronor Irving L. Aronson closed the case on Gloria DuPont. His report said: "Death by drowning, no evidence as to whether criminal, accidental or suicide. And until further evidence is produced, the case is closed."

PART THREE / Conditions in Youth Jails: A National Profile

There is evidence, in fact, that there may be grounds for concern that the child receives the worst of both worlds: that he gets neither the protection accorded to adults nor the solicitous care and regenerative treatment postulated for children.

—*Kent v. United States,* 1966

8/Time Dots of Failure: The Illusion of Treatment

Clyde Perkins, sixteen, lay on his bunk at Fort Grant, Arizona, State Training School for Boys. "Clyde, what are these?" I directed his attention to three indelible marks on the delta of his left thumb and forefinger. "Time dots—each one means time spent in training school."

Clyde had been incarcerated almost constantly since he had first come to Fort Grant at the age of ten. "This time I'm back for parole violation, but hell, I can't find no job because of my record!" According to juvenile delinquency statistics compiled by the state of Massachusetts before it closed down its facilities, young Perkins is a classic case: one of the 88 percent whose family is at or near poverty level; one of 60 percent whose mother or father suffers from serious alcoholism or drug addiction; and one of the 33 percent who come from a broken home. Clyde's "time dots" are themselves national statistics: 74 to 80 percent of all juvenile offenders repeat crimes after punishment.

Clyde was initially charged with a "status offense" (noncriminal), the vehicle by which fifty percent of our wayward children are locked up, thereby removing them from community and

95

parental responsibility. This young man was receiving no professional help to cope with his problems. He had learned to strip a
car during his first visit to Fort Grant, but that education earned
him a return trip to captivity.

As I left the room, I glanced back at the bitter boy, eyes forward, elbows on knees, fingers extended, his right index finger
slowly caressing the time dots on his left hand. "I just got a
hateful suspicion for everyone."

In 1962 the National Conference of Superintendents of Training Schools and Reformatories published a book entitled *Institutional Rehabilitation of Delinquent Youth,* a collection of "the
best thinking of those closest to the problems." In the book the
authors acknowledged the volatile nature of their work:

> The bulk of these boys and girls are not confirmed or hardened
> offenders. They are pliable, impressionable; opportunities to help
> them are great. By the same token, they may be severely warped
> and damaged by exposure to destructive experiences. . . .

The book's rhetoric was also impressive concerning treatment of
children: ". . . It is through clinical services that treatment is
individualized; the necessary information is secured about each
individual's background, abilities, interests, attitudes and problems, in order to plan intelligently for him and to provide certain
types of direct remedial treatment." It further discussed the psychological and medical services and academic and vocational
education that were available to the incarcerated delinquent.

To the concerned and interested reader of the early 1960's, the
book must have stirred much hope. It represented the best thinking and best ideas in progressive social welfare programs for the
child. However, it was all an illusion: If the reader looked closer,
there were more pages devoted to discipline than such treatment
topics as "Clinical Services" or "Academic and Vocational Education." Paradoxically too, the children of whom the authors wrote
are not shaped or molded by professionals paid to rehabilitate
them but rather by other children whose earlier failures and lack
of treatment serve as the pivotal point for further destruction of

hope and positive direction. Indeed, at the close of the 1960's the United States Senate Subcommittee on Juvenile Delinquency quoted the sobering fact that eight out of every ten children under "institutional rehabilitation" return to those same facilities and superintendents with more serious charges.

According to sociologists Wheeler and Cottrell, whose research was used in part by United States Justice Abe Fortas in the historical decision (*re* Gault) that guaranteed "due process" for juveniles, the road to rehabilitation is destroyed at the very onset, when a child experiences injustice within the juvenile court system. Wheeler and Cottrell wrote: "When legal laxness of the Parens Patriae attitude is followed by stern disciplining, the contrast may have an adverse effect upon the child, who feels that he has been deceived or enticed.... Unless appropriate due process of law is followed, even the juvenile who has violated the law may not feel that he is being fairly treated and may, therefore, resist the rehabilitative efforts of court personnel."

When the adjudicated youth enters the penal artery of America, he or she is immediately confronted with the realization that security is first and foremost and treatment is secondary. Those in authority are totally security-oriented. Because state laws mandate some form of general rehabilitation, teachers and social workers are tolerated but have very little voice or influence within the policy structure.

Vermont State Commissioner of Corrections Kent Stoneman's description of the educational programs in most juvenile training schools throughout America as "mere ornaments" couldn't have been more accurate. Through Federal Title I monies, correctional grantsmen have been able to purchase expensive "ornaments" in the form of educational machines and do-it-yourself publications. There wasn't one facility I visited that did not have such expensive equipment, the value of which is, at best, dubious. In Texas facilities prior to 1974, children with an IQ below 90 were considered uneducable and therefore did not qualify for remedial reading programs with their expensive learning machines. In some areas of the country, penal psychologists decline to work with children who have limited verbal skills. During New Hampshire's lengthy history of training schools, less than one percent of its incarcerated population ever finished high school. Few states can honestly say they do much better, all of which violates the compulsory education laws most states have passed.

One cause of the lack of school programs is the time factor. Institutions must function and for that purpose they make maximum use of the student's "stretch" as a source of cheap labor. Training schools are most effective agents for exploiting children: Many teach "commercial skills," but realistically such programs amount to nothing more than a scheme to make the institution self-sufficient. In New York State, children working in a storeroom daily for six hours are rewarded with one candy bar every two weeks. Those who work in the kitchens, laundries and other institutional industries are usually paid nothing.

Theoretically the job of juvenile detention centers is to examine the child's background in terms of personal psychological needs and pass this information on to the probation officer and judge so that during the juvenile court hearing, the latter can make an intelligent ruling to protect both the offender and the community. However, somewhere along the way, reality has eroded theory. Detention centers are nothing more than factories of dehumanization and brutalization and from which the children are shipped out to larger institutions with longer histories of the same processes.

The 1970 national census study out of the University of Chicago (The Pappenfort *et al.* Report) concluded that "detention is a waiting period of enforced idleness that is destructive to the child and of little utility to the criminal justice system." The report substantiated this when it cited that in March of 1966, despite claims that 80 percent of the children held in detention on a given day were emotionally disturbed, less than half had received any psychiatric or psychological evaluation. Twenty-nine percent of the holding units give no examination of any type, 23 percent have no provisions for educating the youths, and only 26 percent have the full-time professional expertise of a trained psychiatrist, psychologist or social worker.

Jails throughout the country score even worse under the study's scrutiny: 86 percent have no exercise or recreational facilities, 90 percent have no educational or vocational programs and half provide no medical services. In 1973, county jails of the Sunshine State of Florida underwent careful investigation by the Division of Youth Services when Bill Hanson, chief of the Bureau of Community Services, did a survey of all jails retaining juveniles. Hanson's study found that, with only thirty-three jails reporting, approximately 2,398 children are held annually (thirty-four facilities lacked adequate records, so the actual total could not be ascertained). Of the sixty-seven facilities, however, not one has any educational programs for children and only six have any recreational provisions. Forty-seven have no "awake night matron on duty," a devastating condition that breeds incidents of abuse and horror that most Americans would rather not face.

The report is filled with such terms as "overcrowded," "dirty," "poor ventilation," "understaffed," "no medical treatment," "no heat," "vermin-abounding," "leaking roofs and leaking plumbing." Wakulla County Jail, where twenty young children were confined, has been condemned. The Florida Division of Corrections has recommended closing the place down. In Lake County a fifteen-year-old died of a heart attack "initiated by exertion, after riding 81 miles on the floor of a patrol car in a straitjacket."

In the spring of 1973, *The New York Times* did an extensive series on juvenile justice in New York City. All the horror stories were told: beatings, forced homosexual acts, rapes, forgotten children shifted from one agency to another without help. But the most depressing aspect *Times* reporter Lesley Oelsner's series documented was the total despair of not only the children but the public officials charged with their care and treatment as well.

"What we've done to kids is just disgraceful," said Judge Phillip D. Roache of the Brooklyn Family Court. "We send them direct to the adult criminal courts, by our inadequacies and our inability to stop them when they start." Retired Manhattan Family Court Judge Justice Wise Polier stated, "I see it as a fraud against the child and a fraud against society." Juvenile Court Judge Florence M. Kelley said, "I don't think we've even tried, really tried, a full schedule of rehabilitation."

Maury Bass, director of the Corporation Counsel's unit for the New York Family Court, commented: "...kids are sent to training schools that don't do much good either. It's a tremendous problem. There aren't enough alternatives." Joseph Moore, director of social services at the Gallagy facility in New York City, commented: "We have a psychiatric staff to do evaluations but not to do treatment." John F. Leis, director of another New York City youth facility, said: "I think the program as it exists now should be closed."

Milton Luger, formerly in charge of New York State's Training Schools, said flatly: "Too many of our facilities don't know how to work effectively with kids." Mr. Wayne Mucci, former New York City director of all children's institutions, confessed: "Eventually, you could probably do away with institutions.... Institutions are doomed to failure and can harm the children who enter them.... The system is really a very damaging one for most kids who get involved in it."

In a remarkably blunt speech before the twentieth annual meeting of the American Academy of Child Psychiatry in October of 1973, Chief Judge David L. Bazelon of the United States Court of Appeals in Washington, D.C., admonished his audience:

> I earnestly submit that your greatest contribution is to be brutally honest in loudly proclaiming that you do not have either the knowledge or the tools or the wizardry to wipe out the afflications of most children in our communities and institutions. It's time for all of us caretakers to stop hiding the smell of society's outhouses. No matter how hidden by bushes or how deodorized, it still smells like an outhouse!

In 1974, historical decisions handed down by two United States District federal judges—one in Texas, another in Indiana—ruled that the incarcerated child has a constitutional "right to treatment." Their strongly worded rulings further negated the illusion of treatment the penal industry has heretofore perpetrated on the American public. Indiana appealed the ruling but lost in the U.S. Court of Appeals in a three-to-nothing vote.

"Right to treatment" litigation grew out of the efforts of young lawyers and youth advocacy organizations investigating treatment and punishment within facilities where professionals were being paid to rehabilitate, train and teach misguided children. Responding to such powerful lawsuits and realizing the public will not tolerate a 70–80 percent failure rate, correctional institutions and officials across the country are currently engaged in various degrees of reform. But I must report that after visiting many states and reviewing current efforts, I have seen nothing more than the cosmetics of reform—long on public relations and short on meaningful performance. I found that facilities in the throes of change got heavy newspaper coverage, but the articles suffered similarities —the praising of a new superintendent, the projection of a "new image"—with very little said about changes that would benefit the inmates.

In the past, physical control was primarily the form of treatment for the incarcerated. However, as the old methods (and even some of the new) begin to fall under public and legal pressures, the juvenile penal system is looking for new ideas. A program gaining rapid acceptance is Behavior Modification, which hypothetically helps a person examine himself introspectively, to recognize and face his faults and/or problems, thereby making it possible to modify his antisocial behavior. Realistically though, many institutions are using this treatment simply to manipulate and control the child for the convenience of the custodians. When the U.S. Bureau of Prisons decided on the program, it made no pretense as to its real purpose; the bureau's "Operations Memorandum 7300.128, 10/25/72" affirmed that the intent was to conform prisoners to prison life. This massive psychological "ripoff" gains impetus even though recent well-documented studies show that in today's prisons, those "most likely to readjust to society successfully upon release are those who are most alienated to prison life during incarceration."

Behavioral Modification at the Arizona State School for Girls outside Phoenix, as described to me by a sixteen-year-old inmate, involves a series of promotions that depend on total cooperation with staff and institutional rules:

A new girl, at level one, is restricted to her room for a week's observation. If the staff decides her behavior warrants promotion, she moves to the second level, a one-week restriction within her cottage, where she is permitted to watch TV and talk with others. Again, on the basis of attitude and behavior within the cottage, the staff agrees to move the girl to the third level for two weeks; there she "is not trusted but yet isn't distrusted." She has to "prove herself"—no more than three infractions during that first week at this level. If she does acquire more than three, she returns to level two. After the second week on the third level, if there are no infractions and all the staff, including security personnel (guards), vote in the affirmative, the inmate becomes a fourth-level "badge girl" for a week. Again the entire staff votes after an infraction-free week and then the girl finds herself on level five, top advancement, "trusted by all and allowed to conduct visitors' tours and even go home on occasional weekends."

The above description was given during a taped interview with two counselors and the deputy superintendent present. All behavior rated good enough to be trusted centered around keeping the institution and its staff free of any hassle from the children. Not once was any mention made of coming to grips with serious behavioral problems. As I was leaving the room, the young trustee drew me aside: "Listen, I play their damned games with one hope, and that is to get the hell out of here as soon as possible."

At the Maple Lane School for Girls in Washington I met Bridgit Carroll, who wouldn't play the Behavior Modification game. Bridgit came from a recently broken family, a fact the girl found hard to accept. Declared "incorrigible" and sent to Maple Lane, she was resentful, saw the Behavior Mod program for what it was and told the staff accordingly. An American Civil Liberties Union lawyer was counseling her at the time about her case and after a few months her mother pressed for legal action too. While ACLU in Seattle was preparing a brief to test the constitutionality of incarcerating incorrigible youngsters, the staff and administrative personnel at Maple Lane found Bridgit's behavioral development unacceptable. After eight months without any weekend visits, the girl requested to spend Christmas at home with her mother. Her supervisor replied on Christmas Eve day: "Request denied. Now, Bridgit, *you* figure out why!" Bridget gave me the following poem she wrote that evening in her room through bitter, frustrated tears. She said she hoped in some way it would "help other children from being used and manipulated."

CHRISTMAS EVE—1972

As I sit at Maple Lane
On Christmas Eve
I'm thinking about my aim,
to leave.

... You have blocked out my aim
and made me wait
Until I play your damned games
I'm not getting out those gates.

Well send me to my room
and strip it while you can
As you're going to hear a boom
Because I don't give a damn.

Handcuffs may hold me down
You may take me in your circles round and round
But let me have one thing to say
You'll never make me stay!

I was introduced to a new form of Behavioral Mod called Positive Peer Culture at the state training school in Boonville, Missouri. A most lucrative program, already being used by a number of states, Positive Peer Culture is designed to alter negative behavior by psychological confrontation in group therapy sessions. A member of Positive Peer Culture staff monitors each session. Changes effected by Behavior Mod are, at best, institution-oriented and scarcely applicable to outside life. Positive Peer further troubles me on two accounts: First, because states like Missouri, which have not addressed themselves to providing adequate care and treatment for the disadvantaged, are holding disturbed and mentally retarded children in juvenile penal facilities. The strong verbal assaults of normal children during the give-and-take of group meetings can only cause further devastation to the minds and egoes of disturbed and slow youngsters, who should not be there to begin with. Secondly, Positive Peer may be listed as new treatment, but it threatens infractions with the same old punishment. Inmates at Boonville who don't cooperate during group sessions are thrown in some of the worst solitary confinement cells I have seen in the entire country.

Progressives like the superintendent at Long Lane in Connecticut lament that "it is impossible to know what is going on every minute when children and untrained and uncaring personnel are locked in their separate cottages. My hands are tied with lack of state support to upgrade the system." Most institutional reformers

and security advocates believe that more intensive and individualized treatment can be given—even on a one-to-one basis—if
there are more funds and newer, larger accommodations. I found
the premise worth pursuing.

I visited the massive, newly constructed $4 million Pierce
County Juvenile Detention Center in Washington State. As we
toured, Director Harold J. Mulholland was obviously proud. Within
the administration complex, most of the offices ringed a pictur-
esque courtyard built for visitation of parents and children. Here,
staff looked out daily on California quail, chukars and mallards
and readily identified some unusual birds—the amethyst pheasant
(a cross between a pheasant and a peacock), the Impeyan Pheasant from India and the great ring-necked pheasant of Chinese
origin—as they pranced about the tailored garden. Some of the
birds were sitting on eggs, and Mulholland was able to give an
account of their progress.

Since the institution had been built for the inmates, I couldn't
help but find gross contrast between the beautiful, esthetic, spa-
cious staff offices and the stark, sterile accommodations for the
juveniles. Subtle as the placement of the barbed wire was supposed to be, my eyes saw it in the rain gutters, draped over roof
angles and wrapped like Christmas lights around supportive
beams. The fence was a source of local pride. Unbreakable, unable to be climbed or seen through—the ultimate in penal fencing
—this corrugated steel wall was designed and patented by Tom
Pennock, superintendent of Maple Lane School for Girls.

Inside, the walls were bare, without pictures or artwork. The
television rooms had TV sets and chairs, nothing more. "Furniture and rugs have been destroyed by the little bastards; well, they
won't get any more," said the director as we hurried through. The
security wing had the latest in electronic gadgets: The locked en-
closures were scanned by closed-circuit TV so that fewer guards
were needed. The large control area in the general population
room was reminiscent of 1930 prison architecture. For the most
part, the children stayed in their rooms. Food was delivered on
trays through the thick iron doors.

I entered one of the cells and closed the door behind me. On
the slab of steel was scratched: "I would rather be dead than
here." Some youngsters had found ways to entertain themselves by

ripping off overhead ceiling blocks and knocking holes in the walls and ceilings. Some of the bare spots on the walls were covered with "mosaic" designs made with wet toilet paper and inspired by boredom and frustration.

A faded purple and gray water color of a dandelion lay on the table in the arts and crafts room. Inscribed on it were these words: "Dandelions are so much like myself,/Just an ugly weed nobody wants."

New institutions, under the guise of reform, still provide the same old illusion of treatment. Until the conflict of security versus treatment is resolved, the costly illusion will remain. And until the smooth veneer of rhetoric and public relations is removed from the penal bedrock of indifference, injustice, mistreatment and corruption, new institutions, new reforms, new administrations and new programs will continue to delude the paying public.

The Man

Hey, hey check out the man
He will do it to you
If you ain't got no stand.

Hey hey check out the man
He'll kick your ass
If he get the chance.

The Man have no regrets
The Man have no sorrows
If he don't get you today
He will get you tomorrow.

—A youth who testified in a Federal Court against
the state of Texas for beating children

9/Legalized Child Abuse: Institutional Punishment

During the early 1970's every major newspaper in
the United States wrote extensively on conditions
within the juvenile penal system. They exposed
the state schools in New York, Maryland, Massachusetts, Connecticut, North Carolina, Virginia,
Colorado, Texas, Arizona, Arkansas, Hawaii, Oklahoma, Illinois and Missouri. Elsewhere, individual citizen groups, state commissions and class
action law suits filled the gap, criticizing their
state institutions for lack of professional treatment, poorly trained, underpaid staff and the
uneasy coexistence of status offenders, mentally
retarded and felonious youngsters. Not a state
was left unscathed. The central issue throughout
was internal abuse: the physical beatings; the sexual violence (juvenile raping the weaker); the

106

harsh treatment and severe punishment of the very young; the violence of boredom.

Running away, which seems to be a barometer of the extent of abuse and violence perpetrated on inmates, is one of the most disquieting problems for juvenile facilities. For instance, during a one-year period at the Gatesville School for Boys in Texas, more than one third of its population ran, even though the boys knew that when and if they were caught, they would be sent to the notorious Mountain View.

Running away attracts adverse publicity to an institution, makes additional demands on personnel and lowers the morale of both staff and inmates. Therefore, punishment is quick and unmerciful. In Arizona, children who ran from the Fort Grant Training School were stripped, even in subfreezing weather, and beaten into submission by the members of the search party. At the Oklahoma Boys School in Helena the heads of those who ran were shaved and the culprits were forced to wear a dress.

Aside from periodic newspaper articles, occasional reports by concerned citizens and a book or two on the subject, very little factual information about life in juvenile penal institutions reaches the general public. Harsh treatment is usually clouded by public relations and charges and countercharges by students, staff and interested outsiders. Officials respond to direct investigation with self-righteous denials. Nevertheless, word seems to trickle out, as it did in Texas for as long as a decade before the Morales trial. Throughout the country, at great risk to their personal safety, children leaked horror stories via letters to friends, family, trusted lawyers and the investigative news media. On the other side of the coin are the unknown numbers who, after crying out for sanity, lower their voices, their hands, their desire to survive, and take their young lives by suicide.

In the system of juvenile justice, punishment is initiated at the time of arrest. Whether the child runs away from home, plays hooky or commits a felony, the law officers snap on handcuffs with no solicitude for the bruises to the "offender's" wrists or ego. The routine strip and search that follows, according to both boys and girls, is even more painful and degrading.

In late 1972 and early 1973 the John Howard Association, a

noted prison reform organization, published a report entitled "Brutality, Politics and Changes at Audy Home." Ninety children, in separate interviews, corroborated that the staff at Audy Home (Chicago) routinely "hit, slapped or kicked boys and ordered over-exercise and standing on the wall [forced inaction]" as punishment. Some told how they were forced to stand outside in the cold. Others were coerced into drinking water from toilet bowls. One boy said a guard struck his anus four or five times with a mop handle.

The Virginia State training schools revealed the same pattern of beatings. One supervisor at the Beaumont School for Boys repeatedly hit a boy suffering from bone disease while he stood defenseless on his crutches. In a Maryland facility a boy was badly beaten by other youths for not bringing back heroin from a weekend pass. The boy was hospitalized and has not been heard from since.

A Harvard undergraduate student, posing as a delinquent at Roslindale, in Massachusetts, before it closed down, recounted his experiences. He testified that children were punished by holding their heads under water or forcing them to run past a line of boys who were required to strike their colleague with closed fists from the waist to the shoulders. Those who didn't or couldn't participate in the striking were made to run the line, too. This same volunteer witnessed an incident in which a child's head was used to mop urine from the floor.

At the Industrial School for Negro Children at Mount Meigs, Alabama, inmates were sexually molested by some of the staff and beaten with fan belts, fists or clubs; some even had hands and feet plunged into boiling water. Treatment programs were nonexistent except to provide cheap labor for local private farms. The situation was so flagrant that when Denny Abbott, a courageous chief probation officer for the Montgomery County Family Court, filed suit as "next of friend" to the abused children, the state of Alabama didn't even contest it. But Family Court Judge William Zhethord was so enraged by Abbott's legal actions that he suspended the young officer for thirty days. Eventually, Abbott had to leave the juvenile court system completely.

Boredom, although not overtly violent, is just as cruel as the beatings and verbal abuse. Sid Ross, an editorial consultant to

Parade magazine, was visiting county and city jails around the country when his attention was drawn to a seventeen-year-old boy at one facility in the Midwest: "Hey, man! How about watering a nice, young human vegetable? . . . You sure get terribly depressed in here. It's nothing, nothing, nothing to do and you get to feel that you're nothing, nothing, nothing." Boredom is bred of several things—all of which further batter the young person's self-image, a factor that contributed greatly to his being incarcerated in the first place: lack of meaningful, interesting programs to provide true rehabilitative direction; the security mentality and regimentation of penal facilities; and the attitude of indifference that slowly erodes tolerance or concern for a person's individuality, especially when that person is a juvenile unable to cope with the adult world. If the child behaves and adheres to institutional rules, he is totally ignored. If he misbehaves for lack of anything better to do or to gain attention, he is usually beaten and thrown into solitary confinement where boredom as punishment is at its most intense.

Following are segments of a long letter a young boy smuggled out of the Audy Home lamenting the boredom:

> You get off the paddy wagon . . . you are told to sit . . . you sit, sit and you sit . . . you listen to the guards talk about dirty jokes at home. . . . If you have cigarettes, the guard says he has to confiscate them, so he takes them, takes one out and lights one up and puts the rest in his top left hand shirt pocket. Then you sit down again and watch him smoke your cigarettes. Then he comes over and asks if you are gay. . . . In the room there are about two dozen kids from the age of nine to eighteen for crimes ranging from stealing three dime bars of candy to strong arm robbery or shooting a person.

Aside from "eating good," the boy said all he did every day was watch TV with all the others until bedtime. He ended his letter: "I myself am good because I don't want the shit beat out of me or stand on the wall for 10 hours. . . ."

"Benching," like "standing on the wall," or forced inaction and boredom, is the main form of punishment at Pruntytown in West Virginia. Here the child is made to sit at attention in a metal chair for six to eight hours a day, seven days a week for three to six weeks in stone silence. During this time, he is isolated from his peers without any counseling, education or recreation. At the training schools in Maryland, where taxpayers pay $12,600 a year per child, youngsters are locked in their rooms for long periods of time and permitted out only to watch TV. When the John Howard Association evaluated the facilities in 1974, they "were struck by the silence around the grounds."

I believe that boredom is the actual catalyst for physical, psychological and sexual brutality among inmates. Without a healthy, continuous outlet for physical, mental and (in adolescents) sexual energies and frustrations, emotional pressures build which sooner or later manifest themselves, oftentimes in a violent or abusive way.

Older youngsters locked within the national juvenile jail structure are in various stages of sexual awakening. Given their close living quarters, lack of physical exercise and inconsistent supervision, sexual frustration becomes potentially explosive, with the powerful stalking the vulnerable. To most who fall victim to staff and inmate exploitation and rape, the effect is shattering. It degrades both body and dignity. Few children will ever forget the experience and many will be socially and psychologically maimed for their entire lives.

Al Brodie, a sensitive minister working with children in South Carolina's Department of Youth Services, wrote me in January of 1974: "I constantly run into kids that have been jailed with adults. I talked to one last week that had been raped three times by an adult. We have state laws prohibiting this; however, it goes on every day and there are so few people that give a damn. No one seems to want to rock the boat!"

John Rowen, former executive director of the Chicago-based John Howard Society, documented the case of a fourteen-year-old boy who was dry-shaved and raped by four adults in the late 1960's. Last year another youngster was raped by a number of inmates and "went into a catatonic state." Witnesses reported he was "ruined for life mentally." Inmates there confessed that up until 1973 virtually every kid coming into the jail was "ripped off on a multiple assailant basis."

Tenacious investigative reporting by Philadelphia newspapers in the late 1960's and early 1970's uncovered that well over 2,000 sexual assaults occurred in the City of Brotherly Love's adult jails.

For some twenty-six months many Philadelphia children were being raped repeatedly in the back of the sheriff's van on the way to juvenile courts for adjudication. As stated earlier, violence is not perpetrated only by peer groups but by personnel as well; Connecticut staff personnel at the Long Lane School for Girls were accused in 1973 of sexually abusing young status offenders, but since the polygraph is not mandatory in that state, it was the employee's word against the child's word in court. Cases were dismissed for lack of evidence.

During the Morales trial in Texas, it was disclosed that psychological testing is available for screening applicants who would be working with children. Although this type of testing would serve to protect a child from adults with serious emotional problems, many administrators choose to forego the screening in order to ensure ample staffing. It also ensures the inevitable—violence.

However, even careful screening cannot totally ensure an end to institutional cruelty. The very nature and structure of the penal system creates its own chemisty for violence. It is my belief, after visiting countless institutions, studying hundreds of abuse cases and talking with young inmates and personnel, that the poorly educated, poorly trained, underpaid guards are also victims of a system that denies everyone therein their humansim. Very few people working in this caldron of violence could successfully elude its effects. For this reason the turnover rate among security people and other youthful correctional personnel is generally high.

Bill Moulden, who left institutional employment after 10 years, told me in February of 1973:

> I started as a correctional officer, a guard, in a juvenile institution. I worked the hole and stripped little boys down and pushed them into rooms that were about six by six, all tile, dark and with a hole in the floor for a toilet that flushed from a button pushed by the guard outside. When the lieutenant wasn't around, I'd bring them out, talk to them, let them watch TV, take a shower, etc. I got in trouble. I had three kids then and was making less than $4,000 a year. I used to hope there would be runaways so I could get some overtime chasing them. I was slowly sinking into poverty. I was a fairly tough guard though, and a kid said to me one day, "What are you coming down on us so hard for—if it wasn't for us, you'd be out on the street looking for a job."

Ed Cohn, assistant superintendent of the Indiana Boys School, spoke frankly about the impetus to violence as I drove out to the school with him. First we discussed what sounded like some very creative programs for the students. Ed was candid and honest when he talked about the effects of working within youth corrections. He and his family live on campus. He said, "You can take it for just so long—being called a mother fucker constantly... having your wife and daughters called no-good whores, etc.— you're human, and you just explode and punch them in the mouth!" But more than half the young inmates in that Plainfield, Indiana, school have committed no serious crime, are human too and can take it for just so long when they, too, explode.

A recent experiment on the psychological effects of imprisonment on both inmates and guards had to be discontinued because of its brutalizing consequences on those taking part. Known as the Stanford Prison Study and conducted by Dr. Philip G. Zimbardo, the subjects were college students from around the country and Canada. Twenty-four males between seventeen and twenty years of age were chosen after extensive interviewing and diagnostic testing. They were paid to role-play as guards and inmates in a prison setting. They had no training except what our culture dictates for the role of a guard or an inmate.

The "prisoners" were treated as such from the very beginning. They were arrested and picked up from their homes at all hours of the day or night, booked and thrown into jail. The experimental guards acted as real-life guards. Violence grew accordingly. The study was to last two weeks but had to be "abruptly terminated after six days because the role-playing had so merged with reality that half the mock prisoners had severe emotional disturbances (uncontrollable crying, rage, disorganized thinking...) while all but a few of the guards behaved consistently in aggressive, dehumanizing ways toward the prisoners." Dr. Zimbardo noted that these pathologies were completely alien in the medical, social and educational histories of the volunteer subjects.

What made the Stanford Prison Study remarkable, according to Zimbardo, was that it was "the first time anyone [had] demonstrated that a prison-like environment could elicit pathological reactions in carefully selected, normal, healthy, average young men." This report on this important social research ended: "It is not possible to resort to a correlation between evil deeds and evil people—our guards were not sadists, nor our prisoners psychopaths. The young men in this prison were all good to begin with, but when they were pitted against the evil inherent in a total environment of imprisonment, the situation overwhelmed the individuals."

In many institutions the daily application of physical and psychological punishment becomes perverted and sadistic. (Again, more than 50 percent of all incarcerated children have committed no serious crimes.) As a form of discipline at the Beaumont School for Boys in Virginia, a supervisor ordered two boys to kill a campus dog with a stick. When they were unable to do so with the stick, the man gave them a shovel to finish the job. On the other hand, in a Texas facility, a child who killed a dog for unknown reasons was punished by forcing him to wear the dog's tail around his neck while chained to a bed for two weeks.

In Massachusetts a boy on work detail had to go to the bathroom. The guard told him to hold it. He couldn't and defecated in the carrot shed. Excerpts from legal affidavits give the reaction of staff personnel:

> The guard grabbed the kid by the hair and dragged him to put his face in the shit. The kid refused. The guard grabbed him by the hair and collar, kicked him to his knees and stuck his face in the shit saying, "That'll teach you to shit in the carrot shed, you cock sucker." The kid got up and tried to wash his face off in the barn sink. Another guard was in the barn and wouldn't let the kid wash his face. Instead he hosed him down from head to foot.

Another boy got sick while eating, but the staff insisted he continue to eat. When he vomited, he "was whacked on the head with a big serving spoon" and was made to do push-ups. The affidavit continues:

> After dinner, downstairs, the guard ordered Smith to do push-ups on the line. Smith felt sick again, asked the guard if he could go to the bathroom, was refused, and continued doing push-ups till he finally threw up again, this time on the floor. The guard ordered Smith to eat his own vomit. Smith kept refusing until the guard started kicking and hitting him. Smith was finally forced by the

guard to eat his vomit until the floor was clean. He ate it all. When he was finally excused, Smith went into the bathroom and threw up in the john.

Part of the same affidavit;

Another time this kid Hill went to the bathroom and took a shit. He forgot to flush the toilet. The guard didn't hear the toilet flush and so he went into the bathroom to check. He then came back out and grabbed Hill by the hair, brought him back into the bathroom and shoved Hill's head into the toilet bowl which was still unflushed saying, "This will teach you to flush the toilet next time."

In Arkansas in the late 1960's, several judges and correction officials created a statewide program they felt would prevent delinquency. With the public blessing of then governor and currently U.S. Senator Dale Bumpers, boys were placed in Cummins Prison, an adult facility, for one day and the guards punished them in such a way that it would "scare the devil out of the delinquent," thus preventing them from ever being tempted to break the law again.

Willie Stewart was about fifteen and weighed approximately 112 pounds when he was taken to Cummins Prison, where in early 1968 three skeletons were uncovered amid reports that hundreds of push-ups, made to jump up and down holding a hoe pressed to the prison records and verified by *The Washington Post*, Willie was "chased by a car as he entered the main gate, shot at, ordered to dunk his entire body in a pool of water, slapped, did 31 minutes of push-ups, made to jump up and down holding a hoe pressed to his head and had his hair clipped ... and [was] dumped on a floor by two guards who decided he was faking an illness...." On the way to the hospital, the young boy died. His mother was told her son "had eaten something that disagreed with him and he died."

Bobby Kendricks told the court of his experiences at the same facility:

There were four of us when I went there, and one boy kept falling down exhausted. We all did at times.... I had to kiss a guard's horse and we had to get down on all fours and oink like pigs....

When the guards said we didn't hoe fast enough, he stuck a pistol barrel in my mouth and told me to suck on it. He did it again later and told me to chew on the barrel and I did.

Kendricks described "Texas TV," a punishment to which he and the other boys were subjected. The inmate leans his forehead and nose against the wall while his feet are a yard or so from the wall, his hands held behind his back. For sport, the guards kick his feet out from under him. During the same day, the inmates were also forced to "wallow in a pool of water and excrement, dunk their heads underneath, scrape up the slime and throw it at each other." Later, during a forced run, the guards would follow on horses and knock them down.

Despite the unusually cruel and sadistic treatment, judicial and public officials in Arkansas thought "the program was good and should be continued." Even after Willie Stewart's death and other extreme incidents came to light, Judge Paul Wolfe (who helped conceive the program) said, "I think it has been successful beyond our fondest hopes, which was to head off young people from trouble again. They go down there flippant, smart aleck, full of talk, but on the way back, they say yes sir and no sir." Some of the 150 juveniles who weathered the preventive program are now serving sentences in adult prisons.

I was interviewing a creative, dedicated youth official in Virginia when I first heard of the CYA (Cover Your Ass) Policy. This particular scheme, which most correctional people regard as religion, has existed as long as the first institutional cornerstone.

On January 13, 1974, the Baltimore *Sun* published a report by Richard C. Monk, a lecturer in psychology and sociology at Mount St. Mary's College, which forced the corrections industry of Maryland to employ the CYA Policy. After spending thirty days at each of Maryland's four training schools and five forestry camps, Monk stated that some of the "institutions altered their report on brutality... elaborate strategies are used to explain the evidence of physical punishment when various neutral outsiders make inquiries.... The staff would use other children to beat upon runaways for bringing disgrace on the cottage." In one report, social workers wrote up a child who was hit with a pool cue and suffered partial loss of hearing. The report was doctored by administrators.

When the report hit the press, the director of the Juvenile Services Agency immediately asserted that there was gross inaccuracy in the study. Later, when pressured by Monk's public astonishment and shock at how the Juvenile Services Agency had ignored the report, the director denied the allegation and told the *Sun* that he "found it helpful in posing questions to inmates when evaluating institutional programs." During that same summer, when *The Washington Post* revealed widespread use of solitary confinement in the Maryland system, the same director claimed he was totally unaware of such a practice.

At Camp Hill, outside Harrisburg, Pennsylvania, I talked to children locked with adults in Mohawk Wing, an isolation area infamous among the inmates. Their whispered correspondence was a familiar refrain—the beatings from guards, the trips downstairs to the hole, etc. But officials at Camp Hill knew I was coming; Governor Milton Shapp had made arrangements. The sticks wrapped in cloth (to prevent leaving marks) that the boys described to me were gone. The downstairs hole was also empty. What remained, though, what could not be hidden, were the deepening lines of hate on the faces of the young, their sunken eyes drowning in despair. These fifteen- and sixteen-year-olders are well on their way to an adult life of crime. Jerome Silo, an adult inmate, told me he was trying to sue the commissioner of Pennsylvania's Bureau of Corrections for lack of treatment for the young boys at the facility.

The Camp Hill scene was repeated when I visited the Audy Home in Chicago. I found little. They, too, had known I was coming. The facility was spotless, nothing seemed amiss, but there was a prevailing undercurrent of hostility toward me from the staff. The tour was fast and I was not permitted to talk with the children, many of whom were lying idle in the fetal position.

Sometimes conditions arise within a penal facility that are impossible to hide, so an investigation is carried out, usually by another bureaucratic department. Few state agencies ever find fault with a sister agency (as we saw in Texas in an earlier chapter). Unless there are courageous, forthright personnel or officials who will support the children in their charges, CYA Policy remains an effective device by which corruption and abuse can flourish undetected by the taxpayers whose children and money are necessary if the system is to grind on.

I arrived at Missouri's Boonville State School for Boys one day in November of 1973. The school was in an upheaval. I took advantage of this and asked to be led to a small section on the grounds which few people ever see or know exists. As we walked to the area, my guides, three young inmates, told me about Boonville and its past history—which was reminiscent of the story of the Tower of London: common punishments were "public" floggings while tied to a flagpole and being chained to a wall in the two brick towers over the mess hall.

They told me about its current history—events occurring at the very time of my visit, stories I have seen, heard, and read hundreds of times: members of the staff having sexual relations with the children, beating them, throwing them into solitary confinement for no substantial reason, pushing drugs, etc. The unfinished symphony of institutional life.

As the boys continued their endless accounts of brutality, I thought back to the story I had read in the St. Louis *Post-Dispatch* when, in the 1940's, Governor Phil Donnelly became so incensed at the violence and killings at Boonville, he personally pulled into the grounds one midnight with a fleet of state patrol cars, removed over seventy-one boys and incarcerated them in the adult prison as incorrigibles. Not even the *Post-Dispatch* could ever find out what happened to the boys. Records are not available.

Finally my young guides and I arrived at a little knoll overlooking the grounds of Boonville. They stopped talking. All was quiet. We were at the school's graveyard. In that chilly midafternoon, I counted fifty-one white markers, only three small ones with names.

Freedom will not come
Today, this year nor ever
through compromise and fear.
I have as much right as the other
fellow has to stand on my two
feet and own the land.
I tire so of hearing people say
Let things take their course.
Tomorrow is another day.
I do not need my fredom when I'm
Dead. I cannot live on tomorrow's
Bread. Freedom is a strong seed
Planted in a great need. I live here
Too. I want freedom just as you.

—Young black girl, State Training School for Girls, Arizona

10/The Sexuality of Punishment: The Juvenile Female Offender

Female care and supervision within the penal system are steeped in sexuality. Although it is true that physical punishment for boys is harsh, brutal and at times even bloody, the young females suffer far greater psychological abuse.

When I began my study of the juvenile penal system, I was unaware of the particularly degrading treatment of young girls within youth jails. However, after visiting dozens of female facilities and witnessing incredible disparities and gross injustices the special problems of incarcerated girls became apparent.

118

A national census of juvenile detention facilities by the University of Chicago (Pappenfort *et al.* 1970) revealed that for a given offense females are incarcerated longer than males and more girls are locked up for status offenses than boys. A similar study done by LEAA in June 1971 had similar findings: Of 44,104 boys and 13,099 girls held within 722 institutions around the country, two thirds of the girls were status offenders compared with one third of the boys. Many of the girls were incarcerated only because they had indulged in sexual intercourse. My own 1974 survey of status offenders in two states showed the following: In Nebraska, only 7 percent of the boys were locked up for noncriminal acts compared with 53 percent of the girls. In Arkansas it was 22 percent for males. Females totaled 78 percent.

Male status offenders in New York State are released from training schools at eighteen; girls are required to stay until they are twenty. In Texas the average length of incarceration for boys at the Gatesville School was 10.1 months in 1972; the average time for girls at Gainesville was 12.4 months. A New Orleans study of detained youths entitled "Where Have All the Children Gone?" revealed that 71.8 percent of all the girls locked up never had any previous detentions, compared with only 56 percent of the boys.

Almost without exception, I found security in the girls' facilities I visited more intense than in the facilities of their male counterparts. Rules were more rigid, fences were higher, confinement cells smaller. Shortly after the Arizona State School for Girls was opened, personnel found that in spite of the very high fence, girls (most of whom were status offenders) were easily escaping by digging through the soft, sandy soil. The Department of Corrections solved the problem by digging a deep well around the entire perimeter of the complex and filling it with tons of concrete. Thousands of tax dollars that could have been used for counseling the children or, better still, providing a constructive community-based program went to a local contractor.

Elsewhere, Florida Director of Youth Services Joseph Rowan said their notorious Youth Hall in Dade County keeps girl detainees in "steel jail cages," and Colorado's Senator Anthony Vollack, in a surprise visit to the Girls Training School in August of 1971, found that the boys' isolation rooms were much larger than the Rose Room, where girls were hog-tied and left lying on the floor for long periods of time.

The East Texas Guidance and Achievement Center, a private facility in Tyler, Texas, houses neglected children from Illinois and Louisiana. I went there about 2 P.M. on a summer day during 1973. At one end of a large house, I found seven or eight boys who shared three bedrooms and who were free to go outdoors and play in the yard under "proper supervision." At the other end eight girls, supervised by a large, masculine woman, shared one large windowless room with a padlock on the door. I entered the hot, airless quarters and found a young girl lying in the fetal position, covered wih blankets. Her eyes were wide open and vacant. Poetry by another young girl I met in a Vermont institution echoed in my mind:

> Be alone by yourself,
> With no one with you,
> Having no one liking you.
> Liking someone, but not
> getting it returned.
> Not knowing why someone hates you
> and calls you names.

There is disparity concerning even food and education for the females. In general, boys are apportioned more food per serving than girls and are allowed to have seconds. Girls are limited to one serving. Brought to light at the *Morales v. Turman* trial was the fact that food at the Crockett girls' facility in Texas was nutritionally so inadequate that more than 80 percent of the inmates were being treated with the antibiotic tetracycline for nutrition-related skin disorders.

Within the educational structure, which is totally inadequate, the girls again fare second-best. In Texas the boys' school at Gatesville had an accredited high school while the girls' school at Gainesville was only an accredited elementary school. The state Public Welfare Department evaluated a girls' training school in Waynesburug, Pennsylvania, in 1973 and concluded that "Vocational-Educational programs were seriously lacking in depth and scope." Until the Chillicothe Girls Training School in Missouri recently changed directors, the girls were forced, in direct violation of the state's rehabilitation and educational provisions, to be servants to the staff while they ate elegantly in dining rooms furnished in John Quincy Adams decor.

In matters of personal hygiene and cleanliness, once again, incarcerated girls suffer greater indignities than their male counterparts. Most female facilities have no individual toilets. An assortment of old pee pots, coffee cans and other crude containers are issued for disposal of body wastes. At Artesia Hall, a private institution in Texas, the girls were forced to urinate in Coke bottles for punishment. The Texas Youth Council publicly hangs a "Monthly Menstruation Report" on the door of all female cottages which lists every inmate (regardless of whether she menstruates or not) and records the onset and finish of each menses. Physical examinations of girls being admitted to the Sheldon Farm for Girls in Pennsylvania determine whether they are virgins or not. Virgins are assigned one color dress; all others wear a different color.

Examinations for venereal disease are carried out with outrageous frequency. Young ladies in custody have been known to undergo as many as three and four pelvic exams for the disease. At some facilities, ten- and eleven-year-olds are forced to submit to "vaginals" each time they are transferred to a new facility, even though they have not been released between placement. In one town in Louisiana two detectives complained to me about the county coroner, who forcefully examined all runaways: "You know when he is working because you can hear the young girls screaming at the other end of the hall."

A fourteen-year-old ward of the state of Illinois who had been shipped to the Meridell Center in Austin, Texas, swallowed paper clips. During the exploratory surgery in November of 1971, a Texas doctor decided, without proper authority from anyone in Illinois, to sterilize her. Richard Laymon, Illinois guardianship administrator who gave permission for the "exploratory surgery," said, "I was not told a hysterectomy had been performed until I wrote for the surgical report two months later." The girl's father, a parking attendant, was not notified until six months later, but Laymon told the Chicago press that there was no legal requirement to do so.

Pat Murphy, the girl's appointed attorney, stated, "They [Illinois Department of Children and Family Services] told us that consent had been given by phone for the hysterectomy and there was a pathologist's report of cancer, indicating the operation was necessary." But the malignancy story was a lie; when records were produced, there was no sign of cancer. Two benign cysts, one in the right ovary, were deemed reason enough for the doctor to sterilize this young black girl. Frank Kopecky, attorney for the Illinois Department of Children and Family Services, voiced his feelings to Carolyn Toll of the Chicago *Sun-Times*: "... frankly, these children whose medical care is paid for by public assistance, are lucky to get any medical service at all."

In the summer of 1973, other wards of the state of Illinois who had been shipped across state lines—to the Mary Lee School in Austin, Texas, and to the Laurel Haven Home for Exceptional Children in Baldwin, Missouri—were administered Depro-Provera, a contraceptive drug. Depro-Provera, manufactured by The Upjohn Company, is prohibited by the Federal Food and Drug Administration to be sold or used as a contraceptive. The 1973 edition of *The Physicians Desk Reference* warned that dogs injected with the drug contracted breast cancer. It's significance with respect to humans has not been established, but repeated injections may cause amenorrhea and infertility for periods up to eighteen months and occasionally longer.

Dangers and lack of Federal Government approval notwithstanding, permission was given to administer Depro-Provera to girls whom Charlene Crump, director of the Mary Lee School, said "refuse to take birth control pills or girls who are chronic runaways." Dr. J. Keller Mack, medical consultant to the Children's Department in Illinois, commented: "If you didn't test the drug on somebody, you would never be able to put it on the market. I thought they might just as well test it on our Illinois girls as girls from anywhere else."

A continuing problem in relation to incarceration of young girls is sexual assaults by their male relatives. It has been estimated that 40 percent of all sexual assaults against girls are committed by fathers, stepfathers, brothers, uncles and other close relatives. Senator Birch Bayh tells the story of one of these youngsters:

Susie, a 12-year-old girl who had run away from home to escape her stepfather's sexual advances, was sent by the juvenile court to a juvenile correctional facility as a "person in need of supervision." Once there, she became the victim of sexual assaults by the older girls as well as the counselors. When she fought back, she was put into solitary confinement in a strip cell for several weeks. She was fed on a meager ration of bread and water, given nothing to read, and only thin pajamas to wear. As her anger increased, so did her custodians' assessment of her unmanageability. She was eventually transferred to a state mental institution, where she is still in custody.

The New York Family Court feels that as many as 10 to 30 percent of the girls in that state who come in contact with the courts are objects of forced incest. Yet in many instances girls who run away from these situations find themselves jailed, then paroled right back into the original life situation.

Senator Bayh's story also exemplifies the flagrant sexual exploitation girls suffer during confinement. An attack which occurred on Easter Sunday, 1974, at the Wayne County Jail in Honesdale, Pennsylvania, is another example. A fourteen-year-old female runaway was raped, not only by the deputy sheriff, but also by two inmates—one an admitted murderer awaiting sentencing—whom the sheriff had released from their cells to participate in the rape.

In Miami, Florida, during a trial of guards arrested for helping females escape in exchange for sexual favors at Dade County Youth Hall, the Grand Jury commented: "We have heard ... a range of incredible abuses that sound more like a prison out of the dark ages.... We have heard tales of young girls being forced to perform all sorts of perverted acts."

Pregnant girls or new mothers who are jailed represent some of the saddest cases I have ever witnessed. Many women find pregnancy or motherhood traumatic—a time for readjusting life-style and setting new priorities. For minors those same conditions, added to the trauma and tyranny of penal confinement, serve to escalate the confusion, loneliness, guilt and bitterness already present in the troubled girl's mind. However, the penal industry—Chicago's Audy Home is an example—often throws pregnant girls awaiting adjudication into solitary confinement as punishment for their pregnancy. An Alabama matron beat one pregnant girl so viciously, she aborted. In Texas female facilities, pregnant girls are forced to agree to abortion or spend time in solitary confinement.

During the Morales trial, Judge Wayne Justice permitted me to sit in the jury box as an observer to the massive right-to-treatment case. Sitting a few feet from the witness chair, I watched a nervous, apprehensive girl, Kitty Trudell, enter the large court room under federal escort. She took the oath and glanced at her attorney, Steve Bercu. Words were not exchanged, but the young girl seemed to be reassured. Biting her lower lip, she lowered herself into the witness chair from which her story would unfold to a strangely silent courtroom.

In January of 1973, Kitty Trudell was incarcerated at the Texas Brownsville Reception Center and later at the Gainesville State School for Girls, where doctors informed her she was three months pregnant. On the evening of January 24, a staff person approached Kitty: "I have some pills to start your period." Although Kitty's oldest sister, who had already served time at Gainesville, cautioned her against taking any medication, all the girls knew that if you were pregnant and refused the pills, it meant solitary confinement. So the girl took the pills and exercised as told.

"On February first, I started bleeding real bad." She informed the nurse, but no one came to see her. No nurse, no doctor, no houseparent. No one. On the night of February 15, the rooms were locked at 8:45 P.M. As usual, the girls were given their pee pots. Kitty Trudell aborted a three-month-old fetus in her pee pot. She placed a towel over the pot and, unable to sleep, kept company with that portion of her dead self during the night. Hours later, when the room was unlocked, she flushed the fetus down a toilet.

Kitty saved one of the pills "to see what it was, because a lot of other girls lost their babies, too." Her self-assurance crumbled when she told the court, "I took the pills because I wanted to go home and not be locked up. I don't like to be locked up behind steel doors."

Young mothers, on countless occasions, pleaded with me to intercede so they could see their sons or daughters. One inmate in the state of Washington told me she hadn't seen her son for seven months. Officials at the Manchester Industrial School in New Hampshire also deny girls permission to see their children.

A baby delivered at the Long Lane School in Connecticut was placed for adoption without permission of the natural mother, who, now in her twenties, is very bitter. I saw "child-mothers" in New York City shelters with stuffed animals and dolls on their beds and their babies' photographs hidden in the bureau drawers.

If American youth facilities foster crime and failure, they also foster, by their very existence, homosexuality. "Institutions make studs," observed one girl at the Waynesburg school in Pennsylvania. She said inmates become homosexual because they are "neglected by their boyfriends, have been raped, or just need someone to be with, to dress up for."

Homosexuality touches almost every incarcerated juvenile at one time or another in varying degrees. Sooner or later, through loneliness, trickery or coercion, many become a participant or an accomplice to a homosexual act or relationship with peers or personnel. For this reason, staff will usually go to great lengths to prevent any friendly contact among the girls. At the Salem School for Girls in West Virginia, youngsters from thirteen to eighteen are locked in their rooms and denied friendships "because they lead to homosexuality." They are also forbidden to converse with visitors. Talk of lesbianism is constantly drummed into them along with lectures on how dangerous and evil it is to society.

The matrons at the Mapleland Girls Training School in the state of Washington did something of a reverse of this. Three middle-aged women who had been busy censuring a student's letter watched as my young guide saw a friend she apparently hadn't seen for a long time and rushed over to embrace and kiss her. The matrons exchanged amused glances, then nodded and grimaced among themselves, seemingly enjoying the lonely despair of girls trying to cope with their emotions, desires and sanity.

A southern Junior League group received a section of transcript and letter from a judge who wrote:

> The transcript reflects the conditions existing when the Junior League came on the scene. I had learned enough from children themselves ... where I had to ask God to forgive me for sending

children to those places, and I had reached the point where I was not sure that He was forgiving me. . . .

———, being duly sworn, testified as follows:

Direct examination by
Mr. Martin

Q ———, would you state your full name?

A ———.

Q How old are you?

A Fifteen.

Q Where are your parents?

A My mother is dead. I don't know where my father is.

Q How long have you been living without your parents?

A I'm not sure, six or seven years, I guess.

Q Have you ever known any parents? Do you remember your parents?

A I remember my mother and my stepfather.

Q In your recollection, have you ever called anyone Mama and Daddy?

A No.

Q Why did you leave [run from] the Satellitic Home?

A Well, mostly because a lot of the girls are lesbians, and they'll come up to you like Janet did. She'd say something like "Well, we got so and so the other night," and they'll tell me what they had done to her. They said "By the time summer comes, we'll have every girl in this house like that. . . ."

Q Did you see Dr. ——— while you were out there?

A Yes.

Q Did he say anything to you?

A Yes, he told me that I was going to be put on two weeks probation. He said if I didn't shape up within those two weeks, that he could snap his fingers, and I'd be up there until I was twenty-one, and that just scared me to death.

Q Was that a reason why you left?

A Yes.

Direct examination by
Mr. Martin

Q State your full name for the record, please.

A ———.

Q Where do you live?

A ———, South Carolina.

Q Are you any relation to the child [———] in this case?

A I'm her sister. I'm actually her half-sister.

Q What sort of relationship over the years have you formed with her?

A I've been just about all the mother she's had. Our mother was an alcoholic. *As far as her fear of Willow Lane, I put it in her.* I ran away when I was fourteen years old with the man that I later married. As a result of that—they sent me out there for eight months. That's when it was really bad out there, and I told ——— about this place. I know what went on out there, because I was there eight months. They can't tell me that these acts aren't committed, because they were tried on me. As far as girls being raped, they are raped out there. I've seen it done. I've seen them get cucumbers out of the garden about that big [indicating] and that big around, and I've seen girls split wide open with them. The nurse, that was my house mother, was queer. She was lesbian. She would take the girls in and take turns. If they didn't sleep with her, they were sent to the detention cell. In the detention cell, they weren't allowed to talk to anybody. They didn't have any clothes on except a long robe. They were allowed to eat no sweets, nothing to read. You were in there for however long they said, and you didn't speak to a single soul. If you did, your time went up that much more. I know these things were done, and I told ——— about them. Maybe I was wrong.

Q From what you told her, would that be enough to scare her?

A I guess so. I still have dreams about it myself. For about six months after I got out, I was scared to wake up in the morning. My mother put a little picket fence about that high [indicating] around the trailer, and I was fifteen years old. When I came home and saw it, I made her tear it down be-

cause I didn't want any fences around me after I had been
locked up for eight months.

Q Being her sister, knowing her all her life, knowing what she's
been through, what she's come through, and likely to go
through, what does ———— need more than anything now?

A She needs love more than anything. She needs a firm hand. I
don't know. She came creeping in my bedroom in the middle
of the night and cried and told me she loved me. She's
screaming for love.

Ann Rittenhouse, social worker and caseworker supervisor at
the Alabama State Training School for Girls for over eight years,
has studied the records of eight hundred girls. In a deposition for
the United States Justice Department, she told U.S. attorneys
that most of the girls placed in the training school are there because Alabama has no other resources. Even then, there is a
waiting period—as long as three or four months—before the girls
can get into state training facilities. So they wait in detention
centers and jails. To the social worker's knowledge, there are no
foster homes in the state created exclusively for girls. Nor are there
any group homes. Eighty percent have committed no crimes
but are in danger of becoming "institutionalized," of "deteriorating" and "regressing."

Unfortunately, Ms. Rittenhouse's study could apply to almost
any given state in the union. In the academic world, there has
been little interest generated and almost nothing written on the
incarcerated female, with the notable exception of *The Adolescent
Girl in Conflict* by Dr. Gisela Konopka.

Regardless of adverse conditions and the seeming hopelessness
of their situation, many of the girls I interviewed around the
country voiced optimism. In three different states, as I left, they
said in effect, "Things are bad here, very bad. But you know,
they're closing them [institutions] down in Massachusetts!"

That state did, in fact, under the forceful leadership of Dr.
Jerome Miller, close all state and county training schools except
one. The Lancaster Girls School, which until 1972 was giving
muscular injections of saline for punishment, at this writing continues to flourish. The old sexist double standard exists, even in
this era of reform.

*I believe it, in its effects, to be cruel and wrong....
I am persuaded that those who devised this system
of prison discipline ... do not know what it is that
they are doing. I believe that very few men are
capable of estimating the immense amount of
torture and agony which this dreadful punishment
... inflicts upon the sufferers.... I hold this slow
and daily tampering with the mysteries of the brain,
to be immeasurably worse than any torture of the
body.*

—Charles Dickens, after inspecting the first American
penal isolation unit at Eastern State Penitentiary in
Philadelphia in 1842

11/The Old Solitary Confinement: Steel, Concrete and Obscenities

Solitary confinement is widely used in juvenile
penal institutions throughout the United States.
Just about every facility I have visited in thirty
states has some form of punitive isolation for
those children who break rules or are otherwise
troublesome. In some tragic instances, isolation
is even used for punishing the mentally retarded.

Solitary confinement consists in locking a child
in a small, highly secure cell by himself for a
period of time—it may be one day, it may be
three months or longer. The rooms are dirty,
damp, vermin-infected, vile-smelling, cold in the

129

winter and hot in summer. They usually have a bare mattress on the floor and a toilet or hole in the floor. Total silence is the rule. No talking, no reading, no visitations.

Most of the children I saw wore only underwear. Behind heavy steel and iron doors they would sit in whatever little sunlight was available; if the door had bars, they'd rest their arms and hands on the floor beyond the cell, as if reaching out to freedom from this institutional hellhole. I would stop to talk, to make conversation, but found passive, frozen faces, concealing hurt, rage, determination or hopelessness.

The rationale for using solitary confinement sounds reasonably justifiable from the standpoint of correctional personnel. They claim it is used basically to protect the child from inflicting physical or psychological injury on himself or others. However, Dr. Danilo Ponce, child psychiatrist and consultant at the Diamond Head Mental Health Center in Hawaii, believes that protecting a child capable of self-harm or destruction with "isolation per se, doesn't accomplish anything.... It may make things worse. By depriving the kid of stimulation and human contact, you're really creating more problems than you are solving. Somebody needs to be with the child. It's vital." I personally feel, after visiting staff and talking with students, that solitary confinement has only one major purpose and that is Control. It is the staff's trump card; it is a substitute for comprehensive and dedicated treatment and rehabilitation.

On October 2, 1975, at the Alabama Industrial School for Boys outside Birmingham (currently called the Roebuck Campus), I was shown the worst isolation cells yet by George M. Phyfer, Director of Alabama's Department of Youth Services. Beyond a locked door in the cellar of a boys' cottage were two small cages constructed of steel mesh and reinforced with thick, rusty iron grating. These cells were built sixteen years ago at the cost of $900. Hanging from the iron ceiling were pieces of material. They were remnants of makeshift hammocks made by the boys with whatever cloth was available to them—someone had even used the plastic mattress cover—to escape the rats that crept into the cages as the children slept.

No one outside the institution knew these cells existed until late summer of '75, when one runaway lad refused to return to Roebuck Campus* for fear of being punished in the iron cages. His voiced fears led to an investigation and the cells, which only recently had been made more comfortable by installation of toilets, were ordered closed by Director Phyfer.

In the United States, three important events prompted national interest in the subject of solitary confinement. The first was the 1933–35 United States Antarctic Expedition, during which the long, cold nights of close confinement caused schizophrenia to strike a member of Admiral Richard Byrd's research team. But perhaps what precipitated intensified study of the subject was this country's preoccupation with the effects of close confinement and long periods of isolation for our space program astronauts.

Modern research has been conducted with animals or with adult humans. The findings of how isolation affects animals is quite startling. Dr. Francis Vincent De Fuedis and other researchers at the Indiana University School of Medicine found that the brain chemistry of animals placed in isolation actually changed. In mice, Dr. DeFuedis claims, "behavioral change correlated directly with a marked decrease in the incorporation of carbon atoms of glucose (energy sources) into their brains." Even though the mice had ample food and water, "the effects of confinement made them violent and aggressive to their fellow mice once they returned to their colonies."

Macaque monkeys, isolated for the first six months of their lives, all had difficulty adjusting to monkeys who had not been secluded. As with mice, "isolated monkeys seemed to be unwilling to expose themselves to new or complex situations, and if this occurred, violent behavioral reactions followed." Follow-up research revealed that "social aggressiveness, self-threatening behavior and abnormal sexual behavior were commonly displayed at maturity." Females were "marked by indifference and brutality toward their offspring." The same was true of chimpanzees.

Human experimentation with isolation and solitary confinement

* At the same facility stands Bush Chapel, erected in 1923. The building's paint peels and its wood rots even though there exists a $400,000 special endowment fund designated for its upkeep.

clearly shows that forced isolated imprisonment has a devastating effect on the human mind and body. Research conducted over the last twenty years corroborates that normal people who are confined for periods of time, generally no longer than a two-week duration, suffer decreased visual skills including impaired color differentiation, slowed motor coordination and poor auditory ability. There is an inability to concentrate, to think clearly. Subjects are bored, highly restless and suffer speech impairments. Many experience hallucinations and perceptual distortions of human faces. A participant of Bexton, Heron and Scott's study in 1954 reported: "The wall bulged toward me and went back; the experimenter looked short, then he suddenly got taller, then he closed up again; the whole room is undulating, swirling; things don't stay put; people appear roughed."

Russian researchers discovered that "respiratory rate and blood pressure began to decrease while the heart rate increased in men who were isolated for sixty days." Other studies indicated that solitude, whether at sea or in polar climates, causes one to be "lethargic and withdrawn, progressively more irritable, depressed, have changes in body-images and lose contact with reality." The U.S. Department of Defense found that American soldiers who endured enemy captivity similar to that used by our juvenile penal system experienced psychoses and, in some instances, adrenal gland collapse, resulting in death.

It was formerly believed that because solitary confinement resembles the act of sleeping, the body would have increased resistance to skin disorders. However, the opposite is true, which perhaps explains why 80 percent of the girls at Texas youth facilities were treated for skin disorders in 1972.

In 1964, Russian investigator Y. Nefedov confirmed earlier research of 1944, that the frequency of electrical (alpha) waves within the brain progressively slows down as the duration of isolation lengthens. Dr. DeFuedis went even further, stating that isolation affects the supply of glucose in the blood and that "brain energy metabolism depends rather exclusively on a continued supply of glucose from the blood . . . and changes in these biochemical agents within the body and blood will alter brain function and behavior."

Dr. Walter L. Wilkins, scientific director of the Navy Medical

Neuropsychiatric Research Unit in San Diego, recently described volunteers who spent months and years in isolation research as "men of heroic conduct."

The U.S. space program has pointed out that to cope successfully with solitude, man must have "emotional stability, composure and stoical compatibility." In one major laboratory-controlled experiment to prove the effects of solitary confinement on grown men, more than one third dropped out because "they could not take it." A study made of these men revealed they tended to be smokers, nonreaders, watched a lot of television and were younger than the other volunteers. This description typifies the children in our jails, detention facilities and state training schools. However, there is one disparity. Here, there is no quitting. Here is only the daily threat and reality of solitary confinement behind massive iron doors. As one ex-inmate puts it: "I was ready for anything when the state got me. I was reaching out. They put me in 48 hour solitary. My wound, which was open, closed, and the infection was locked inside me for 18 years."

What effect does extended isolation have on a child? Scientifically speaking, no one really knows, for there has been little research on isolation as it pertains specifically to the young. However, some leading authorities have made their thoughts known. During the *Morales v. Turman* case, Dr. Gisela Konopka, Nazi concentration camp survivor and current director of the Center for Youth Development and Research at the University of Minnesota, testified that isolating young children for any period of time is "wrong and demeaning because it only increases anger, fosters alienation and can do great harm to the child." Dr. C. Jack Friedman at the Philadelphia Psychiatric Center asserts that "if a child is mad when he is placed in lock-up, then the experience of total isolation from fellow students and staff serves only to reinforce that madness."

Those within the penal industry have supported the above statements. Superintendent Leonard F. Gmiener of the Montrose School for Girls in Maryland told how one of his charges in lockup pulled a radiator off the wall. William Kelley, ex-employee of Green Valley, a private facility in Volusia County, Florida, described the desperation and rage of one of their children for State Attorney Investigator Thomas Loadholtz:

... I watched this student who was thrown in our bomb shelter
without food for over four days and this was authorized. I don't
know who authorized it, but it was called therapy—starvation
therapy ... I listened to him pound on that metal door and I know
it's a matter of record there's a welder who had to repair that metal
door on that bomb shelter from the rattle that that boy gave it.*

I myself saw a cinder block wall that had been clawed by a sixteen-
year-old boy in Arizona. In his madness to climb toward an iron
window sill, he ripped the flesh of several fingers down to the
bare bones.

Institutions who claim they no longer have solitary confinement
have simply adjusted their terminology, deceived or lied outright.
Casual observers now hear such esthetic terms as Crisis Intervention Room, Security Treatment Room, Quiet Room, Meditation—
Separation—Time Out—Psycho Room. For girls it may be called
the Rose Room. Chicago's Audy Home refers to it as the Blue
Room. All the aforementioned titles have originated with the
staff and professional people. The inmates' labels are more graphic
for they are based on experience and not public relations: the
Hole, Black Hole, Hellhole, Jug, Coffin Box, Cockroach Play-
ground and Looney Room.

A recent survey of fifty residential treatment centers within the
states of Iowa, Minnesota and Wisconsin, though, revealed that
old ways do not die by changing names or even concepts. In the
questionnaire 40 percent of the centers admitted they used solitary
confinement under the label "control room." Sixty percent denied
the practice. However, in lieu of a questionnaire, on-the-site
surprise inspections may give a very different reading.

Early in 1970 the New York State legislature passed a law
limiting solitary confinement to one day and eliminating it completely for children under thirteen. It also directed that "each
isolated child must be examined once in each 24-hour period by a
licensed physician." In response to this legislation, the commissioner of social services complained to Governor Rockefeller:
"... the most frequent reasons for isolation of girls are hysterical
and uncontrollable behavior and attempts at self-destruction, and

---

* U.S. Senate investigators later found that the boy's mother was billed ten
dollars for the welding job.

among boys, the most frequent reasons are extreme aggressive behavior and persistent running away.... The bill allows little room for discretion."

On May 20, 1970, Nelson A. Rockefeller exercised his executive power against the children of New York State and vetoed the bill. Since that time, the same legislation hasn't even got out of committee. About the only changes visible in the solitary confinement procedure concern metal hand- and leg-cuffs. They have been replaced by disposable plastic restraints which are tighter, consequently hurt more and can be removed only by cutting with a shears.

In 1971 a federal court hearing in New York State revealed that 81 inmates at the Brookwood Center for Girls had been placed in solitary for a total of 369 days. The then-director of clinical services and acting principal of the education programs said this treatment method provided the girls an opportunity to get hold of themselves and to think through their problems. An ex-inmate put it differently: "Did you ever try sleeping on a cold, bare floor, with your stomach aching from hunger and your head filled with thoughts of suicide, hate and revenge?" Federal Judge Morris E. Lasker issued an injunction against the state training schools to discontinue the "cruel and unusual punishment." Eight months later a legal aid lawyer visiting Brookwood found children still in solitary confinment.

This is not unique. Nor is it uncommon for those in charge to feign ignorance of policy abuses. In Maryland before a child can be placed in isolation, the state director of youth corrections must be notified in writing and give his approval. Nonetheless, Robert C. Hilson, director of Maryland state juvenile institutions, was "shocked" when reporters found that during 1973 at least 226 children had been locked up for more than forty-eight hours in 1,213 different instances. Hilson told the press, "I'm going to raise holy hell with those who have been abusing the policy." But when the local press died down, so did the holy hell, and everything was back to normal.

Hawaii long ago outlawed solitary confinement for adults, but children were unaffected by the order. When Murry Engle of the *Star Bulletin* recently exposed the frequent lockups at Koolau's Youth Correctional Facility, Beadie Dawson, spokesman for the state department of social services, countered: "Now isolation is just a place for the child to cool off and is similar to a parent sending a naughty child to his room." Even states with national reputations for progressive reform still have solitary units. A lawyer from Oregon wrote me, "I have toured the state training schools and was appalled at their isolation units—they're cell blocks, pure and simple."

"Man in isolation is man in stress," wrote Dr. Roland Radloff, program director of social psychology at the National Science Foundation. Truer words were never spoken for two youngsters handcuffed to a bed in solitary confinement at the Glen Mills School for Boys in Pennsylvania shortly before Christmas 1973. A fire broke out in their seven by eleven room at the private, non-profit school. After some delay, the boys were released but were badly burned and in need of hospitalization. Edwin Snider, with burns covering 45 percent of his body, died five weeks later. Rodney Hallman of Reading, a rather nervous, shy boy was charged with murder and arson. The Snider-Hallman case is a classical study of the tragedy and institutional insanity surrounding the practice of solitary confinement.

Rodney was in isolation because of uncontrollable behavior at his cottage. Edwin had escaped from Glen Mills but voluntarily returned because "it was too cold in the woods." While officials at the school said the boys were not handcuffed as reported by the press, employees told state investigators that a few days before the fire, they saw Snider "escorted on the grounds in a straitjacket by staff people" and later "handcuffed to the Hallman boy."

One of the boys lit a fire to get the attention of the guard with hopes of getting out of the cell. It was not until two highly flammable mattresses burst into flames and short-circuited the lighting that the guard responded to the youngsters' screams. Even then, the supervisor had no key on hand to open the isolation door. When he finally found one, it was too late for Edwin Snider.*

---

* Sleighton Farms, sister institution to Glen Mills, saw a tragic parallel when, in 1972, sixteen-year-old Henrietta Brown was placed in solitary confinement. Her mattress caught fire. Rescuers, unable to open the heat-buckled door for more than ten minutes, were too late. On June 19, 1972, Henrietta died from "extensive second and third degree burns of the face, neck and extremities."

Three months before this misadventure, a conscientious probation officer, Vincent Mirigliana, reported to a Philadelphia juvenile
court:

> I feel in my conscience I should inform the court that Glen Mills
> represents an antiquated system. [He described their isolation cells
> as follows.] There are four concrete walls and a latrine that does
> not flush unless it is flushed from the outside. There is a concrete
> slab, upon which a mattress is placed on which the boy sleeps.
> There is no light in the cell room itself, hence the boys are kept
> in total darkness. There is no supervision other than a man who
> brings up food and who is allowed to give the boy a shower. Boys
> remain in the dungeon for days with no reading material and
> nothing to keep them occupied other than the four concrete walls.

His words were met with judicial indifference.

A quiet and unpublished state welfare investigation after the
fact revealed that "boys were placed in the detention cells
[solitary confinment] on 394 occasions for a total of 2,044 days
during 1973. The average stay was over five days. One boy was
confined for 35 consecutive days. We have a report from another
youth who jumped from a third floor window in the detention
facility in March and was hospitalized with back and arm in-
juries for more than two weeks." Pennsylvania State Investigator
James M. McGrory found that the supervisory arrangement emphasized staff convenience to the point of child neglect.

The Glen Mills School immediately and successfully sought
protection against rumored reprimand from the state department
of welfare (which doesn't even have the power to enforce licensing of Glen Mills and other such facilities). On January 24, 1974,
the Honorable John Justus Bodley of the Court of Common
Pleas in Bucks County wrote the following letter to the superintendent of Glen Mills:

Dear Mr. Novick:

Thank you for calling my attention to the publicity and apparent
irresponsible reporting which grew out of the unfortunate fire at

---

Her death was never reported to the Pennsylvania Department of Welfare as
required by law, nor was it reported to her sentencing judge, Joseph Bruno.

your institution on December 21, 1973. I can offer little consolation by saying that, assuming your review of the events to have been accurate, as I do, the sensational big lie technique is never set aright by those who employ it. This is an unfortunate truth which we find in our modern mass media.

Having had occasion to commit boys to your institution in the past, I am aware of the good work that you have done and I trust that those in our Department of Welfare who hold the view that juvenile delinquents should not be committed to institutions will eventually learn that there is a crying need for more facilities like yours. I trust that you will be able to secure the kind of cooperation from the Department which you deserve.

You will note that I am sending a copy of this letter to the Secretary of the Department so that she might become aware of the fact that you have support among the judiciary.

> Sincerely yours,
> John Justus Bodley

JJB:amr
cc:Mrs. Helene Wohlgemuth, Secretary
   Department of Welfare

Three days before this letter was written, Rodney Hallman, charged with murder and arson, told McGrory, "You got to get rid of that detention. It climbs a man up the wall."

Dr. Karl Menninger of the Menninger Foundation in Topeka, Kansas, recently responded to my question on how he felt about solitary confinement:

> Do I have any thoughts on the effects of keeping young people in confinement? I get so mad and hysterical I can't think anymore. When I think of the savage, brutal and uncivilized way they are treated, I think it's near absolute evil. I feel sure it's only done where there are especially strong reasons to keep the public from finding out about it. Expose it if you know about it and don't let anyone say, as a German citizen of Weimar did to us when we went into Buchenwald, that they didn't know what was going on in there.

Dr. Menninger's outrage is justified. There was nothing in my travels to equal the depressive, unhealthy, uncivilized aura of isolation. Here in stark solitude, the young lie (often in the fetal position) or lean against the walls covered with others' names, dates and poetry of obscenities, expressing separate and collective rage against the darkness of the night.

But most powerful, most glaring, most deeply etched in the walls of the bricks and stones, most deeply carved in the wood and scratched on the metal, is that four letter word we all know and use ourselves from time to time: H E L P. It is an obscenity too, because we as a people and a nation permit it to go ignored while the dreams of these children, generation after generation, perish in the dust of their forgotten youth.

I am afraid, comfort me. I fear this place with walls.
Your hard drugs dope me. With your lies, others
blame me. I am alone yet my friends are with me.
I have clean water to cool me, green grass to dance
for me, tall trees to sing softly to me, the sun and
moon as a light in the back of my mind, to guard me.

—Fifteen-year-old-girl,
Minnesota

12/The New Solitary Confinement: Thorazine to Electro-Cell Implants

In 1953, chemotherapeutic treatment of the mentally ill made notable progress with the introduction of tranquilizers. Chlorpromazine (Thorazine) was one of the earliest drugs to achieve prominence in relieving aggressiveness, noisiness and agitation among the disturbed. For the first time in years patients enjoyed activities and relationships that would have been impossible without its benefits.

By today the consumption of tranquilizers as well as barbiturates (sedatives) and amphetamines (stimulants, which we will not discuss here) has grown out of all proportion to their benefits. Pharmaceutical salesmen, fully aware of staffing problems, training problems and the entire realm of difficulties that beset juvenile institutions, realize they have a bonanza market.

Administrators bent on maintaining a smooth-sailing ship at all costs, are thankful for the supportive custodial role psychotherapeutic drugs play in minimizing fighting, running away and general mayhem, as well as for its use in controlling and punishing problem children.

Physicians and psychiatrists attached to juvenile facilities often fall into one of two categories. Either they are too incompetent to maintain a private practice or they are supplementing an already overburdened lucrative practice. Therefore, they may find that the liberal administration of mood drugs is useful. A tranquil institution puts fewer demands on the doctor's time and/or talents.

For these reasons incarcerated children are now forced to endure not only the old methods of isolation but the new as well. Locked within four small walls behind metal doors, they find themselves in a frightening, bewildering state as medicine injected into their bodies takes hold of their minds. The evils of yesteryear, brutal punishment and solitary confinement, combine with the evils of modern drugs to further enslave these children to their keepers.

Martin Cole, eighteen, was one of eighty children dumped into mental hospitals by Chicago schools, parents and state agencies, because there were no other facilities for neglected minors. These eighty, along with hundreds of others already incarcerated in five different state hospitals, were subjected to regular medication every day they were confined.

Martin was admitted to the Chicago-Read Mental Health Center late in 1972. He came from the Tinley Park Mental Health Center, where during a three-year-confinment the hospital staff continually asked his state guardian to place him outside the hospital. On the day of Martin's admission, the examining physician ordered a daily dose of Thorazine (a tranquilizer), 150 milligrams, and Stelazine (a sedative-stimulant), 2 mgm., which he received for over three months. On February 6 a technician requested an order for Amytal Sodium (a sedative), 7½ grains, IM (intramuscularly), PRN (whenever needed). The request was granted over the phone.

On February 16 the physician increased the Thorazine to 200 mgm. and Stelazine to 15 mgm. daily because Martin was "agitative, disturbing and hyperactive." On March 14, Martin was given Amytal Sodium, 7½ gr., IM. A progress note entered on

April 29 indicated "no behavior problems," but medication continued as before.

On May 29, Cole refused oral medication and was given another injection of Amytal Sodium. Simultaneously, the doctor ordered the Thorazine increased to 450 mgm. a day and Stelazine to 30 mgm. a day, the maximum recommended dosage. On May 30 he again increased the dosages because of an "increased tendency to become belligerent."

On July 19 the Thorazine was increased to 600 mgm. a day and the Stelazine remained at twice the maximum recommended dosage. On July 20 it became necessary to prescribe Artane to combat the side effects of the antipsychotic drugs that were being administered in such heavy dosages. On the same date, however, Navane, another powerful antipsychotic drug, was given intramuscularly. Progress notes between July 26 and 28 said that Martin was "really out of it."

On July 31, at the request of a mental health technician, the doctor ordered by phone 100 mgm. of Nembutal. On August 2 the Thorazine dosage was increased to 800 mgm. a day and the staff was given discretion as to whether Nembutal should be given. On August 7 the physician prescribed the tranquilizer Prolixin (zombie juice, as the inmates call it), 20 mgm. a day (the maximum recommended dosage), an intramuscular injection of Valium, an oral dose of chloral hydrate, a hypnotic, 400 mgm. of Thorazine, 100 mgm. of which were given IM, and full restraints were applied. For the first time during Cole's stay, the doctor called for psychiatric evaluation. Consultation lasted less than ten minutes: the psychiatrist continued the level of medication.

On August 16, 30 mgm. of Prolixin was ordered, 50 percent more than the maximum recommended dosage. Cole began to develop abscesses on his buttocks from the intramuscular injections. Penicillin was initiated but discontinued after serious adverse patient reaction. On the following day Martin got three times the maximum recommanded dosage of Prolixin, two thirds the maximum recommended dosage of Valium and the maximum recommended dosage of Elavil, an antidepressant.

A psychiatric examination given at this time advised that Martin was desperately in need of close personal contact with a therapist.

Despite this recommendation, on September 13, another psychiatrist prescribed the maximum recommended dosage of the most powerful antipsychotic drug, Haldol, and Thorazine, 200 mgm. a day, to be given at the staff's discretion. On October 22 the physician ordered Haldol, 21 mgm. a day, the dosage exceeding by 50 percent the maximum recommended for adults. The doctor entered a note that Cole's temper "... often babyish, too ... may have been triggered from boredom from his long institutional stay." During this entire period, Martin Cole, who was at Chicago Tinley Park simply because he was a "neglected minor," also spent more than twenty-five days in the old form of solitary confinement—a small strip cell—with nothing to look forward to all day save interruptions for massive dosages of drugs.

As of August 1973, more than two thirds of the patients at the Chicago Tinley Park Mental Center were unnecessarily hospitalized. Almost half of the children at the Chicago-Read, Elgin State, and Madden State facilities should not have been incarcerated, either. Yet because two thirds of all "direct-care staff" were nonprofessionals, and because their job was to control the behavior of the child, well over 70 percent of the inmates were on psychotropic or narcotic drugs by order of a staff physician.

What do these drugs do? Tranquilizers and barbiturates in excess cause drowsiness and slurred speech and preclude the user from normal activities. Prolonged overuse of tranquilizers can cause jaundice, liver and kidney deterioration, respiratory problems, ulceration of the bowels, intestinal hemorrhage or brain damage. Prolonged use of barbiturates can cause addiction, the withdrawal symptoms of which are severe nervousness, body twitchings and convulsions. Either sudden withdrawal or an overdose can cause death.

Pharmacist Milton Silverman and Dr. Philip R. Lee, authors of *Pills, Profits and Politics,* state that as many as 30 to 40 percent of all hospital patients suffer adverse drug reactions and as many as 160,000 die annually due to legal drug dosages. "It [misuse of drugs] ranks among the top causes of hospitalization ... and kills more victims than does cancer of the breast." According to Chicago pediatrician Dr. Robert Mendelsohn, "we simply do not know what the effect is on the child's body, especially if several drugs are given simultaneously."

One would presume that if a child is given a single drug—
Thorazine, for instance—the doctors and personnel who should
be aware of the effects of such a drug could protect the child
according to his medical history and physical condition. But all
too often, in the heat of crisis or institutional policy to quiet a
troublemaker or a child who is going berserk in solitary confinement, the needle is quicker than a timely review of his medical
records. Such was the case of Anthony Jones, a nineteen-year-old
asthmatic at the Sheridan, Illinois, Training School for Boys, who
was given daily injections of Thorazine for misbehaving. Had
those responsible for medicating the young man read the warnings
enclosed with the vial, they would have known that Thorazine is
contraindicated for asthmatics. Anthony Jones died of strangula-
tion caused by Thorazine-induced respiratory inertia.

The gross misuse of drugs as witnessed in the cases of Martin
Cole and Anthony Jones caused Chicago Legal Aide attorneys
Patrick T. Murphy and John D. Sullenberger to file a hard-hitting
class action lawsuit against the Illinois State Department of
Mental Health late in 1973. They alleged that the state hospital
"utilized psychotropic drugs solely to control patients rather than
in a therapeutic fashion for purpose of treatment." Four months
later in the Circuit Court of Cook County, Chicago, a nationally
prominent mental health judge, Joseph Schneider, ruled that
future use of psychotropic drugs must be part of an overall treatment plan, not indiscriminately used for institutional control of
the child. He called for an end to placing poor and neglected
children in inferior facilities while well-to-do children have benefit
of far superior state and private institutions. The judge also ordered an independent ombudsman to review the treatment of
wards of the state in mental hospitals.

Another major class action suit (*Nelson* et al. *v. Heyne* et al.)
in the United States District Court for the Northern District of
Indiana documented that poorly trained and nonprofessional personnel were permitted to give daily injections to children solely
for the purpose of control and punishment. Its premise, as documented by attorneys Tom DiGrazia of the Youth Advocacy Program and John Forham of the Legal Education Program in
South Bend, Indiana, maintained that inmates at the Indiana

Boys School were subjected to prolonged solitary confinement, corporal punishment and indiscriminate use of powerful tranquilizing drugs. The youngsters were placed in solitary confinement "bird cages," as the inmates called them, four by eight feet, thirty in all, for as long as ninety consecutive days, including Christmas and New Year's Day. There the guards gave them IM injections of Thorazine and Sparine, which the "doctors rarely prescribed because they were not there."

After months of litigation, Federal Judge Robert P. Grant ruled:

> The court finds as shocking to the conscience and violative of the Plaintiffs' [boys'] 8th and 14th Amendment rights, the Defendants' [correctional personnel] present policy with respect to tranquilizing drugs ... policies are far afield of minimal medical and constitutional standards. Accordingly, the Court orders the immediate cessation of tranquilizing drugs which are administered without the specific authorization of a physician.... It is further ordered that defendants prepare and submit for the court's evaluation a formalized policy governing use of tranquilizing drugs. The proposal must include detailed provisions governing the prescription of drugs, the administration of drugs, and procedures to insure psychological and medical evaluation of those to whom the drugs are given.

Though the landmark decision by Judge Grant left no doubt concerning drug abuse of children, the state of Indiana appealed to the second highest court in the land—the United States Court of Appeals for the Seventh Circuit. Never before in American history had a right-to-treatment case for juveniles gone that high in the judicial system.

On January 31, 1974, Senior Circuit Judge Roger J. Kiley and Circuit Judges Thomas E. Fairchild and Robert Sprecher handed down their decision which supported Judge Robert Grant:

> We are not persuaded by Defendants' arguments that the use of tranquilizing drugs is not punishment. Experts testified that the tranquilizing drugs administered to juveniles can cause: the collapse of the cardiovascular system, the closing of a patient's throat with consequent asphyxiation, a depressant effect on the production of bone marrow, jaundice from an affected liver, and drowsiness, hematological disorders, sore throat and ocular changes.

They further ordered, as had judges Schneider and Grant, a state policy of minimum medical safeguards, to protect the child from drug assaults by unauthorized personnel.

However, rulings by courageous state or federal judges will not stop the wanton, abusive use of psychotropic drugs. The problem is complex, and hidden professional corruption is rarely touched by class action court orders. For instance, back in 1971, in *United States of America*, ex rel. *Alton Stewart v. Coughlin*, a judge, after reviewing the dangers associated with Thorazine in the pharmaceutical company's literature, ruled:

> If there is any warning that I might give, it is a warning to this pharmaceutical company that this drug [Thorazine] is not to be used for control of prisoners ... and that juvenile petitioners not be submitted to the use of Thorazine or any other tranquilizer whatsoever for purpose of mere control, and certainly that they not be submitted to the use of Thorazine or any other tranquilizer for the purpose of punishment.

That ruling was made a year before I started research for this book. I have yet to see any warnings by said pharmaceutical company directed to personnel of juvenile penal or mental institutions, but I have seen doctors ordering the above mentioned drugs without ever seeing the child.

The pharmaceutical industry is both rich and powerful. With vast financial resources, they field an army of lobbyists, marketing specialists and well-paid, generously commissioned sales people. Incentives are offered for physicians and psychiatrists to prescribe medication liberally. High profits for the drug industry, lucrative commissions for salesmen, bargain trips and gifts for the physicians and an easy solution for institutional staffs insure that biochemical restraints will remain an accepted mode for replacing and/or supplementing the old forms of solitary confinement in years to come.

The future is even more frightening. Medical experts like Dr. Mendelsohn feel that we are about to see a third and worse form of solitary confinement—restraint by electrodes and radiation implants on the cortex and brain cells. Dr. Mendelsohn believes that not only will biochemistry prove to be too expensive, but that,

The New Solitary Confinement/147

once all the facts are known as to the dangerous side effects on the body, it will be judged unlawful.

The case of Eddie Sanchez illustrates Dr. Mendelsohn's warning quite well. Eddie Sanchez became a ward of the state of California when he was four and took the all-too-familiar route of bounding in and out of foster homes, ending up in prison. He was chosen for a trial Behavior Mod program called START, which he helped to sabotage by destructive behavior. From then on, he was labeled a serious troublemaker. A letter from Sanchez describes what followed.

> I was supposedly misbehaving. At first I was put on Prolixin in pill form. I had to take it three times a day. The effect was I'd suffer muscle spasms that felt like cramps, and I seemed to have lost a lot of my coordination, as my arms would not swing when I walked.
>
> But the officials did not think this helped me as I still got in trouble. So one day several guards came to my cage and escorted me to the shock-treatment floor.
>
> I was put on a bed and my sleeve was rolled up on my right arm and this doctor got this needle.... He hits me and I right away feel a tingling sensation in my whole body, sort of like when your foot goes to sleep, then like somebody pushed a 200 lb. weight on my chest. All my air is driven from my body, then my muscles all relax, even my eyes until I can't move nothing.
>
> After a while, the shot wears off and I am led back into the hole. This was done several times. I never consented to it or signed a permission slip as I was seventeen.

While Eddie Sanchez was under the influence of Anectine, a muscle relaxant, he was given electroshock treatment. After eight such experiences, he took the suggestion of a fellow inmate who told him that if he threatened the life of President Nixon they would send him to a federal prison. Shortly thereafter, the Chicano boy wrote the Secret Service and threatened to kill the President. That did it. He was convicted of a federal offense and turned over to federal authorities.

We as a society have chosen physical imprisonment as the treatment for our troubled and neglected youth. Modern drug technology has further sophisticated this captivity through the overuse and misuse of behavioral drugs by untrained and semi-skilled professionals for staff convenience. And in experimental stages, research goes forward to replace expensive drugs with more moderately priced electrode and radiation implants, which, too, will make youngsters who do not conform to institutional standards, docile "robots."

There is a crack in the Earth
And I'll have fallen in.
Down in the darkness where I have never been.
People are looking, staring at me;
I lie here and wonder what do they see?
Shall I be here forever
I can not climb back
Rotting and dying in this horrible crack
Am I alive or am I dead.
Oh God, who will save me from
This crack in my head?

—Sixteen-year-old female suicide,
Illinois institution

13/Beyond the Free World: Suicide

When Richard Garber, a district justice in Bucks County, Pennsylvania, asked Gary Stoloski where he lived, the boy screamed: "I have no address! I have no address! You'll have to kill me to send me back to jail!" But for the fifth time in a period of six weeks, Gary went back to Bucks County jail on a misdemeanor charge. The next day, on June 13, 1973, a few days after his eighteenth birthday, he was found hanging in his cell—death by suicide.

Gary Stoloski's death had several things in common with most juvenile suicides: it occurred within the first twenty-four hours of confinement and it appeared to have been spontaneous. It was also part of a growing national trend. Over the last decade, suicide among children between the ages of fourteen and nineteen has increased by 200 percent and is now the second-ranking cause

149

of death for Americans between the ages of fifteen and twenty-four. (Suicide for the entire U.S. population ranks tenth as a cause of death.)

Gary Stoloski is a classic example of the boy from the "other side of the tracks" who crossed over and found himself victim to the politics of professional power. Gary had been dating the daughter of Frank Bolduc, executive director of the New Jersey Bar Association, for over two years. The young couple were serious and for Stoloski, raised without any real family ties, it was the first good thing that had happened to him. However, the boy's alleged involvement with drugs and the dating of his daughter worried Bolduc and he filed numerous charges against the boy with the local police.

While being constantly harassed by the law, Gary wrote "... I went out with her [Jayne Bolduc] for over two years. Then the father decided that he didn't want me to go out with her anymore after Jan. 1, 1973. ... I am really confused ... I mean, all I want is love which is not really hurting anyone, is it? I don't see what I did that was so bad to deserve something like this."

William Ford, Bucks County juvenile officer, commented on the boy's record: "There are trivial complaints and some drug involvement, but there's nothing in his file that would place him as a criminal." Local chief of police Charles Ronaldo also commented: "He really wasn't a bad kid as much as a mixed-up kid who didn't have a home and was raised by grandparents. Most of his involvement with our department was in executing complaints signed by Mr. Bolduc. We advised Gary to stay away from the Bolducs' and Jayne until they both became of age. He chose to ignore that advice."

The executive director of the New Jersey Bar Association wined and dined local, county and township police officials. In June of 1973 the Pennsylvania legislature passed a new penal code dealing with "harassment by communication." The law was only six days old when Bolduc formally charged Gary with making some 300 telephone calls to his home. (Police had confirmation by Pennsylvania Bell Telephone of nineteen calls.)

Gary was again incarcerated in the county jail and made another call to his girl friend. When the father complained, the warden assured him that the young man would make no further calls. Nor did he, for he was dead by his own hand within a few hours. (Ironically, during this time, Frank Bolduc was helping New Jersey draft its proposal for juvenile delinquency reform which would prohibit the incarceration of juveniles in a county jail.)

Though few writers disclose actual identities in an effort to protect the names of the youths in question, I feel compelled to do so. Gary Stoloski, Darrel V. St. Cyr, Jerome Andrew Price, Frank Sproule, Marvin K. Aki and Nathaniel Johnson were incarcerated juveniles whose fear of death capitulated to their greater fear of life and who resorted to suicide. Their deaths, more than representing individual decisions, were closely related to the existing laws that bring about insensitive placement and to the treatment policies of our institutions, particularly the practice of solitary confinement. If these suicides are to have any meaning, an examination of conditions that lead to such an awesome act must be made from a wider perspective than that which sloughs them off as merely nameless children whose despair was strangled by rat poison or the sheet from which they hanged in a bare isolation cell.

The most severe punitive method for control in our juvenile jails is solitary confinement. There is a proven high correlation between solitary confinement and suicide, attempted and successful. In spite of this damning correlation, correctional people continue to use solitary confinement as a means of punishment after court orders, investigations and riots urge and command them not to do so.

Because often guards, teachers and administrators believe that attempted suicide is an effort on the part of the child to manipulate, it is treated with a quick visit to the infirmary and then back to the madness of solitary confinement. During the *Nelson v. Heyne* federal court case in Indiana, it was established that corrections personnel placed attempted suicides in straitjackets and put them in solitary confinement for extended periods of time. This is not an uncommon practice and conflicts directly with the views of Dr. Bruce L. Danto, who has worked closely with the suicidal-prone and flatly states they should not be kept in isolation. In a letter to this author, Dr. Danto enlarged on the theme:

The leper role of a child placed in solitary confinement can only be viewed from the standpoint of sadistic management.... In my opinion, if a child is placed in solitary confinement and commits suicide, we are dealing with homicide and this is placed on the staff, as they have left the child no other alternative by which he can assure himself of his humanness and individuality.... I think that mental health professionals must speak out against this heinous psychological crime which has been imposed upon the administratively exploited child.

(The National Association for Mental Health, Inc., responded as follows to my inquiry on its opinion of extended isolation: "The ...Association...has taken no formal position on solitary confinement of children or any other penal practice, nor do we have any data on the effect of solitary confinement on the growth and development of children or such confinement leading to suicide or on suicides within juvenile penal facilities.")

Very little is known about what inmates call SIDEWAYS—suicide among penal inmates. One of the country's earliest theories on the subject of suicide attempts was written around the turn of the century by a then well-known prison warden: "Suicide in prisons is instinctive imitation, craving curiosity, mischievous desire to elicit alarm, an attempt to create sympathy for favors and a certain abnormality inducted by pernicious practices." This attitude has not altered appreciably. Most superintendents I talked with felt the act is "just a means of seeking attention." Harold Mulholland of Pierce County's Juvenile Detention Center in Washington State, for instance, told Peyton Whitely of the local newspaper: "There have been no suicides here in recent years. There have been attempts, a situation more common with girls than boys, sort of an emotional thing, trying to get attention." All the records I have read on the subject, especially in Texas, give the same opinion about suicides.

However, many experts in the area of suicide see these attempts as a "crying out for help." Witness below, for example, excerpts from signed affidavits:

One morning at 9:00 he went into the maintenance shop, turned on a 9-inch table saw and shoved his throat into it two times cutting through his trachea.

From the Gainesville State School for Girls:

> Barbara Bode: 6-29-72—tried to choke herself with hands while in solitary confinement; 8-7-72—tried to choke herself with a sheet; 8-31-72—choked herself with torn mattress; 11-29-72—choked herself with her blouse.... Wrapped a belt around her neck; 12-27-72 —swallowed a needle while in solitary confinement.

Others have cut their wrists with sharpened shoe polish cans and drunk window cleaner and different combinations of cleaning liquids and insecticides.

In 1966 the research team of Teicher and Jacobs observed: "More often than not, adolescents who adopt the drastic measure of a suicide attempt as an attention getting device find that this too fails... and the adolescent is then convinced... that death is the only solution to what appears to him as the chronic problem of living."

Where jails and prisons are concerned, the cure has become the cancer. In the United States the death rate by suicide is 10.5 per 100,000; in our county jails, the rate rises to 57.5 per 100,000. More than nine times as many girls attempt suicide as boys. But possibly because our culture dictates that the male figure is not supposed to cry or reach out for help, twice as many boys kill themselves as girls. Within the past few years, however, the number of self-inflicted death in females has risen—most markedly among black females—by as much as 183 percent in the last decade. In the general black population, male suicide rate is 10 percent; for incarcerated black males, it rises to 20 percent.

Among American Indians, particularly males between fifteen and twenty-four years of age, the suicide rate is twice the national average. On some reservations the rate is five or six times greater. Causes, according to the National Institute of Mental Health, are many, but chief among them is the fact that the average Indian "has often been jailed at an early age, has spent time in boarding schools and has been moved from one to another... and is under the influence of alcohol." At a tender age, when they most need the security and stability of parents, tribe and reservation, young Indians are transported many miles away to boarding schools organized by and for the convenience of the white bureaucrats. Is this not too a form of isolation, of solitary confinement, albeit in a different form and under better conditions?

Basic similarities exist among children who take their own lives. First, there is usually a deep sense of helplessness, hopelessness and loneliness. Everyone experiences some of these feelings occasionally, but when all three occur simultaneously, the probability of suicide greatly increases. Such was the case of Darrel V. St. Cyr, a sixteen-year-old Louisiana boy with a history of neglect and abuse. Diagnosed as severely depressed and possibly suicidal, he was dumped into the Louisiana Training Institute in Baton Rouge because there was no room in a hospital. Here he was put in isolation for walking into his counselor's office without permission. Four days later (in February of 1974) Darrel methodically ripped up a sheet and wove it into a rope and hanged himself.

Often there is absence of a significant other—someone to trust and admire. In many cases preoccupation with death is related to drugs or lack of involvement in daily constructive activities, or an unusually strict and demanding code of performance. (A study of worldwide suicides during the nineteenth and twentieth centuries found that old Prussia and the present-day states of West and East Germany consistently had the highest suicide rates. Interestingly enough, the fact that the German suicide rate has remained the highest in the world is attributed to its rigid rules of conduct and resultant fear of punishment which were characteristic of Prussian society.)

The Spartan standards of Germany, past and present, are not unlike those found in America's juvenile penal facilities. So severe and uncaring, so authoritarian and dehumanizing are conditions in most penal institutions, especially isolation units, that children are forced into suicides with what I call a high determination factor. For instance, at the Koolau Youth Facility in Hawaii, Marvin K. Aki, aged seventeen, was thrown into solitary confinement "for asking for a cigarette" from an employee. Marvin hanged himself with such unrelenting determination that he had to assume a sitting position while suspended from a doorknob. After his death the report noted: "When his body finally was removed, rigor mortis set in so that the sheeted shape on the stretcher was sitting upright."

Dr. Karl Menninger claims "suicide is murder in 180°." In "Mourning and Melancholia" by Sigmund Freud, the psychoanalyst wrote: "It is true as we have long known, that no neurotic harbors thoughts of suicide which are not murderous impulses against others redirected upon himself." Such would seem the case of Jerome Andrew Price, who was sent to county jail in Conroe, Texas, for playing hooky for seventeen days. After serving time he reappeared with his mother before the sentencing juvenile judge, who gave him another day in jail and scheduled him to report again the next morning. Mrs. Price said, "The judge thought that an extra day in jail might help him [Jerome]." But instead, Jerome tied one leg of his trousers around the window and the other around his neck and hanged himself. His death was an echo of the past: the boy's father had killed himself ten years earlier in the same jail.

Suicide is a most sensitive topic for administrators of both public and private facilities. Many explain away responsibility for suicides by listing them as natural or accidental deaths. For instance, when sixteen-year-old Nathaniel Johnson committed suicide, officials at Youth Hall in Miami, Florida, told the local paper: "He might have accidentally strangled while faking a hanging so that he would be moved to a hospital where he could escape." Other penal facilities minimize the data by not reporting them. Still others employ such ambiguous classification systems that self-destruction is subsumed under other categories of death. Richard Esparza speculates in *Jail House Blues** that "if suicide reporting in jails parellels the reporting of suicide in the general population, we may assume that a very large number are not documented ... [and] could be ten times as high as the actual number of recorded deaths."

Dr. Rosemary Sarri, Project Director of the National Assessment of Juvenile Corrections, wrote of her attempt to ascertain the actual number of suicides and acts of self-mutilation within juvenile facilities for the National Assessment of Juvenile Corrections: "All of the agencies contacted indicated that such acts occurred, but no one had any data on their frequency." Nor could

* Epic Publications, 1973.

I find any evidence of research into the subject by universities or national mental health facilities. I asked Dr. Edward F. Zigler, former United States Chief of the Children's Bureau and Director of the Office of Child Development under the Nixon Administration, why this was so. He answered candidly, "Because nobody has cared enough to investigate it." This is tragic, for without full knowledge of the dimensions of the national rate of suicides among incarcerated youth, they will continue to be ignored, along with the brutal and sadistic punishment and treatment that prevail at every level of the juvenile penal system. As Dr. Zigler said after he resigned his national post, "This is the only country I know that permits the legal abuse of children."

The state of Texas is typical in its attitude toward the incidence of suicide among juvenile prisoners. New York State Legislator J. Edward Meyer wrote to Texas at my request, seeking the number of suicides, attempted and successful, within its youth facilities during the last ten years. Mary Ann Stubbs, statistician of the Texas Youth Council, wrote back: "Regarding attempted suicides within the Texas Youth Council Training Schools during the past ten years, we can report only one attempt, which was not successful." Yet during the Morales trial in that state in the summer of 1973, the U.S. Justice Department reported that the FBI found the names of twenty-two juvenile prisoners who attempted suicide thirty-three times since January 1, 1972, in Texas.

Texas was not alone in its falsely optimistic reply to inquiries: Indiana, Delaware, Connecticut, Tennessee, Georgia, Nebraska—all disclaimed any suicide in the last ten years; Arkansas had "no successful suicides"; Wisconsin and Michigan had three and two attempts respectively; Arizona admitted to two between 1964 and 1971; Nevada and Illinois had no information; and South Carolina never answered the questions. Massachusetts placed its figure at fifteen reported suicides.

During the summer of 1973, I experienced what I felt was a deliberate cover-up. In Pima County, Arizona, I met Ray Delpo, chief probation officer at the county detention center, where a highly authoritarian administration had recently been replaced by a more progressive group. Delpo promised me the files on three suicides I found especially interesting. One had occurred in 1969, the other two in 1972. He placed the latter files in the top drawer of his desk until he could secure the record of the 1969 suicide. In short order, the files disappeared and apparently were destroyed. At any rate, Delpo has never seen them again.

In both suicide instances, the victim, a young boy, had been placed in solitary confinement at the center, outside Tucson, for a minor infraction of rules. The first child went mad, ripped out a lighting fixture and used the wiring to hang himself. The second boy scratched the following on the thick wire glass of his door before his suicide: "As you are I was once. As I am you shall be." He then climbed to the upper bunk, pushed the bed out from the wall so that his legs could hang over, placed his head under the arched safety bar and violently flipped his body over the bed, breaking his neck. It was necessary to cut off the bar to remove the boy's body.

The third file was later found and I had the opportunity to acquire what I believe is an insight into typical forces that drive such youths to suicide. Frank Sproule, adjudicated for chemical intoxication (glue sniffing) and running away, was released from the Job Corps camp in Oak Glenn, California, in December of 1968 because "he was so homesick that he simply could not adjust." In 1969, Frank's probation officer, Richard Quinn, called his employer, to say the young man was quitting his job and was going to run away. Quinn and a colleague went out to look for Sproule. Quinn reported:

"... on the South side of the Benson Highway is a small store. We observed Frank sitting in the shade there with a suitcase." Frank saw the probation officers, took off for the desert and was caught, but because of his determined struggle to get away, the police were called. After three additional men came to help, according to the report, the boy continued to struggle and cry and it took five officers to subdue him. "They told him to put his hands behind him because they were going to handcuff him, and with that he really went berserk and the officers had to hit him on the head with the handcuffs before they could handcuff him." A latter affidavit by Quinn stated: "One of the uniformed sheriff officers took his handcuffs, and holding them like you would a pair of brass knuckles, took about a six-inch swing at Frank's head, hitting him on the head. . . ."

Frank Sproule was treated at the Pima County General Hospital for laceration of the scalp at 2:45 P.M. and released (He told attendants at the hospital he had been treated there three years earlier for attempted suicide.) In less than three and a half hours he would be back again, this time DOA. He had been returned to the detention center, where he hanged himself.

The National Center for Mental Health, created by the U.S. Congress in 1957, recommends that anyone contemplating the act of self-destruction should go to one of many "Crisis Intervention Centers" now being developed around the country. Experts all urge the establishment of more "hot lines" for persons to turn to for help in coping with suicidal impulses. They also urge the disturbed person to seek out clergy or anyone else who will listen. It is most important to talk to a concerned and sympathic listener in order to relieve destructive psychological pressures.

However, given the conditions of solitary confinement and incarceration in general, it is impossible for a child about to commit suicide to go to a crisis intervention center or make a hot line call. There are no hot lines for the isolated youngster. There are no clergymen or counselors or friends to keep him company. There are no rehabilitation programs. A suicidal incarcerated child is left alone to cope with his own worst enemy—himself.

In Connecticut a fourteen-year-old boy penned his last thoughts, discovered four days after his suicide. His tragic eloquence indicts the madness of institutionalization:

> The Lord's purpose for putting me in the population was for me to learn about the world and its inhabitants. I have only been alive for 14 years. But in that short period of time I have learned too well perhaps, the ways of life. I have learned more about people than quite a few grown men. Which means I have fulfilled God's wish.

> I consider myself as mentally stable as anyone. I had dreams of finishing high school, and then perhaps going on to college. Those things, in my case would be highly improbable, since at this early age I have seen the insides of too many institutions.

> To the many people who have tried to help me during all this, I wish to express my sincere thanks. To the others, may they rest in peace, also.

Where rigid control and inhuman brutality substitute for treatment and human concern, where corrupt and sadistic jobholders and money-makers substitute for dedicated professional personnel, there you will find the exploited and tormented child, broken in spirit, stunted in psychological development. There you will find, under the public relations, the evasions and the lying, records of children who were driven to madness and death. And finally, there is where you will find those people who should be held accountable for institutional homicide.

PART FOUR / The Politics of Corruption

In this lonely world I walk, and in heart I try to talk.
I sit in my lonely detention room and dream! I see
  visions of a
World that is not a candy-coated
nightmare of hatred, lies, pain and corruption.
This is my world and I pray that someday my dream,
  my world will become reality.
But someday never comes.

—Tom, age fifteen
detention home, Nebraska

14/Jobs, Kickbacks, Million-Dollar Contracts and the Wells Fargo Line

Political influence is the foundation upon which a pyramid of jobs, contracts and corruption is built to entomb our troubled youth. Many politicians who have been entrusted with elected power, wield that power to help supporters, friends and clients realize salaries or vast corporate profits. Using that same power, they also collaborate to conceal crimes against children as a means to an end—that end being profit. In the name of children's services and juvenile justice, millions of dollars are made and thousands of jobs are justified and young lives, passing through the revolving doors of incarceration, are irrevocably altered. Roughly, only two out of every ten ever escape unscathed.

One example of the politics of crime in institutions centers around the death of Danna Hvolboll, a rather plump, blue-eyed girl with a toss of blond hair and a drug problem. "Send us your daughter and we will return you a lady," read the slogan on the bottom of the application for Dr. Joseph D. Farrar's Artesia Hall, a private, profit-making school for disturbed children, outside Houston, Texas.

At the campus, Danna was placed in solitary confinement after being caught with her boyfriend. On her seventeenth birthday, unable to stand the madness any longer, she drank roach poison and became very sick. Farrar began to slap the girl and pull her hair as punishment for faking an illness. She was given something to induce vomiting and forced to walk the grounds. Early in the morning of November 12, 1972, Danna Hvolboll began to convulse. Farrar had her tied into a straitjacket. Finally, he took her to the hospital. It was too late. On November 14 she died at Ben Taub Hospital in Houston. The autopsy stated she died as a result of bronchopneumonia, following ingestion of pesticide (carbonated).

The hospital ruled her death "accidental." However, a year later, after investigation of the strange circumstances surrounding her death, Dr. Joseph Jachimczy changed the "accident" to "homicide." Farrar was indicted for murder by a Liberty County grand jury in June of 1973. His supporters began to squirm.

Farrar, who had dubious professional credentials, founded Artesia Hall under a cloud of controversy. Ruth Urmy, Welfare Regional Licensing Supervisor, who knew about conditions at the school, struggled against powerful politicians to prevent the state of Texas from granting a license to operate this institution for troubled children (at $600 a month per student). Farrar, in turn, hired two lawyers, Price Daniel, Jr., who later became speaker of the Texas State Legislature, and a recently retired member of the State Board of Public Welfare, W. Kendall Baker, to help in his battle against Mrs. Urmy. With such skillful legal assistance, Farrar was able to counter Mrs. Urmy and State District Judge Clarence Cain, who stated publicly, "I am not going to have a concentration camp in Liberty County," and Farrar was awarded a license to operate the school.

Mrs. Urmy was demoted from supervisor with staff to a clerical worker who had to obtain permission to go to the ladies' room. She was later suspended from her job for reasons of "inefficiency and being a disruptive individual." During her hearing in the

Texas Welfare Department, she wasn't permitted to discuss the Artesia case. And although it was denied that political influence was used in the Welfare Department's decision, Mrs. Urmy's boss, who dismissed her, suffered a memory lapse on twenty-two questions dealing with how and why the license was granted to Artesia Hall and Dr. Farrar.

In 1972 a Liberty County police sergeant told Farrar he was illegally licensed and his business was suspicious. But other police officers kept quiet because the owner of the school was paying them a bounty of twenty-five dollars for returning runaways. Children here were punished in a "cooler"—a four-by-four-by-six-foot wooden cage fitted with barbed wire—or were forced to stand in garbage cans filled with ice water while staff gave them GI baths with wire brushes. Students whom Farrar had referred to as "ancestors of dogs" in turn referred to his school as "an insane place" and scores tried to escape in four- and five-hour treks through the adjacent swamp filled with alligators, snakes and bobcats.

In the summer of 1973, Governor Dolph Briscoe visited Artesia Hall and called it "unbelievable." What he and law enforcement officials found opened a massive can of worms concerning licensing procedures for private child care facilities in the Lone Star State.

In Pennsylvania Larry Barker, Commissioner of the Office of Children and Youth, was an extremely effective, hard-driving innovator who cared about children. He wanted the Pennsylvania Department of Welfare to conduct regular inspections of the institutions that served incarcerated youths. He was especially concerned about a facility near Pittsburgh called Oakdale.

Oakdale is a private facility, valued at $1,997,213, which houses public wards of the state. A 1971 evaluation revealed some problems: children in solitary confinement, questionable practices of child labor, and staff accused of stealing personal belongings from the students. A position for Director of Treatment was created but never filled. At that time, in a long letter to the Office of Children and Youth, Superintendent Charles Bugbee promised there would be changes.

Commissioner Barker had his doubts. A year later he took a

team out to Pittsburgh to re-evaluate Oakdale. They checked into a motel and conducted a training session. Each member of the team was instructed on what to look for in specialized areas. By the time Barker's evaluation team left Oakdale, Superintendent Charles Bugbee had left town.

The report Commissioner Barker submitted to the governor and the Oakdale board of directors was devastating: Some of the cottage managers and parents appeared to be functional illiterates; rooms were still being used for solitary confinement; monies were missing from the boys' accounts and treatment was nonexistent. There were rats in the kitchen and filthy conditions in the toilets. Finances were so questionable that the team recommended that the office of the auditor general of the Commonwealth should conduct a full investigation and audit. When the board of Oakdale Boys Industrial Home of Western Pennsylvania heard the entire report, they asked how they could "close down quietly."

The victory was also the beginning of the end for Larry Barker. He visited the Girls School at Waynesburg, a dumping ground for "misbehaving girls." Not one child there had a criminal record. He suggested that the place either be closed down entirely or used for handling serious problems, like alcoholism in adults. For the patronage jobs earning up to $12,000 a year, his proposal was threatening. Barker had made more enemies.

Commissioner Barker began to develop a plan that would train interested citizens to conduct his "Oakdale Team Evaluations." He also convinced Secretary of the Welfare Department Helene Wohlgemuth that the entire child care service in Pennsylvania was expensive (a half billion dollars) and badly organized. He recommended that those services be streamlined for the sake of the taxpayers as well as the children. On November 22, 1972, Mrs. Wohlgemuth wrote every juvenile judge in the state that the Department of "Public Welfare was embarking on a new policy." In short, she told the judges that since a number of judges in both eastern and western Pennsylvania were sending children to the opposite side of the state and since the department was footing the bill, public welfare would subsequently make the placements.

The child industry of Pennsylvania is vast and influential and the pressure must have been great. By January of 1973, Mrs. Wohlgemuth caved in and wrote all juvenile judges again: "This is to advise you that I immediately order a halt to implementation of policy changes announced in my letter to you of November 22, 1972 affecting the operation of youth institutions administered by the Department."

The outspoken Commissioner Barker reacted quickly to his boss's letter. He publicly stated: ". . . large sums of money have, for all intents and purposes, transformed a social service into a profit making industry."

Barker's recommendations to visit and evaluate other facilities around the state were now rejected and he was told not to visit the state legislature. His idea of training private citizens to evaluate state-supported child care institutions took on greater importance as he felt increasingly frustrated by bureaucratic and political realities. In the spring of 1973, while developing these private child advocacy groups, Larry Barker was demoted and that summer he was dismissed from public service.

The operating budgets for private, county and state agencies dealing with delinquent juveniles totaled over $50 million for Pennsylvania's 1973–74 fiscal year. When all sixteen thousand children were combined, along with their service budgets of $50 million for delinquency, $50 million for neglected and welfare expenditures and $351 million for mental health and mental retardation, the industry Larry Barker wanted to unify by reform is not small or powerless.

The Commissioner himself realized it when he said, "We have heavy investment of resources in buildings and maintenance staffs. We have the political interest when a Youth Development Center is the economic base of a community." And Barker knew that, because of the political interests, it is impossible to redirect monies into new and workable programs for youthful offenders. To this day, almost all Pennsylvania juvenile delinquency monies go into existing institutions instead of community-based programs with proved success records.

The most common justification for political clout within the child care industry is simply to protect the hundreds of thousands of jobs it provides. As more and more reformers call for community-based programs that take the children out of institutions, the politics of jobs takes on ugly dimensions. I witnessed this firsthand in the spring of 1974 but was unaware of the power play until much later.

Forty select persons from around the country were invited to attend a conference on deinstitutionalization at the Academy for Contemporary Problems in Columbus, Ohio. I was in attendance when Dr. Jerome Miller, director of Children and Family Services for the State of Illinois, and Dr. David Fogel, director of the Illinois Law Enforcement Commission, complained about union jobs in institutions being discussed. They pointed out that the purpose of the conference was to help children, not provide jobs, hence, they should be discussing what to do for children and not job security for guards and other custodial personnel.

After studying the politics of jobs in Massachusetts, it is easy to understand Miller's comments: "It is just too difficult to reform these institutions because most are based on political patronage and the institution becomes more important than the child."* A review of some budgets proves Miller's point.

At the Hampden County Training School, the superintendent, his wife and daughter had salaries totaling $29,698. In 1971 the superintendent of Middlesex County Training School had the following credentials: former florist, former Middlesex County treasurer, no college education. He, his wife and son—who was director of athletics and recreation at $13,606.76—all worked at the school. Together the family was making $37,114.76 a year. They had two free county cars and occupied an eleven-room home on the grounds, for which they paid $290 a year.

But they weren't alone in this. Ninety other employees were making $820,947 a year, sixty-nine of which were upgraded or reclassified, with salary raises, in a three-year period. (Small wonder it cost over $12,000 per student per year!) Two men were drawing $8,687 each as plumbing foremen, but there were no

---

* Joseph Leavy, who replaced Miller, discovered that the Springfield Probation Office was carrying on its payroll as "on sick leave" a probation officer who was serving time in the Massachusetts adult penitentiary for sexually black-balling boys on probation—sexual privileges or prison again for parole violation. While in prison the man had to be placed in protective custody because many of the adult inmates had once been victims of his sickness. When the man left prison, his old job would be waiting for him. Fortunately, Commissioner Leavy intervened.

plumbers working under them. The school's budget revealed that
only $13,500 was designated for "books and educational meterials."
More was paid out for a barber than all "medical, dental and
laboratory services" combined.

Also present at the meeting and taking notes was Linda Tarr-
Whelan, director of Program Development for the American
Federation of State, County and Municipal Employees. Upon
returning to Washington, D.C., she informed the president of her
union, Jerry Wurf, of the anti-union sentiments expressed by both
Miller and Fogel. Two days later, Jerry Wurf flew to Chicago to
demand that Drs. Miller and Fogel resign or he would have Governor Daniel Walker fire both men for "advocating policies aimed
at dismantling state institutions."

Wurf also read before a gathering of Illinois public employees
a memo that Ms. Tarr-Whelan had prepared which called Fogel a
fool and a failure and said both men wanted to close down
prisons and hospitals, which would abolish thousands of jobs. Any
such plan, Wurf said, would be contrary to Governor Daniel
Walker's promise not to lay off state employees. Four months later
Dr. Jerry Miller was no longer director of Children and Family
Services; he was kicked upstairs as consultant to the governor. Six
months later Miller was fired.

Jerry Wurf went after Dr. Miller's job and career for more
than anti-union talk at a conference. Wurf knew that Miller came
from Massachusetts, where he had been instrumental in emptying
most of the juvenile training schools. He had been the leading
advocate and enforcer of this policy. He fought against patronage
priorities of politicians and union leaders. He was honest, tough
and very effective. To Wurf he was frightening.

In the spring of 1974, I received a call from William J. Ensign,
commissioner of the Ohio Youth Department, former mayor of
Toledo and friend and political appointee of Governor John J.
Gilligan. Ensign wanted to acquaint me with his "excellent program" for youth, which he hoped I would praise in this book. It
took a little scratching to find, however, that beneath Commissioner Ensign's smooth political rhetoric lay a public relations
attempt on behalf of his governor, who at the time had Presidential aspirations. Actually the Ohio Youth Department was totally
and disgracefully political.

Ensign's administrative assistant, Denny Gilbert, mailed out to all the departmental staff at least once a year little green computer card reminders of their obligation to the political party that gave them their jobs. Training-school superintendents were expected to pay the Democratic party $500 annually; employees making from $15,000 to $20,000, $200; those drawing $10,000 to $15,000 sent checks or cash for $100; and even clerk-typists were expected to donate $10 a year.

Personnel were hired, not on the basis of qualifications, but whether they were party Democrats. This policy cost a young boy his life when he placed a towel over his head and sprayed deodorant into his lungs. I was told the youngster could have been saved if a doctor or nurse had been on duty. However, the position of nurse had not been filled, according to Public Relations Director Corrine Smith, because the department couldn't find a registered Democrat at the time. The boy's lungs froze, and so did disclosure of his death and the way political patronage had helped bring it about.

About the same time Ensign called me, a boy took his life at TICO—Training Institute of Central Ohio. "But it never got out," Corrine Smith told me. "We got the mother in and agreed to pay all the bills."*

Ultimately, the people of Ohio paid the price for the political corruption, especially a Roman Catholic couple, who died on their knees clutching a crucifix and rosary as a parolee of the Ohio Youth Department emptied his revolver in their heads. The boy was released in October of 1973, after serving time for murder, and by February of 1974 his frightened mother reported to officials of the Youth Commission that her son had broken parole, was hatefully hostile and carried a gun. And again, according to Corrine Smith, "the attitude of the department concerning the mother's warning was, 'Screw it!' "

The power of training schools at local and state levels has been so strong that they have freely ignored recommendations of Presidential commissions starting with the Wickersham Commission in 1929–31, which condemned the incarceration of children and urged alternative programs for rehabilitation.

---

* Burial expenses.

The most significant recommendation of the Johnson-appointed National Crime Commission in the 1960's was its urgent call for emphasis on community-based correctional programs, with a corresponding de-emphasis of the institutional alternatives. In January of 1974 the National Conference on Criminal Justice Goals and Standards urged the "phasing out" of state juvenile correctional institutions. To date, only Massachusetts has shown itself willing to follow that recommendation. However, there is still one facility operating in that state, and the others, although empty of children, have not closed. Maintenance people and counselors report to work each day where guards watch over empty cells and corridors while they play pinochle, at a cost to Massachusetts taxpayers of over $2.2 million a year. Until state officeholders have the courage, the human decency or the political sensibility to again reverse the role of institutions—from placating jobholders to helping children—the outdated and sadistic sacred cow with a union collar will continue to be carried by the taxpayers.

Cook County, Illinois, maintains a patronage system under the guise of Division of School Attendance, worth between 2.8 and 4 million tax dollars a year. A special report in 1973 said that this operation, manned by a lawyer for the Chicago School Board, a chief school attendance officer and 355 "Mayor Daley soldiers," supported the most frivolous jobs in the system.

Ed Carter, social worker, became an imminent threat to the "frivolous jobs" when he was hired to review students' records before they went to truancy court. Carter was bright and efficient. He found that many children had legitimate excuses for truancy: hearing problems, poor vision or emotional problems like those of one little boy whose mother had died the day school started. Ed Carter cut the truancy judge's work load by 25 percent. But this threatened the job machinery. The next school year the social worker was transferred for "budget reasons."

John Brown, assistant attorney general for the state of Washington, told me of his struggle with the Association of Washington State Superior Court Judges when he drew up legislation to eliminate noncriminal children from the entire judicial structure. The judges knew that without truants, runaways, etc., filling their courtrooms, there would be smaller case loads and they would be let go. And as one judge told Brown during a heated debate:

"... Sonny, I kissed a lot of asses to get this job." During the last ten years the average annual salary of a full-time judge with juvenile jurisdiction has increased 85 percent—from $12,493 to $23,187.

Though it is clearly wrong, one can nevertheless empathize with unskilled employees who use whatever political clout they can muster to hold their jobs. I understand their fears about competing in a job market where modern technology has considerably reduced demand for unskilled labor. What is not understandable is the way the professionals—doctors, lawyers and other well-educated entrepreneurs—are ripping off troubled children.

For instance, in Connecticut, there is a group of judge-appointed "panel attorneys" who defend juveniles. It is a lucrative appointment. A panel lawyer receives $100 per child even if he appears and the case is postponed. One lawyer made $1,000 in one day in this way. Information given me by New Haven attorney Sue Ann Shay indicates that panel attorneys can make as much as $40,000 to $60,000 a year. However, lawyers who follow due-process-of-law procedures for their juvenile clients and cite on the Gault decision, which guarantees legal representation for children, are seldom recalled for service. Those who help expedite the judge's case load by reviewing a child's record and determining his fate unemotionally over coffee and Danish prior to court appearance are called back repeatedly.

Another matter that cries out for investigation is the relationship between pharmaceutical companies and those medical authorities working for state institutions who order restraining drugs for children as described in Chapter 12. Amanda Spake, in "Prescription Payola,"* allowed that thousands of doctors are receiving attractive kickbacks for ordering large quantities of drugs. In 1972 the pharmaceutical industry spent roughly $5,000 per doctor in the United States in an effort to encourage doctors to prescribe more drugs.

One company gave G.E. portable TV sets to those who prescribed enough Ethaquin to qualify for an award (Ethaquin is a drug that dilates blood vessels). Pfizer and Lederle Laboratories, according to Ms. Spake, were in keen competition to sell Diplo-

* *New Times* magazine, June 26, 1974.

vax, a polio vaccine. One company offered doctors a cassette tape recorder if they administered 250 doses of Diplovax, a Craig electronic calculator for 500 doses and an upright freezer for 1,000 doses. The same company also ran a bonus point system for more expensive prizes, including color TV's and stereo sets.

Other companies give fishing rods, Sony desk radios, Bulova Golden Girl watches, pool tables, microwave ovens, all-expense-paid trips to New York City, including fancy hotels, restaurants and tickets to Broadway shows. Larger drug companies pick up the tab for low-cost trips to Bermuda, Hawaii, etc. How many incarcerated children are administered drugs on the basis not of their needs but rather of the material greed of doctors and state representatives?

For many professionals, the name of the game is grantsmanship and large contracts. The University of Michigan received a most generous grant from the Justice Department's LEAA (Law Enforcement Assistance Administration) to study and create new juvenile standards for the country. With the money came high hopes that some useful information would result. Two years later, after $1.5 million dollars had been spent by members of the university faculty, LEAA had to pump an additional $1 million into the research project to save it. Dr. Buddy Howell, director of the Institute for Criminal Justice, U.S. Justice Department, said at that point that "they had not even agreed on their research objectives and all of the money was gone."

In California the Council on Criminal Justice requested $522,128 over a period of three years for the Hidden Valley Ranch Project. Of the $214,128 allotted for the first year, $91,000, or 41 percent, of the funds was earmarked for the research firm who wrote the proposal.

Some professionals turn entrepreneur and work the juvenile system in the areas they know are weak, such as treatment. Dr. Ivan H. Scheier has filled such a vacuum. His company, PSI, Probation Service Institute of Boulder, Colorado, provides probation officers and juvenile courts with psychological evaluations and recommendations for children awaiting adjudication. The basis for the computer data is Dr. Scheier's composite experience as a "volunteer worker with over 2,000 cases in Boulder, Colorado's, Juvenile Court over a period of nine years." The child takes a forty-five-minute multiple choice test, the results are fed into Dr. Sheier's computer and, within seconds, the psychological profile is on a pink readout sheet.

PSI has come under professional criticism. Many experts doubt the scientific validity of the computer and express fears that the 15-cent test and seven-dollar readout evaluation could damn a child forever in a permanent file. Dr. Scheier told *The Washington Post*: "Insofar as my judgment is poor, the program is poor; insofar as it is good, the program is good." But Dr. Lee Gurel, president of the American Psychological Association's Division of Psychologists in Public Service, said, "... the computer printouts make general statements that have the P. T. Barnum sucker effect —like bump readers, tea leaf readers and palm readers." He also feels that the computer's answers are "hostile to the child."

Still, Scheier's evaluation is much cheaper than a $100 psychologist evaluation, and apparently more and more courts are attracted to the fast-moving, fast-talking computer, even if a heroin addict tests "a great deal healthier on heroin than off heroin." If Maryland adopts the program, which it is now considering, it will be the sixteenth state to buy into PSI's services.

If one could scrutinize the financial structure of juvenile facilities with their immense budgets and multiple institutional needs, one would find most of them riddled with conflicts of interest and naked corruption. Clear-cut examples of this include some Georgia jails that have "turn-key fees" and refuse to release children until their parents paid the local sheriff room and board. Dr. Jerry Miller, former director of Youth and Family Services in Illinois, told me that before Illinois Governor Dan Walker's administration, memos would come down from the governor's office commanding the Youth Department to send children to select private facilities because their census counts were low. Children were herded off like cattle to enhance profits enjoyed by the business cronies of local politicians. So powerful was this group, they successfully lobbied the state legislature to include in the state budget a line item on the amount of state funds that "must go for private facilities."

Perhaps one of the most flagrant examples of conflict of interest that I saw was at the Fort Grant Industrial Training School in Arizona. Fort Grant is no longer an all-purpose training school for boys, but in its heyday, the politics of corruption flourished there. I visited Fort Grant twice in 1973. The first time, I was permitted to stay overnight in the home of the recently fired superintendent, who was under investigation for some forty-six charges made by the state attorney general.

Superintendent Steve Vukcevich was one of the early innovators of "distributive education" within youth corrections. He felt that rather than sit around in cells all day, the inmates should be out working—and work they did. Former Speaker of the Arizona State Legislature Tim Barrow told me how the boys would work as cheap laborers on nearby ranches and farms; yet investigators found that not one boy left Fort Grant with a cent of his earnings. The scheme for taking the boys' monies was locked into Fort Grant's harsh disciplinary policy. If the youngsters ran and were caught, they were placed in solitary confinement and fined twenty-five dollars or more—the amount depended on how much the boy had in his account.

Most of Fort Grant's staff lived in comfortable low-rent brick homes provided by the state. A state audit revealed that employees and their families enjoyed full course meals for fifty cents. And all their auto repairs were made gratuitously in the institution's auto shop.

William Dixon, an assistant attorney general for Arizona, and members of the state auditor general's office found "falsified inventory records and totally inadequate record-keeping on special funds." They also found that the school cattle herd and hog herd exceeded "available grazing land and the school's dietary requirement.... The dairy herd also exceeded school dietary needs, resulting in milk being given away to employees." However, the assistant attorney general of the state found "no records on cattle butchering" and the students were "fed poor, starchy food and little fresh meat."

The underwear-clad boys in solitary confinement were fed the following menu day after day: cold cereal and a half cup of milk for breakfast; no lunch; one wiener with a half bun, three potato chips, a half cup of milk, a half cup of cheese macaroni with a hard roll for dinner. Records substantiate that one mentally retarded child received that basic diet while in solitary for two hundred and three days!

Not far from the school is the Buckskin, a dude ranch with bar and swimming pool—owned by the former superintendent of Fort Grant. I visited and interviewed Steve Vukcevich. His spread is quite beautiful! It was alleged that the Buckskin was the scene of "regular after-hour drinking and gambling stag parties by employees." Rumor also had it that many local and state politicians and judges found their way out to the ranch to be entertained. (State investigators found that one local politician had his political brochure printed at the school print shop.) Vukcevich denied the testimony of former employees on all these points.

One person who frequently visited Buckskin ranch was Seymour Heller, a Phoenix Industrial Chemicals salesman. Heller testified that while he was there, he saw "the swimming pool paint, insecticide and weed killer purchased [from him] with state vouchers for the school." He also testified that Vukcevich solicited gifts like "boxes of fishing knives, pen and pencil sets, steak knives and barbecue sets." Heller finally refused when the superintendent asked for sixty sets of gold-plated silverware for the ranch. Heller's sales at the state training school immediately fell from a high of $2,500 per visit to $200.

When fired from his position, the superintendent decided to fight, and many people, including most of the staff at Fort Grant, rallied to his defense. In October 1973 a benefit golf tournament was held "to let Vukcevich know who are his friends." T. J. Mahoney, a Pinal County superior court judge, was in charge of reservations for the successful fund-raiser.

Later, after a very long hearing, the state dismissed thirty-two of the charges against Vukcevich, but forty-six charges remained, upholding the firing. However, a Cochise County superior court judge, Lloyd Helm, overruled the state of Arizona when he stated that "charges against Steve Vukcevich were ridiculous"* and ordered him reinstated. About this time, it was quietly discovered in Phoenix that for years state correctional people in the central office were returning to the state treasury a million dollars annually that was earmarked for rehabilitating incarcerated children. Small wonder (based on information by Arizona senate research-

* In the fall of 1974, Vukcevich was elected to Arizona's Eighth District State House of Representatives.

ers) that 80 percent of all adult inmates then serving time at the state prison were graduates of the Fort Grant Boys' Industrial School.

One of the most colorful characters I met in the child industry was Brother Lester Roloff, a maverick, Bible-carrying Evangelist, crusading against worldly goods. Brother Roloff had homes for delinquent teen-agers in the Corpus Christi area of Texas and in Hattiesburg, Mississippi, and a home for alcoholics and drug addicts at Culloden, Georgia—all under the corporative umbrella of Roloff Evangelistic Enterprises.

To observe him preaching against the evils of the state at giant rallies was an unforgettable experience. Two million followers who listened to his hell-fire and damnation preaching on well over one hundred radio broadcasts across the country bore witness by sending Reverend Roloff an average of $7,000 in "Love Messages" each morning. His faithful gave their spiritual leader, among other things, a $60,000 home, a maroon Cadillac, a private airplane, a mink coat for his wife, and 273 acres around his Georgia home. But during the summer of 1973, his world started to crumble.

On April 29, 1973, while Mr. and Mrs. Daniel Hanson were at Roloff's Rebekah Home for Girls visiting their daughter, they heard wild, uncontrollable screaming. Mr. Hanson investigated and in a room found "three male subjects holding a girl and slapping her. One of the subjects was holding the girl by her legs, upside down with her head on the floor." Mr. Hanson took his daughter and the family left Rebekah Hall for good. He then went to the police.

At a Texas state legislative hearing, children from the home told how staff people would beat them and "not know how to stop." Some would climb into bed, sit on the children and beat them unmercifully for being "witches, demons, whores, etc...." Some girls took photos of the beatings immediately after they were administered and these were dramatically presented at the hearings in the summer of 1973. Of all the affidavits in my files on institutionalized child beatings, the ones concerning Roloff Evangelistic Enterprises outnumber all others. It is by far my heaviest file, filled with heartless, vindictive physical and verbal assaults.

Brother Roloff, with Bible in hand and self-righteousness in his voice, took on the state of Texas for trying to place his $2.8 million girls' home under state licensing guidelines. He did not deny his disciplinary tactics: "Better pink bottom than a black soul.... We whip 'em with love and we weep with 'em and they love us for it. We never leave a mark on them."

While Mimi Crossley, a young reporter from the Houston *Post*, was covering the Rebekah Home beatings, she overheard an old black cleaning woman say, almost to herself: "What I can't figure out is where do all the babies go?" Mimi Crossley went to work. At Roloff's Girls Home in Hattiesburg, where unwed mothers from the Rebekah Home were sent to give birth, Crossley documented how the babies found new homes and parents in Roloff's national gray market. The infants were shipped to Georgia, Tennessee, Alabama, Florida, Ohio, Indiana, Michigan and Louisiana. The adoptive parents paid between $600 and $900 and many gave large "love messages" to Roloff Enterprises in exchange for a baby. State laws on proper adoption procedures were disregarded. Mrs. Roloff herself flew a child into Kansas in one of Roloff Enterprises' three private planes.

I heard Brother Roloff defend his gray baby market: "We always place them with the Faithful. We've never placed a one in a home where there was ever a drink taken or a cigarette smoked." And he spoke of Mimi Crossley: "She is a Jezebel, a harlot, and an agent of the Devil."

The Fort Grants and Brother Roloffs of this country pale to near insignificance, however, if you study the wealth and record of Father Flanagan's Boys Town, the famed Catholic home for little waifs in Nebraska. Father Flanagan borrowed $90 back in 1917 to give homeless boys shelter, education and direction in life. The good priest was not always successful in his attempts to put his home in the black; for decades he floundered near financial bankruptcy. Then in the late 1930's, Hollywood made a film on the famed orphanage starring Spencer Tracy and Mickey Rooney. Tracy got his Oscar and Father Flanagan got an ace fund-raiser named Theodore Miller from Mooseheart, Illinois. After seeing what a friend called "the damnedest movie," Miller called Father Flanagan and shortly thereafter he was in Nebraska, designing what was to be the most successful fund-raising letters ever mailed out in this country.

"He ain't heavy, Father... he's m'brother." For years, my wife and I received the annual Christmas and Easter letters with that line which touched our hearts and pocketbooks—along with millions of other Americans. What really turned out to be heavy was the stock portfolio of Boys Town. Thanks to the 1969 Internal Revenue Law, in April of 1972, a small Nebraska weekly newspaper, the Omaha *Sun*, was able to obtain Boys Town IRS form 990. From these records the nation discovered what not even the board of trustees of Boys Town knew about—its immense wealth and vast stock investments, all top blue chips. So great was the wealth that if it were a profit-making business, it would have been 372 on *Fortune*'s list of the top 500 businesses in the United States in 1972.

By 1974, Boys Town's net worth was $266 million and still growing. The high population of 900 boys decreased year after year to a low of 550 in 1974. In 1972, fifteen hundred boys who knocked on the doors of Boys Town were turned away, many because their IQ's were below 80. Those who were turned away ironically echo the institution's own letter for funds, which reads: "Spring—a happy time for most boys—will find many homeless and neglected boys with their hearts filled with agony and bitterness. Abandoned..."

The former director who told Nebraska newspaper reporters earlier, "We're so deep in debt all the time," changed his tune when the Omaha *Sun* published the true facts. Father Nicholas Wegner now offered: "This is a business. No business ever stops trying to save for unknown contingencies. If we go into the retarded business, we'll need the money."*

The seventy-five-year-old director, who carried a million-dollar life insurance policy, was finally telling the truth. Every aspect of Boys Town is an effort to make money, and care of children is secondary. The financial octopus swamps everything. The stock portfolio brings in over $8 million annually. The biannual mailings

---

* In the late 1960's, Vice President Hubert Humphrey participated in groundbreaking ceremonies for a mental retardation program at Boys Town which had been proposed twenty-six years earlier. In 1976 it still does not exist.

realize $18 million. Father Wegner even solicited Title One funds (federal monies for educationally disadvantaged children) totaling $100,000 per year for the hard-pressed institution. The cafeteria, which made close to $40,000 from visitors, was given $10,000 annually from Uncle Sam's school lunch program. State governments were asked to help and Boys Town took monies from welfare departments for children who were entitled to its benefits. The Illinois Department of Child and Family Services placed thirty-one boys in Father Flanagan's and $41,000 annually in the general kitty. The school has outside interests too. It owns 120 acres of land nearby, an office building in Omaha, a summer camp in Iowa and ranch land in Wyoming. As I found in most juvenile institutions I visited, the best program at Father Flanagan's was the art program. Here, creative art teachers are able to tap the anguish and eloquence of unwanted children. The gift shop, which sells "authentic pottery and leather goods by the boys," grossed $71,343 in 1970 alone.

In October of 1973, Father Flanagan's Boys Town got a new director. Father Robert P. Hupp found a deteriorating custodial-care orphanage, rampant with nepotism and feather-bedding. The poorly kept dormitories had no air-conditioning and in some instances even toilet paper was unavailable. The director of public relations admitted that most of the boys ran away at one time or another.

According to Michael Casey, who was hired by Father Hupp to improve conditions at the famous institution, "There is so much slush here, it's unbelievable." For instance, he and his aides discovered one staff person who showed up for work one day a month and drew a full salary; one large family with ten members on the payroll; and another counselor who removed twenty horses from the grounds for his personal use. The board of directors included a banker who handled all of Boys Town income, an architect who designed every new building, and a department store official who sold the school all its clothing and furnishings.

Children were subject to corporal punishment, mail censorship and rules that, according to Casey, "came out of somebody's prison manual." Father Hupp told Paul Critchlow of the Philadelphia *Inquirer* in June of 1974: "I suspended a counselor a few weeks ago for smashing a kid in the face. I had a minor riot from the teachers. Some of them just don't know any other way to deal with the kids." In 1972 it was suggested to the then director, Father Wegner, that Boys Town bring in the standard-setting Child Welfare League of America to evaluate its program. Father Wegner scrapped the idea, saying the $10,000 cost of evaluation "appeared prohibitive."

Michael Casey felt that the problem had started when Father Flanagan died: "When he died, everything stopped here but the cash registers." Those of us who gave and became "Honorary Citizens of Boys Town" really did believe that the little boys sent us the Christmas letters—not the 125 ladies who work on four floors of the Wells Fargo office building in downtown Omaha. The mail solicitations from Theodore Miller, the small-town boy with a very humble beginning, had the master touch of Madison Avenue—pseudo-sincerity. The man who first wrote, "He's not heavy..." left at his death an estate of $4,166,617.

Under pressure to diversify, Boys Town recently hired a New York-based consultant firm, which recommended that they move the institution into two new areas. Proposed was a $30 million Boys Town Institute for Learning and Communication Disorders on Creighton University's Omaha campus, and a $40 million fund to build and develop a new Center for the Study of Youth Development with research branches at Stanford University in California and Catholic University in Washington, D.C.

The new proposals present a problem. Old-guard elements at the school have threatened law suits if Father Hupp attempts to dip into the $266-million treasury. In the meantime it is back to the letter writing and those ladies on the four floors of the Wells Fargo building, cranking out the solicitations again—for the new proposals and, of course, for the old.

Dear Mr. George Ray:

*... you didn't give permission for me to go home
this summer. ... I hate to run away from this place
but I will if I'm forced to live here. I just want to go
home with my mother and family. You all up there
just don't understand, why someone be forced to live
somewhere they don't want to be. ...*

Your Surely,
D.C.

—Letter to an Illinois official from a banished child in
Texas, September 1971, discovered during investigation,
summer of 1973

15/Interstate Commerce of Children

There is in this country a mushrooming multimillion-dollar industry that thrives on the interstate commerce of dependent and neglected children. In air terminals across the land, these
children, over 15,000 in number, usually poor, of
minority background and rejected by local private
child-care facilities, stand with their state guardians, waiting to travel hundreds, even thousands
of miles away from family and friends: Virginia
sends them to Idaho; Idaho sends them to Virginia; Arizona ships them to Texas, California
and Colorado; Colorado sends them to Arizona.
Alaska sends its legal wards to five different states
In all, I have found twenty-eight states who admit to interstate commerce of children. Theoretically, the youngsters' destinations are private
treatment centers where they will have a home
and care. In reality, this care amounts to
that given to cattle or a precious commodity,
assuring the continuation of a profit-making
scheme.

182

Banished too are the mentally retarded and American Indians. As discussed in the chapter on the runaway, the Bureau of Indian Affairs (BIA) has established boarding schools for Indian students far from their families and tribes. For instance, the Chilocco Indian School in Oklahoma boards more than 600 Indian youngsters from twenty-five states, and 1,500 Navajo children are shipped more than five hundred miles to an off-reservation BIA boarding school, the Intermountain School in Brigham City, Utah.* The abuse and punitive treatment these forgotten children receive, supposedly under the guise of education, has much in common with the treatment of criminals in detention centers, training schools and county jails.

Banishment, with or without economic motives, has always been a form of extreme punishment. In the Bible, the Lord banished Cain when He said: "... a fugitive and a wanderer shall you be on the earth," and Cain answered: "My punishment is too great to bear." In ancient Rome, Greece and Palestine, the common punishment for crimes and political offenses was state-imposed exile. Even today undesirables are deported from our country, and other nations send great numbers of criminals and political opponents to distant parts where they are forced to provide the state with a cheap source of labor to develop new lands.

After three years of research in this area, I am convinced that unless steps are taken to reverse the trend, neglected and non-criminal children, many of them victims of internal family problems, will continue to be banished in greater numbers. They will become cheap labor for developing additional private residential treatment institutions at exorbitant costs to the children and the taxpayers.

For some children, out-of-state services are imperative for extensive and/or specialized treatment, and reputable, well-established institutions such as Pennsylvania's Elwyn Institute and the

---

* The boarding schools are in direct violation of treaty rights made with the Navajo tribe in 1869: "... and the United States agrees that, for every 30 children between said ages of six and sixteen years who can be induced or compelled to attend school, a house shall be provided, and a teacher competent to teach the elementary branches of an English Education shall be furnished, who will reside among said Indians, and faithfully discharge his or her duties as a teacher."

Menninger Foundation stand ready with quality facilities. For other institutions, however, the motivation for transporting children is at best questionable. Illinois, Louisiana and New Jersey are three states that I believe have suspicious systems for transporting their wards across state lines. Banished children from these states, numbering in the thousands, are followed by millions of hard-earned tax dollars to fill the private coffers of adroit businessmen who operate the so-called treatment centers.

To my knowledge, this practice of child commerce was first established in the early 1960's in Chicago when, as the civil rights movement grew and racial pride was interpreted by some as militancy, many private and state bureaucrats turned their backs on minority children. These black and Puerto Rican children, along with poor white youths flooding into the Chicago area from Appalachia, were labeled as "hard to place," "emotionally disturbed" or "high risk" by the social workers and courts.

For the next ten years, until the summer of 1973, thousands of Illinois children were sent to fifty institutions in seventeen states including Missouri, Oregon and Texas. Louisiana is currently spending $3.8 million per year for out-of-state care of 750 neglected, retarded and emotionally disturbed children, 95 percent of whom end up in Texas. In 1975, New Jersey spent $7.5 million to send more than 1,000 of its neglected and emotionally retarded wards to eighty-eight institutions in nineteen states and Nova Scotia.

Why are so many children sent to Texas? When Governor Dolph Briscoe raised the question to his attorney general, John L. Hill, the latter submitted his investigative findings in a report accompanied by the following typically bureaucratic letter of transmittal which concluded:

There can be little doubt that the placement of a large number of out-of-state children in private profit making child care facilities in Texas caused somewhat of a boom and expansion of such establishments. Such privately owned facilities have risen to financial success by setting up legal facilities, insofar as Texas' inadequate licensing standards are concerned, and the accepting of out-of-state children from those states who could not or would not accept such children for a variety of reasons, including a lack of facilities which could meet their state standards, which were higher than those in Texas. This raises serious policy questions which perhaps need discussion and resolution on the national scene.

The child-care vacuum of the early sixties was filled when two Texas businessmen, Wayne Lippold and Gregor Cruickshank and two officials from the Texas Public Welfare Department, Everett Woods and John Robinson, shrewdly projected a vast market for interstate traffic of such children. They, and a host of paid child psychiatrists, using children from Illinois, Louisiana, New Jersey and two other states to a limited degree, created an empire including Meridell Achievement Center and two spin-off centers— the Wimberley Children Center and Abilene Youth Center. From 1969 to 1973 these institutions realized over $4 million from Illinois alone.

Wayne Lippold, Meridell's founder and president, was proprietor of a small loan company in the Austin area for twelve years, before entering the child-care business. Gregor Cruickshank, also founder and treasurer, was a businessman with vast experience in Texas real estate and real estate management. Both men were married to registered nurses with some background in psychiatric nursing. Woods and Robinson were moonlighting at Meridell while employed by the Public Welfare Department (the state agency that regulates such institutions as Meridell), but later, as the empire became a financial success, they left their civil servant jobs for the more lucrative child business. That business was brisk and growing. In 1972 the Wimberley Center developed a grandiose concept for a new showplace campus and planned to borrow $300,000.

Like any business operation, the Meridell chain was out to make profit and that meant cutting operating costs to the bone. So outdoor living—the Camping Program—became very popular and profitable. Overhead expenses were nil. The children cooked their own food and saw to their own shelter. School was not required, eliminating the need for professional staff. Investigators have estimated that the actual per diem cost for each child in the camping program was between $3 and $4, while Illinois was paying about $23 per child per day. The taxpayers of that state spent $29,100 to keep one little boy in the program for three years without a day of education. Two South Dakota children were there for six years without any schooling. The records simply stated that these children "were not ready for school." One employee requested better camping equipment, including winter sleeping bags because the temperatures fell below freezing at certain times of the year. The request was rejected as "unnecessary cost."

Meridell's expediency was seldom scrutinized because of its tax-deductible entertainment policy. Visiting officials were frequently treated to sumptuous meals at the "Barn," a popular and expensive steak house on Balcones Drive in Austin. They were also provided plush motels for their stay. A former high-ranking Meridell official explained: "We would get these 22-year-old girl welfare workers in from Illinois and wine and dine them and snow them on our treatment.... We used Meridell's credit cards and there was never any limit on the expense account....* Attractive female staff members were also paired with visiting male officials.

One way to protect one's business is to have the right people looking out for your best interests. According to John L. Hill, the "right people" for Meridell were high-ranking state public welfare personnel:

> The Meridell Center and Meridell combine have had many close connections with the DPW [Department of Public Welfare] through the employment of several DPW personnel as consultants and part-time workers.... James B. Harvey [formerly administrator of the Austin region for the Department of Public Welfare and responsible for licensing such facilities as Meridell] provided officials of the school with "feedback" about the 1971 legislative session's consideration which might affect it and was paid $600. for his work in February–April of 1971.

Though Meridell never submitted an annual audit report until 1974, a direct violation of state law, it had no problem obtaining

---

* Not "snowed" by Meridell staff was a lawyer for the Chicago Legal Assistance Foundation whose report noted: "No treatment plan, psychiatric or psychological evaluation or progress note appears in a resident's file except, perhaps, for occasional notations entered by staff at Meridell.... No evidence of physical and dental checkups appears in files... clearly inadequate for placement of children."

license approvals for increased child enrollment. In August of 1964 it was licensed for 36 children; in November of 1968 it was licensed for 110 children, and in April of 1973 the figure was up to 285 youngsters. John Robinson, who worked for the state public welfare department from 1959 to 1971 as supervisor and later administrator of the Austin division (which issued the above licenses), was also receiving $300 a month as consultant to Meridell. He later became social services director at the school.

Another person involved in the Meridell combine was Dr. George Willeford, an Austin pediatrician, consultant for Meridell, part-owner of Wimberley, and former Texas State Republican Chairman. According to Dr. Alex Munson, a psychiatrist at St. Jude's Hospital, when Dr. Willeford was accused of harassing a former Meridell employee for talking with the press during the height of a state investigation into private child-caring facilities in the summer of 1973, he confided to Dr. Munson: "If one commode overflows it can stink up the whole house."*

In the early spring of 1973, Meridell's Illinois bubble burst when eleven boys from the Abilene Youth Center were picked up by Dallas police. A police officer noticed a weaving auto during a sleet and rain storm, stopped it and found that it was stolen. The boys were attempting to drive home to Chicago. All eleven were placed in a Dallas hospital for symptoms of drug withdrawal from tranquilizers administered at the Abilene Youth Center. Their tales of abuse and subsequent investigations and lawsuits by Pat Murphy and staff† prompted the then director of Children Services, Dr. Jerry Miller, to bring most of the Illinois children home from Texas.

Wade Wilson, a former administrator of the Meridell chain and presently a doctoral candidate in the field of special education at the University of Texas, outlined the systems at Meridell (which are common to many private, residential, child-caring facilities) in a reflective article, "Self-Cycling Dilemmas of Residential Treatment":

* On October 31, 1974, Dr. Willeford was given a three-year appointment by President Ford to the National Advisory Council on the Education of Disadvantaged Children.

† Pat Murphy headed up the Chicago Legal Assistance Foundation. The foundation was responsible for breaking the Texas-Illinois Connection scandal.

Unfortunately, there exist institutions in which program and staffing are held to a minimum for conscious financial gains. Many times there are long lists of advertising professional persons listed on letter-heads and advertising literature. These "consultants" range from psychiatrists to lawyers and bookkeepers. Many times these "consultants" have little or nothing to do with the program of an institution but spend one or two hours a week for an hourly fee of $40 in exchange for the use of their name and degree and signature on medical reports.... Modern buildings, swimming pools and landscaping are also examples of "parent catchers."... While a few children are lodged in new modern buildings, many more are often in make-do structures which hopefully can be disposed of or repaired by the time a licensing agent inspects.... Many of the administrators of these agencies are experts at telling placement resources and parents what they want to hear... many referring agencies send out inspectors to "approve" these programs but the administrators and owners of such Residential Treatment Centers can often snow the inspector by rapid whirlwind tours....

Wilson feels, as I do, that the fault lies not with the private owners but rather with state legislatures that, failing to provide children of their state good local programs, send them off to distant facilities and then are unable or unwilling to inspect these facilities adequately. In a letter to me in December of 1974, Wade Wilson wrote: "The legislators, in response to parents and mental health professionals, fund expensive programs out of state, while businessmen, whose business it is to make money, take advantage of the opportunity, and *children are abused.*"

And abuses abounded. Illinois children in Oregon were hand-cuffed together around trees and left out overnight. Fifty-eight Texas children—some normal, some above average—were unwittingly subjected to untested birth control drugs in Missouri. In Illinois, students were forced to sleep in their own urine in closed 4½ by 4½ isolation rooms after their requests to use the toilet were denied. Some were forced to eat odd assortments of food like peanut butter, hot sauce and mustard. Others caught smoking were forced to eat the cigarettes. Runaways were given injections of Thorazine followed by a "short shot of alcohol to sting." Heads were shaved. Phone calls and mail were censored. A boy suffering from Osgood–Sclatter Disease* was allegedly forced to "stand for hours in a cold water tub and crawl about on his knees" as punishment for joyriding in a car. The same boy was also forced to camp out in the cold without proper medication.

In a facility for Louisiana children called the Heart of Texas Home, in Bangs, Texas, medicine was dispensed by the cook and no medication records were kept. In one room of this institution there was a section "caged for uncontrollables," and the fence surrounding the back area of the play yard was electrified. The Wood Acres Home for mentally retarded children, which was supposed to send its out-of-state Louisiana wards—most of whom were trainable or educable—to the Conroe, Texas, public schools, never bothered. At Harris County Halfway House, fifteen retarded girls from Louisiana were abandoned when the director simply walked out, leaving the youngsters alone and uncared for (emergency food and supervision had to be organized). Some of these centers administered the drug Aventyl to curb sex problems of the children. Aventyl is an antidepressant that decreases libido, but it can also be especially painful for males in that it causes swelling of the testicles.

Many children are abused by economic exploitation. A seventeen-year-old Illinois girl was sent to the Haven Acres School for the Exceptional in Oregon and worked with retarded children for $10 a month. At the same time, Haven Acres was receiving $13 a day for her care. The owner of the Dyer Vocational Training Center in Leona, Texas, also paid his thirty-two mentally retarded children from Louisiana $10 a month to work in the various enterprises he owned. These included two service stations, a grocery store, an eighty-acre farm and a welding shop. He, in turn, was receiving over $50,000 to provide treatment for these youths. One form of punishment at Dyer was to withhold the children's wages. At the Mary Lee School outside Austin, Texas, investigating State Representative Lane Denton discovered Illinois teen-age girls "making clothespins in a filthy, abandoned shack full of snakes and old refrigerators."

A particularly crippling abuse was the lack of education

---

* Manifested by the destruction of the growing ends of a child's bones.

the incarcerated children, a lack such as experienced at the Wood Acres Home. It was left to the discretion of each institution to determine whether a child was ready for education. More often than not, for economic reasons, the schools determined they were not. Of the few on-campus schooling programs that did exist, not one was certified. Illinois Department of Children and Family Services staff member Ralph Baur said: "The most frequently identified need by the children themselves, is educational services followed by job training and job placement." Not only were the children and taxpayers of the states sending the children misled, but so were the taxpayers of Texas. "More than $1 million a year in state special education funds was being pumped into the private facilities, some of which pay little or no state taxes," revealed the Texas Educational Agency.

The abuse of the legal rights of all children living under state imposed exile is staggering. The activities of their keepers are criminal: child abuse and neglect (warehousing children without proper treatment, education or food); official misconduct and malfeasance (use of public funds and facilities for self-interest rather than for children's welfare); battery and aggravated battery (drug assaults, corporal punishment, severe beatings, etc.); and denying children the privileges of the first article of the Bill of Rights—freedom to worship in their own way.

These abuses can flourish only because there is total lack of supervision by the sending states that send their children to other states. Rarely do they visit the facilities unannounced, nor is there any record that child-expert teams seriously inspect and evaluate out-of-state placement centers. Sidney J. Gomez, chief of the Louisiana child placement section of the Division of Mental Retardation confessed that his office does not inspect out-of-state schools but does make certain they are licensed. As far back as 1967, letters were exchanged between Illinois and Texas state officials arguing whose responsibilities it was to monitor the child care institutions in Texas. Each state accused the other of not living up to its legal and professional responsibilities; then the letters ended and no serious follow-up or tough inspection ensued. The issue was ignored for almost a decade, while Illinois children continued to be shipped south and placed in dubious institutions, including Wimberley Center, which had no approved license, even by the lax Texas standards.

New Jersey also had children at the Texas Meridell Achievement Center and at a facility in Virginia called Edgemeade. Edgemeade was evaluated in the recent past by the Federal Military Program called CHAMPUS.* Because of the poor services and facilities found at Edgemeade, CHAMPUS withdrew support and informed parents to remove their children from the facility. I have since interviewed Jersey officials who confirmed that they, along with eight other states now sending their children to Edgemeade, were unaware of the CHAMPUS decision. Nor have they bothered to monitor that or any other institution now serving the needs of New Jersey children placed far away from home.

When former commissioner of Pennsylvania's Child and Youth Services, Larry Barker, made his systematic investigation of Oakdale Boys Home outside Pittsburgh in 1972, he found seven New Jersey boys living there at a cost of $760 per month per boy.† When Barker (who subsequently had the home closed down) informed the Garden State of conditions at Oakdale, an official responded: "We intend to screen subsequent possible placements for Oakdale with extreme care ... and to closely review the status of each of the youngsters and will, in all likelihood, work out alternative placements, during a diplomatic period of time."

Total negligence in supervision can almost be forgiven when compared with the instances in which officials inspect and evaluate placement centers and deliberately falsify their findings. I observed one such instance personally. In the summer of 1973, Louisiana officials visited the East Texas Guidance and Achievement Center and reported to their superiors back home that children at the center were getting "excellent care and total individualized attention." I visited the operation about the same time, along with Representative Lane Denton and Bill Aleshire, his administrative assistant. Regional Public Welfare Administrator

* Civilian Health and Medical Program of the Uniformed Services.
† Funds were provided by a triangle of sources: $400 from the Bureau of Children's Services, $210 from the State Department of Education and $150 from a private foundation operating out of East Orange, N.J.—the Turrell Fund.

Charles E. Jenkins gave us the background history of the institution. He said the place should never have been licensed. Records revealed that the sewage disposal system didn't work and human waste was flooding onto school property. A neighbor filed a criminal complaint against the owner and well over 125 citizens petitioned the Department of Public Welfare to withdraw the school's license. Former teachers and students came forth with many horror stories, the worst of which told of two boys who threw gasoline on a third student and set him on fire, burning his shoulders and face terribly. The incident was never reported to the police for fear of bringing bad publicity to the school. Still, the school was relicensed because of pressure by politicians—the out-of-state child industry is a lucrative business.

At the Dyer Vocational Training Center, where the children were working in assorted gas stations and welding shops for $10 a month, the visiting Louisiana team also reported: "Impressed with Dyer, especially its organization and structure." In their annual report they chided the critics:

> Mention should be made of the publicity concerning children placed in out-of-state facilities, and particularly in Texas. A great many accusations were made in the press about various institutions used by Louisiana and most of these turned out to be either exaggerated or inaccurate. Unfortunately, retractions, if there were any, did not receive the same space and emphasis that the original accounts were given.... As it turned out, all institutions used by Family Services except one were given a clean bill of health. There was no evidence that any child placed by this division was abused or mistreated....

In recent years, thanks largely to the efforts of attorney Patrick Murphy, who, with a team of colleagues, doggedly hounded and filed suits against the Illinois State Department of Children and Family Services, the state of Illinois has begun to recognize the full dimensions and tragic consequences of placing children out of state. Instrumental in this recognition was "An Illinois Tragedy: An Analysis of the Placement of Illinois Wards in the State of Texas," an investigative report by DePaul University lawyer Patrick Keenan. Its conclusion was powerful:

> Alas, the worst fears are realized. The children and money were banished to and wasted in Texas by an efficient, responsive, mind-

less, heartless bureaucratic monster inexorably grinding its way through children's lives. And the cogs which made it up helped piously, righteously and without vision or liability. Everyone is responsible. No one is or will be accountable. No one meant for it to happen. It just did. Too bad.

Illinois has admitted that it lost track of some fifty-five children —banished and vanished forever. Four returned home in coffins;* others, to paraphrase Erik Erikson, came home with the most painful of all possible scars—the mutilation of their spirits.

New Orleans lawyer William Rittenberg has filed a civil class action suit (*Gary W. v. the State of Louisiana*) in the United States District Court of the Eastern District of Louisiana against the Texas facilities housing Louisiana children. It is hoped that Rittenberg's suit not only will answer legal questions surrounding modern day banishment of children but will protect the future rights of children from interstate greed merchants.

One of Rittenberg's plaintiffs is thirteen-year-old Joseph G., who at age three was taken from his mother solely on the charge of poverty. For the last ten years, Joseph has been subject to out-of-state residential treatment centers—the last being East Texas Guidance and Achievement Center. His case, like those of thousands of other children, clearly shows how the state may destroy whatever is left of the family structure for dependent and neglected children. For example, in Illinois, a family on welfare gets only $40 per child per month. If that child is taken by the courts, the state will pay a foster home $140 per month. If placed out of state, the same child is worth $750 per month to the receiving center. The long-term human cost of such a practice as out-of-state placement is immeasurable when you consider the impact it has on the child and other members of the family. As Pat Murphy said, "A child should be able to get help from the state without being taken from his family and the family should also be able to get help without being destroyed."

Sadly, but in a positive vein, of more than 250 children returned from Texas to Illinois, 80 percent were placed back with their

---

* Keenan's state investigation team stated that the deaths of three of the four children "warranted at least superficial criminal investigations" and that all four should have had autopsies. All the deaths were termed "accidental."

family or relatives. But as one parent told me, "At first we're not fit to take care of our children and then they say we are!"

A national inquiry into the interstate commerce of children is imperative. And it should be carried out at the federal level. Investigations by Texas Attorney General John Hill and by Patrick Keenan both failed to answer many questions and neither could find history of "payment, inducements or kickbacks" of a criminal nature concerning placement of out-of-state children.* Louisiana has never conducted a serious investigation. Until I turned over my information on children in out-of-state facilities to the New Jersey Crime Commission, that state was unable or would not provide the numbers, cost or placement centers to the speaker of its own state legislature.

Back in fiscal year 1972, there was a freeze in Illinois on all funds and rate increases for the care of institutionalized children. Yet all the out-of-state institutions Illinois used were given up to 50 percent of their requested rate increases, and Meridell, the East Texas Guidance and Achievement Center, the Wimberley Children Center and Summit Oaks (which opened a Chicago branch office) were awarded a 75 percent rate increase.

Tulane University's Dr. Dorothy S. Randolph conducted a survey of Louisiana child care facilities and found that with the "exception of highly specialized treatment," the state could provide qualified care to all the 1,812 children subjected to out-of-state placement. Why then has Louisiana not had any referrals for more than two years? Why are they going to Texas at four times the cost? Why does the Dyer Vocational Training Center in Texas take only Louisiana referrals from the placement office of Sidney Gomez (Division of Hospitals—MR Division). Why is it that until the Texas Connection story broke, in-state Louisiana facilities received a fixed rate of $125 per month per child while the state paid the Meridell Achievement Center in Texas $1,125 per month per child?

Why are these children deprived of family relationships and involuntarily taken away to distant accommodations, some times

---

* It is here that this writer takes exception to an otherwise enlightening report ("An Illinois Tragedy"). Keenan's investigation team covered a decade of business in Texas and sixteen other states in thirty days.

to remain for years? Why is involuntary servitude and peonage tolerated? Why are tax dollars given to institutions in the name of treatment while children waste years of their lives in year-round camping programs?

What constitutes criminal fraud?

... the fact the committee should find most fearsome is that CHAMPUS was created by and is, in fact, Congress' Rosemary's Baby. And until you steel up and give federal guidelines some teeth to enforce criminal laws against the offenders, the horror stories of young Americans being used to perpetuate the child industry will continue unabated.

—From testimony by Kenneth Wooden—rejected by Senator Henry Jackson's Permanent Subcommittee on Investigations

16/The CHAMPUS Scandal: Greed Merchants, Pentagon Brass and Senate Hopefuls

During the summer of 1974 the U.S. Permanent Subcommittee on Investigations, chaired by senators Henry Jackson of Washington State and Charles Percy of Illinois, held nationally televised hearings. The American people heard shocking tales of child abuse, including stories of youngsters who were buried alive as punishment or whose bloodstreams were injected with their own urine.

At the height of the hearings, while flashbulbs popped and cameras ground, a witness explained to Senator Jackson the function of the leg irons, handcuffs, chains and bullwhips that he held up, one by one, for the mass media. Senator Jackson left the room. Senator Percy entered and the entire procedure was repeated. It was a great show and, in my opinion, one more abuse of the children who endured the inhuman treatment at the Green Valley School in Florida and University

Center, Ann Arbor, Michigan—to name a few. Once the TV lights went out, the kids were forgotten. I know. I broke the CHAMPUS story while researching this book, having decided I could not wait until publication to expose the horrors I had found and to prod the Congress to act. This chapter is my story of investigative research and orchestrating political action while I watch the greed merchants, pentagon bureaucrats and ambitious politicians dance around a national scandal—and finally almost bury it by their consuming self-interests.

I first heard the term CHAMPUS—Civilian Health and Medical Program of the Uniformed Services—in June of 1973, shortly after a murder indictment was handed down against Dr. Joseph D. Farrer of Artesia Hall, a CHAMPUS-approved facility. Texas Representative Lane Denton called from Austin and asked what it was. I hadn't the foggiest idea. A few weeks later, I went to Austin to act as Denton's research assistant in his investigation of child care abuse at Artesia Hall, a CHAMPUS-supported institution. For me it was an excellent opportunity to learn something about CHAMPUS.

A federal program, enacted by the Congress in 1956 and operating out of the Pentagon and Fitzsimmons Hospital, Denver, CHAMPUS is a national health program that provides total medical coverage to dependents of active or retired military personnel. In 1966, Congress amended the legislation to include psychiatric treatment. More loosely interpreted, this covers an area that encompasses from mildly emotionally disturbed to severely retarded children. Since there were no limitation provisions for professional fees or guidelines for treatment, the military children have supplied raw material for a very lucrative enterprise. Sixty percent of all CHAMPUS-funded child psychiatric facilities never existed prior to 1966. These are the private institutions to which I will address myself.

During our investigation of Artesia Hall, we had calls from parents in Central Texas about an expensive facility called Lebe Hoch, located a few miles from the LBJ Ranch near Johnson City, Texas. I visited the institution unannounced in late June of 1973. The entire staff gathered in a small conference room to hear what I had to say about "alternatives to incarceration." After I had asked several pointed questions about the care and treatment available at Lebe Hoch part-time psychiatrist Dr. W. Ash stood up and asked: "Just one minute, how many children are you going to send us?" When I answered "none," the entire staff got up and left.

However, no one prevented me from touring the facility and talking with staff, children and visiting parents. I learned that despite the fact that Lebe Hoch had no state license and had failed a thorough examination by Denver CHAMPUS inspector Lieutenant Colonel Janet Rogers, the institution had enough political clout to continue operating as usual.

On the grounds, I noticed a strange structure with heavy black plastic covering all the windows. That evening a former house parent told me it was the private domain of a Dr. Snap, who believes that children are not retarded but that their intellectual development has been aborted by birth. Dr. Snap believes he has restructured the mother's womb in these totally darkened rooms, and he places the retarded child here to grow. This, the doctor believes, along with deep pressure therapy on the spinal cord and buttocks, will result in a normal child.* Donna Perish came close to dying in her "womb." When her parents removed her after four weeks in this atmosphere, they found her body covered with sores.

Before leaving Texas, I encouraged the legal counsel to the state House of Representatives' Committee on Human Resources to investigate the facility. They did, and written testimony submitted to the hearings said Lebe Hoch was totally lacking in professional management and that the general conditions of the physical plant, medical records, personnel records and financial records indicated gross neglect and incompetent management. Two of the facility's psychologists weren't even licensed in Texas, and "medical records," according to investigator Benny Britton, "do not agree with the financial records of several patients reviewed."

I flew to Denver. The staff at CHAMPUS headquarters was very helpful and concerned about the program but totally frustrated by their Washington superiors. They had tried to close

---

* Dr. Snap is still in business in Texas. He now has a private plane and occasionally flies out to the program's Denver headquarters to lobby for higher CHAMPUS rates.

several CHAMPUS-approved institutions like Lebe Hoch and Green Valley in Florida, but for unexplained reasons, the Pentagon, who sets the policies, reversed their decisions. Colonel Rogers and Captain Lamont Peterson were particularly outspoken and agonized over the lack of accountability in the program. In the months ahead we were to be drawn together by a common bond of increasing anger and frustration.

After I returned home, someone mailed me a list of sixteen institutions "that should be visited and evaluated by an outsider like [myself]." According to my unsigned source, these institutions were "making a fortune from the U.S. Treasury, riddled with conflict of interest and poor and inhuman conditions all under the guise of treating the emotionally disturbed." The letter also contained computer readouts on facilities and patients. I began to see how vast the operation was: CHAMPUS was another version of interstate commerce of children, only this time it was big money. United States taxpayers were paying anywhere from $1,000 to $6,500 per child per month at eight hundred private facilities. In my attaché case lay two lines written for me by a young girl at Lebe Hoch who was judged to be mentally retarded. I realized it was a poignant insight into the plight of many CHAMPUS children:

> From the cities dark and gray
> They send their children far away.

Late in the summer I decided to try to interest both the U.S. Justice Department and the U.S. Senate in CHAMPUS. I met with Senator Jackson's staff and they could not believe that conditions I described existed in the United States. They dismissed me with: "When and if you have more information, come back...."

In the early fall of 1973, I set up an intinerary that would take me to Florida, New Mexico, Colorado, Illinois, California, Michigan and Pennsylvania to investigate conditions in CHAMPUS-approved schools. I left a very chilly Pennsylvania and landed in a warm Daytona Beach, Florida. My first facility was the Green Valley School. The information I would glean from that visit would ultimately touch off the most expensive inquiry ever conducted by the Senate Permanent Subcommittee on Investigations.

Green Valley, under the directorship of Reverend George Von Hilschimer, had recently been the subject of adverse publicity from an investigation by the Florida state attorney general's office. Raids in the late sixties and early seventies had also revealed an assortment of child-control devices, including electric cattle prods, shock collars, shotguns, leg irons and much more. Von Hilschimer was charged with practicing pharmacology and medicine without a license and engaging in unusual therapy, including human experimentation. On October 21, 1968, the Volusia County board of health sent a letter to CHAMPUS, calling the Green Valley School "unsanitary" and stating that a "bomb shelter was being used for solitary confinement."

State investigator John Upman and I talked with students at Green Valley, all of whom told of physical beatings, solitary confinement and easy access to drugs and sex. One boy told us that he "saw Reverend Von Hilschimer drunk many times" and that he would then make students "show movies backwards three and four times." Another complained of getting injections of Prolixin, which made him shake. With every "not very good meal," unlimited vitamins were handed out.* (I saw them discarded on the ground around the campus.) Upman and I wondered aloud how Von Hilschimer stayed in business after the investigations by the attorney general's office. "My father read about Green Valley in *The Washington Post*† and was impressed," one boy told us.

Embarrassed by the negative publicity and raids by the attorney general's office, the CHAMPUS headquarters in Denver wanted the operation at Green Valley terminated. The Pentagon, however, sent its own Dr. Kenneth Babcock (also consultant to the Joint Commission on Accreditation of Hospitals—JCAH) to evaluate the facilities. After all the revelations by state officials about torture devices, suicides, solitary confinement and poor health conditions, Dr. Babcock still gave Green Valley a favorable report, and the Pentagon denied the request to take the school out of the program. It was not until 1973, when JCAH set forth specific requirements for psychiatric hospitals, that Green Valley

* Each vitamin Von Hilschimer pushed in his mega-vitamin program cost taxpayers one dollar.
† *The New York Times* also advertised Green Valley.

was removed from the CHAMPUS program—but that was $1.2 million later.

From Green Valley I went to New Mexico, Texas and Arizona, then on to a facility called El Cajon Reading Achievement Center, in San Diego, California. Here former staff substantiated what a Denver source had told me—that staff were paid $100 for each child they found and enrolled in the CHAMPUS program. Hunger for the hundred-dollar bills grew to a point where employees were going door to door in search of military personnel who had children with reading problems and CHAMPUS benefits. FBI agent Charles Kellerman's report (Bureau File #46–61316, Oct. 20, 1972) also confirmed this evidence, which he turned over to the U.S. Attorney in California, but criminal charges were never filed against anyone at El Cajon.

University Center in Ann Arbor, Michigan, was a private hospital for mentally retarded children. Big CHAMPUS money changed all that, in 1966: it then became a private psychiatric hospital for emotionally disturbed youngsters who were the children of military parents.

I went to the University Center unannounced and found the only two staff persons on duty working on personal projects while the students were left to entertain themselves with TV. Recreation equipment lay in the cellar gathering dust and rust. The medical area was disgracefully unsanitary. Students told me that drugs abounded in the vicinity of the facility and were easily accessible. I was taken to visit the "quiet rooms"—solitary confinement. They were filled. One thin boy wrapped in a blanket and sitting like an old man on his cot had been locked there for buying a can of beer the night before. He was staring blankly out the window while another boy in the nearby "playboy room" (for good behavior) was loudly playing a record by Led Zeppelin called "Stairway to Heaven."

A youngster came up to me as I was about to leave University Center and asked, "Why are you here? Dr. Kambly loves money —are you giving him some?" Of course I wasn't, but Dr. Arnold H. Kambly, the owner of University Center—an institution that the Michigan State Board of Health decreed could not be called a "hospital"—was receiving an average of $2,700 per month p child. One child was drawing in $3,150 per month for the docto

By the time of my visit CHAMPUS had already dumped well over half a million dollars into the center.

Although visits to two CHAMPUS facilities in Pennsylvania uncovered nothing comparable to conditions at Green Valley, Lebe Hoch, Artesia Hall or University Center, I felt I had enough information to approach Washington again. I made appointments with Senator Jackson's legal counsel, Joel Merkel, and U.S. Deputy Assistant Attorney General James P. Turner. Turner was interested and wrote that he had asked attorneys in the Office of Institutions and Facilities of the Civil Rights Division of the U.S. Justice Department to investigate my charges and to work with me if the charges merited in-depth study.

Joel Merkel, on the other hand, was interested but skeptical. He wanted more proof and felt that letters from around the country urging the senator to investigate abuse to children enrolled in CHAMPUS would lend credence to my request. Within days, I had Representative Denton, parents of CHAMPUS children, and staff, professional and nonprofessional, writing Jackson, requesting and demanding an investigation. A week later I was back in Jackson's office, again asking him to act by virtue of his membership on the Senate Armed Services Committee.

His office set up an appointment for me to meet with John Walsh, senior investigator of the Senate Permanent Subcommittee on Investigations. Walsh, at the time, was busy completing his report on the Russian wheat deal but lent a sympathetic ear and then asked if I would cooperate with the subcommittee—share contacts and files from my own CHAMPUS investigation.

I left Washington elated. I knew I was no longer dealing with politicians on The Hill but with a highly professional investigator who instinctively knew I was telling the truth. My excitement was intensified by two packages my wife handed me when I arrived home. I found five unpublished and restricted* audits on CHAMPUS by the comptroller general of the Committee on Appropriations for the House of Representatives. They were dated March to July of 1971.

---

* The cover of each audit read: "Restricted—Not to be released outside the General Accounting Office except on the basis of specific approval by the Office of Legislative Liasion, a record of which is kept by the Distribution Section, Publications Branch, OAS. . . ."

I pored over the documents. Up to this point I was convinced I had a national scandal on my hands, but the data in these five documents confirmed my suspicions and lent solid irrefutable substance to my investigative research thus far. I knew I had been right to contact the U.S. Senate and Justice Department.

The material in these documents was devastating, not only to CHAMPUS but to the medical profession as well. The dimension of their greed was shocking. Since the policy makers in the Pentagon had never set guidelines on what CHAMPUS doctors could charge, the sky was the limit—as high as $153,000 for one doctor. Of thirteen physicians who received over $50,000 from CHAMPUS, eight were psychiatrists, the highest of these pulling in $106,000 for such treatments as "adjustment reaction of adolescence," nail-biting and overweight. Another doctor, from Virginia asked $106,000 for 772 consecutive daily visits to one patient; others elsewhere were charging $37,000 and $32,000 per patient.

With this sort of billing, costs of the CHAMPUS operation rose every year. It had started with a budget of about $26 million in 1956; by 1973 the figure was at half a billion a year. General Accounting auditors had found that CHAMPUS patients were charged roughly $43 per day for treatment compared with $32 in private psychiatric hospitals and about $5 in state mental hospitals.

Here too, kickbacks allowed a little "pin money" for the doctors. For example, some private firms were selling enuretic conditioned-response training equipment to CHAMPUS officials for $220 to $445 per machine. (The same enuretic devices can be bought at Sears for $20—deluxe model is $33). Physicians who pushed models for the private firms were rewarded $5 to $15 per device. Some of the doctors admitted they had never even seen the bedwetting patients.

In December of 1973, I stopped all travel and hid away at the home of Massachusetts Assistant Commissioner of Youth and Family Services Ed Budelmann, in Shutesbury, to begin writing. In early January 1974, John Walsh and Bill Knauf, two professional investigators employed by the Senate, visited me, and for nine straight hours we scrutinized my files on Lebe Hoch, Green Valley, University Center (all CHAMPUS accommodations) and

204/The Politics of Corruption

sixteen other facilities, and the computer readouts I had collected. We listened to tapes of families and children who were subjected to the greed merchants. It was stimulating to work with such highly professional investigators. As I had decided, I did not share with them the audits from the comptroller's office, but as it developed, it didn't matter, for they already had them, too. The investigation was snowballing and I felt it was in safe, nonpartisan hands.

Prodded by Investigator Walsh's frequently expressed concern about what the Justice Department was doing—"if there was ever a case of people needing their civil rights protected, it is these children who are subject to CHAMPUS-supported commercial jails"—I continued pushing the Justice Department, which finally agreed to send two lawyers up to Massachusetts to review my files and see if there was "a potential violation of federal law." On April 9, 1974, Jack Anderson, referring to the $500 million probe in his "Washington Merry-Go-Round" column in *The Washington Post*, said: "The importance of the study is indicated by the fact that Sens. Henry M. Jackson (D–Wash) and Charles H. Percy (R–Ill.) have diverted senior investigators from their vital Fuel Crisis study to looking into CHAMPUS." Bill Knauf informed me of their plans, which called for major, extensive congressional hearings in the fall. The hearings were to last three weeks. He asked if I would be willing to testify. It was a rhetorical question.

By early June, however, an extensive three-week national hearing was being chopped down to two or three days by Jackson's subcommittee chief counsel Howard Feldman. Conditions at only two facilities, Green Valley and University Center, were to be made public. Politics was raising its ugly head, and a highly professional investigation was going to be short-changed. The collapse of the Nixon Administration was imminent and both Jackson and Percy were running hard in hopes there would be an election for the job that President Nixon would be forced to give up because of Watergate. I was upset and asked for a meeting with Feldman, which could not be arranged until shortly before the scheduled hearings in July.

Feldman informed me he did not want me to testify or be present at any press briefings. Period. I later learned that an opening statement prepared by the investigators for Senator Jackson, giving an account of my role, had been deleted by Feldman. Only after great pressure was applied, did he permit a watered-down version of this statement. Still, I wasn't allowed to testify. The reason was simple: Jackson's top press and political strategists viewed the hearing as great national publicity and wanted to share credit with no one. I also met with Senator Percy briefly early in the hearings, but his staff, too, decided against letting me testify.

It was a hellish four days. The hearings did, in fact, illuminate the problem of abuse at Green Valley and University Center, and the articulate evidence presented by the investigators was effective in cutting off CHAMPUS approval of these institutions. Senators Jackson and Percy both got good wire service and TV coverage. *Time* magazine carried a full page on the hearings and I overheard Jackson's press secretary joyfully exclaim, "Christ, the Judicial Committee impeachment hearings are on the air and we are still getting prime coverage—beautiful!" But Jackson had ensured coverage when, on the first day of the hearings, he told Feldman to inform ABC they were not giving the chairman enough footage —the chairman being Mr. Jackson.

Unfortunately, there is a big difference between a shallow grab for headlines and honest determination to effect change. The chairman wasn't even present the entire last day while the top brass of the Pentagon testified, and his closing statement was read by someone else. The TV lights were gone and so was Senator Jackson. I left Washington with my family and my untried testimony.

Still it was not a total loss. Within days after I returned home, both the Pentagon and Denver CHAMPUS headquarters phoned. The Pentagon called out of concern—in their words, "We hear you are writing a book." The Pentagon CHAMPUS staff wanted to discuss what they were doing to improve CHAMPUS. Denver, on the other hand, had called to continue what I believe was a sincere effort to clean up fly-by-night facilities—against the tremendous obstacles of political influence and the bureaucratic inertia of the Defense Department. Denver CHAMPUS wanted the names of establishments they could visit unannounced.

At this time, the Justice Department moved in to investigate and litigate CHAMPUS offenders. U.S. Attorney Louis Thrasher, an excellent courtroom lawyer during the Morales trial, was back from Harvard University after a year's leave and was appointed to a new position at the Justice Department, Office of Special Litigation. He called and I put him in touch with Senate investigators Walsh and Knauf, who made the committee's files available to him.

Still another positive by-product of the hearings was revealed to me by Genevieve Tarlton, from the staff of Texas Lieutenant Governor William Hobby. The Morales trial had damaged the image of the Texas Youth Council and the state wanted some reform alternatives. Governor Dolph Briscoe had appointed Robert Lanier, of the Lanier Foundation* in Houston, to come up with some new ideas for dealing with problem youths. Lanier had been flying state legislators down to witness a "wilderness" program at Green Valley and they had been on the verge of finalizing arrangements to have Texas children put under Von Hilschimer's care when they viewed both him and his institution in a new light on national TV. Needless to say, the shocked legislators and Robert Lanier withdrew their commitment.

Realizing that Jackson and Percy no longer had any interest in CHAMPUS, I decided to postpone my deadline on the book and continue my own investigations. I flew out to Denver again. The staff was more cooperative than ever before because they felt that the senators' committments were "thinner than air." Mrs. Ann Presley, a CHAMPUS evaluator, gave me information on Redding Ridge, an Alabama facility.

Mrs. Presley visited Redding Ridge and found it overrun with

---

* The Lanier Foundation indirectly supported the Green Valley School through the Korczac Memorial Medical Clinic of Orange City, Florida, a private group of doctors who represented the specialties of psychiatry, internal medicine and allergy immunology, and who were funded to work with George Von Hilschimer. One of the doctors, William Philpott, was formerly under indictment for manslaughter in the deaths of two people who underwent his carbon dioxide (CO_2) inhalation therapy for alleged allergic and mental disorders in Massachusetts. Children at Green Valley were receiving the same therapy. Although Lanier never returned my phone calls or answered my letters, he did meet with Senate investigators in Louisiana and sadly reported that his own mentally retarded daughter had been treated at Green Valley and in Dr. Philpott's facility in Massachusetts.

cockroaches, the floor littered with food, dirt and fifty twenty-year-old mattresses. In one little boy's medical folder a part-time psychiatrist had written: "Johnny doesn't react so violently to homosexual advances anymore." When Mrs. Presley told an administrator of the private facility that she would strongly recommend closing it down, he told her they were expecting $40,000 from their claims officer shortly and "isn't there some way we can reason this out together?"

Shaken by both the little boy's folder and the not-too-subtle bribe, Mrs. Presley went to the first pay telephone booth to report back to her office. When the office answered the phone, she was unable to talk. She just wept.

The psychiatric treatment program under CHAMPUS was designed to actively help those children who would benefit from such treatment on a short-term basis. It is not a custodial program. Audit reports clearly state that "approval is required for more than 90 days of care." However, as I searched the CHAMPUS files in Denver, I found one thick file that clearly showed that someone has had approval many times. The daughter of Mme. Claire Chennault, wife of the Army Air Force general of Flying Tiger fame, has been confined under custodial care for more than thirteen years. Over $100,000 has been paid by the taxpayers on this case. When effort is made to stop CHAMPUS payments, according to Colonel Rogers, pressure is brought to bear and approval is given. The last approval was given when a letter dated April 26, 1974, from Dr. Robert Health, chairman of the Department of Psychiatry and Neurology at Tulane University's School of Medicine, stated: "Miss Chennault's mother, Mrs. C. Chennault, is unable at this time to assume the full financial burden for treatment." Mme. Chennault could not be reached at this time because she was in the Orient on business. She is a major stockholder, member of the board of directors and Vice President for International Affairs of the Flying Tiger Line. In 1972 and 1973, Flying Tiger had the highest profit margin of any airline company in the world: 17.3 percent or $30.6 million in pre-tax profits.

Although Mme. Chennault has been unable to assume treatment costs for her daughter, she can afford to reside at the expensive Watergate complex in Washington, D.C., and she made major contributions to former President Nixon in 1972.*

The Denver office was becoming increasingly resentful that the Pentagon was trying to place all the blame on Denver for not finding child abuse in facilities that office had visited. But when I visited Herbert Hainer, executive director of the CHAMPUS program at the Pentagon, after the hearings, I found that although he and his politically appointed boss, Vernon McKenzie, wanted the abuses uncovered, they had no inclination to stop them. I asked Hainer what had been done about the fifty or more recommendations the Comptroller General of the United States had made to improve, update and correct past abuses in the program and was surprised and shocked by his reply: "If this is all GAO [General Accounting Office] can do, I don't ever have to worry about them." Apparently he was right, for in January of 1975, as the Comptroller General was busy preparing his sixth audit on CHAMPUS since the Senate hearings, I was told by persons working on that audit that for the sixth time they would include the same comment: "We have not obtained written comments from the Department of Defense on matters discussed in this report...."

The Defense Department told me that, at their orders, all CHAMPUS psychiatric facilities must be approved by JCAH or similar professional evaluating groups. I found JCAH housed in the Hancock Building, Chicago. The division for evaluating psychiatric facilities serving children and adolescents had been established as recently as February 1974 and was administered by a registered nurse, Margaret Murphy. Eight part-time physician-evaluators were paid $550 per day.

I discovered that when the evaluators rate an institution, the children are to be asked no questions about treatment. Nor do the

* In 1968, Mme. Chennault contributed $5,000 to RMN. In 1972, according to Rosemary Wood's private list, she contributed another $5,000 prior to the campaign reporting date of April 7. After that date Mme. Chennault wrote four separate checks of $2,500 each to different subcommittees of CREEP (Committee to Re-Elect the President), including Media, Radio and TV. Five hundred dollars was donated to the Republican convention gala and $1,000 to Senator Howard H. Baker, Jr.—a total of $16,500 in 1972.

evaluators have any standards by which to judge what illnesses should be treated and how, or what is the minimum amount of time a professional—e.g. psychiatrist—should spend with the children.

If JCAH rates a facility unsafe or unhealthy, there is no follow-through to notify local health or fire authorities or the CHAMPUS fiscal agents who pay the bills. Many times, those who set the standards for juvenile psychiatric facilities are the very ones who are treating the children. This is what those in the trade call "peer review"; it is akin to letting the rabbits guard the CHAMPUS lettuce! Some of the facilities that have enjoyed the Joint Commission's stamp of approval for two and three years have been rejected and disapproved by evaluating teams out of the Denver CHAMPUS office. These facilities include University Center.

Every large organization has a chart listing their chain of command. CHAMPUS's chart is headed "Defense Department." Next to that box sits "The United States Senate," a bold red line connecting the two. I was later to learn the purpose and influence represented by that red line.

On September 9, 1974, Captain Lamont A. Peterson of the Denver office of CHAMPUS made an unannounced visit to Joya Real Youth Ranch in New Braunfels, Texas, and found over-drugged boys in solitary confinement, poor health conditions, little treatment—at the cost of $1,500 per month per student. Peterson's report read: "It is recommended that this facility no longer be CHAMPUS-approved, based upon the fact that there has been a deterioration of the physical plant including safety and fire hazards, as well as the over-use of the seclusion and isolation room as a treatment modality." A similar evaluation was written for St. Jude's in Austin, Texas.

Letters affecting CHAMPUS withdrawal were about to be sent out to Joya Real and St. Jude's when Hainer called from the Pentagon and said they must be re-evaluated before closure. The offices of three congressmen and a senator had intervened. Two were from Mississippi, two from Texas. Why Mississippi? Because Joya Real Youth Ranch was about to be sold to a Mississippian for one million dollars. Those intervening were Congressman

Trent Lott and Senator John Stennis, both of Mississippi, and Representative O. C. Fisher of Texas. Representative Jake Pickle intervened for St. Jude's.

Both the facilities knew the evaluating teams were coming the second time, but Joya Real still failed. However, Hainer told Denver officials that Senator Stennis directed that it not be closed.

Colonel Horace Corley, Captain Peterson's superior, could no longer take what he called "the no-standards administrative nightmare of the Pentagon." He asked a friend, a public nurse in Texas, to visit Joya Real. She found the patients "super drugged—in a stuporous state." She interceded with the doctor who originally gave permission for drug use at the facility. Convinced by the public health nurse of the abuses occurring, he agreed to withdraw his permission to administer the medicines. Without support of medical approval, the facility caved in, and Corley was ready to close it down no matter what the Pentagon said—or did.

During the days preceding the July hearings, an early memo* from Feldman to his boss, Senator Jackson, made clear that the intensive investigation hoped for was not to be:

> I have talked preliminarily about this inquiry with Sterling† and we both feel that this might make an excellent investigation which could be completed in a rather short time and be the basis of a good one-day hearing highlighting abuses of children and inefficiency of this program of the Department of Defense.

Once it had a fortress of facts, the Jackson staff built a moat between itself and all others associated with exposing the CHAMPUS scandal.‡ Feldman, learning that Justice Department lawyers were working closely with Senate investigators, demanded a meeting with Justice Department attorney Mike Thrasher of the Special Office of Litigation. When Thrasher confided to him that

* Memo given me by a source on Senator Jackson's main office staff.
† S. Sterling Munroe, Jr., administrative assistant to Senator Jackson.
‡ Subcommittee Minority Chief Counsel Stuart M. Statler told me that much of the information that came to light during the hearings had been withheld from his staff by Senator Jackson's staff during the investigation period. This was a clear violation of the first rule of procedure of the Permanent Subcommittee on Investigations: "The ranking minority member shall be kept fully apprised of investigations and hearings."

he planned to litigate to test the violation of constitutional rights of children being shipped to out-of-state CHAMPUS facilities, Feldman brushed him off by saying there was a long history of back-stabbing between the Justice Department and the Permanent Subcommittee on Investigations. Thrasher told me that when he discovered Feldman's attitude, he wanted out of the case.

The upshot of the meeting was that Senate files concerning the CHAMPUS investigation were no longer available to the U.S. Justice Department. The children of whom Senator Jackson had spoken with such concern during the hearings were left to fend for themselves because an important investigation of their legal rights was stymied. Feldman performed the *coup de grâce* to the Justice Department's investigation with the full knowledge that neither would his own committee continue to investigate. It was an arrogant and callous abuse of power.

The Permanent Subcommittee on Investigations under Senator McClellan was apolitical during his eighteen years (1955–73) as chairman: the Senator had no aspirations for higher office. Hearings were for the purpose of carrying on investigative work. The senators themselves actually carried out the investigations. There were no press releases, only announcements as to the date, topic and names associated with proposed hearings.

According to one Senate investigator, things are different today: now, two senators competing for headlines quote freely to the press about something they have merely been briefed on by their staff, who have been briefed by investigators. "Is the subcommittee becoming too political?" I asked another investigator. He answered, "You've got two very ambitious senators and when you've got a tool [Permanent Subcommittee on Investigations], you're going to use it."

Was the subcommittee used as a tool to further political aspirations? I think so. I believe that close examination of the expressions of concerns during the CHAMPUS hearings will prove them nothing more than a dose of common political rhetoric.

The following quotes made during the hearings, considering what has transpired since then, will illustrate my point:

> SEN. CHARLES PERCY: It is my hope and belief that these hearings will go further than simply exposing grave problems in the

CHAMPUS program.... Let us learn from the CHAMPUS experience and make our new health insurance program effective, responsive and most importantly—humane.... As the French novelist and essayist Albert Camus once movingly wrote: "Perhaps we cannot prevent this from being a world in which children are tortured, but we can reduce the number of tortured children. If we do not do this, who will do this?"

SEN. WALTER D. HUDDLESTON of Kentucky (also a member of the subcommittee): I hope they [the hearings] will focus attention on the problems of mistreatment and abuse of institutionalized children and suggest means not only to preclude such mistreatment in facilities receiving federal funding, but in all facilities which are permitted to operate in this country.

SENATOR HENRY JACKSON (chairman): I said it seems to me that we need to amend the CHAMPUS Act to make it a federal crime for anyone who has a contract with CHAMPUS through the Department of Defense to follow a course of treatment and conduct such as has been testified to here: the gross mistreatment and shall I say premeditated mistreatment of children and youngsters....

Jackson's closing statement included:

As far as the federal role is concerned, I am directing staff to draft appropriate legislation which will make the abuse of any child whose treatment is funded by CHAMPUS monies to be a federal offense with appropriate penalties.

The chairman gave the Defense Department thirty days to come up with ideas and programs to strengthen CHAMPUS and provide some form of outside accountability. I gave the chairman and Senator Percy six months, then checked back on their performance. All those questioned during my two days of searching in Washington suggested I see Senate investigator John Walsh. But Walsh told me he wasn't proposing any legislation for Jackson and that little, if anything, was happening on that score.

Percy's staff directed me to "minority investigator" Jonathan Cottin, who told me the Senator had written a letter to the Pentagon expressing his concerns about CHAMPUS. I asked to see the letter, but Mr. Cottin later replied, "After checking it out, we cannot release the information to you." Then he confessed, "There wasn't much in it anyway."

The hearing did have some positive results. Even though their investigation was cut short, the professional investigative staff remained interested: One investigator leaked information concerning certain individuals around whom the hearings centered to both the FBI and the IRS and the independent goading action of other investigating staff members has led to pending state and federal indictments.

Presently, the Defense Department has completely revised CHAMPUS standards. However, these new standards are based on facility approval by the Joint Commission on Accreditation of Hospitals—hardly a firm guarantee against future child abuse, when those conducting the accreditation visitation are not allowed to speak to the children. University Center and Green Valley have both been closed since the hearings but the mechanics for the closings had been set in motion by local press, state claims officers and Denver CHAMPUS evaluators long before the gavel opened the hearings.

There had been no follow-up at all. I marveled at how well the CHAMPUS staff had pegged the entire scenario months earlier. They had never feared the possibility of vast upheaval.

I was distressed by another aspect of the Permanent Subcommittee on Investigations. For the first time in its history, there has appeared a "minority investigator," clearly indicating the dawning of partisanship in that committee.

I questioned Investigator Knauf, who had recently left the subcommittee for a position with the State Department. According to him, "New people brought on board now come as Jackson or Percy people—it has become partisan.... There is a gulf here and it's widening under the charade of working together as a unit.... The ambitions of the leadership has put tremendous pressures on the staff and on the focus and orientation of the Committee.... It has made us cautious and it stunts the operation of the Committee.*

Many, I know, will feel that politicians in Washington use every Senate and House committee assignment to further their own political aspirations—it's the name of the game! Not so with

---

* Other Senate staff verified Knauf's statement but did not want to go on record at this time.

the Senate Permanent Subcommittee on Investigations. As governed by the rules of the United States Senate, this committee is extremely powerful. It is a permanent entity, well financed, with a large full-time professional staff of criminal and civil investigators.* It is vested with the power to subpoena public and private records and people. And the power to subpoena is the power to destroy.

Because of this, the CHAMPUS scandal represents more than the greed of merchants who take advantage of children, more than a poorly administered federal program. It points up more than the all too common peddling of political influence to protect the profit sources of friends and contributors. Ultimately, the worst revelation of the CHAMPUS scandal concerned those individuals who sought, by virtue of their leadership role on the investigative committee, to gain greater political power.

Senator Jackson and, to a lesser degree, Senator Percy both, perhaps unwittingly but without question, transgressed the fine line of integrity when they used the frightening power of that subcommittee as a tool for their personal political advantage. The potential for abuse is too great, the people who are ultimately harmed are too vulnerable.

* Staff of the $1.1 million committee has recently been enlarged and Senator Jackson's top international affairs adviser, Dorothy Fosdick ($35,000), and chief defense and arms control adviser, Richard Perle ($30,000), are both paid from committee funds.

PART FIVE/Alternatives and a New Bill of Rights for Children

He who dries his brother's tears
will never weep alone. . . .

—Anonymous

17/"Till Two Years After Eternity" and Other Successful Programs

Mrs. Chessie Harris of Huntsville, Alabama, is in her seventies, but she still carries food and children's clothing in a shopping bag slung over her arm. It is a matter of habit and the mark of concern of a remarkable woman haunted daily by the sight of children cooking meat bones on trash can lids and living and sleeping in alleys and old abandoned cars. Chessie Harris and her family have given unstintingly to neglected and dependent children.

Born around the turn of the century, Mrs. Harris grew up on a sharecropper farm, working the cotton and corn fields. Her father was a friend of Booker T. Washington, and education was important to the large family. Her own five children have graduated from the best colleges and universities in the country, but none has forgotten the training and compassion of their parents.

In 1954, when Mrs. Harris wanted to do something for the children with "the same hungry look as starving sharecroppers had in 1909," agreement among her husband and children was unanimous. They sold a family farm in Ohio, and their property in Huntsville, Alabama, became known as the Harris Home for Children. Without any help from government or social agencies, the

218/*Alternatives and a New Bill of Rights for Children*

Harris family took in unwanted children. Since then, the Harris Home for Children has pooled its modest assets into a private foundation that supports small group-homes and apartments, with all facilities and land legally held in the name of the children they serve, "till two years after eternity."

Whenever possible, the Harris Home involves the real families of their wards and attempts ultimately to reunite them. Children without any family are quickly assimilated into a larger family structure. Young married house parents (many of whom attend college) have two to seven children within their families. Where there was once a total void, there are athletics and culture, warmth and opportunity—all in an effort to tap and develop the potential of every child.

The Harris Home uses no fancy brochures, rhetoric or public relations, boasts no showpiece structures, just a solid record of saving young human beings from the vacuum of not being wanted. In 1974 its first neglected child graduated from college—Alabama A&M. Children thought to be mentally retarded are now married and raising families. Of more than one hundred children helped by the Harris Home, more than 90 percent have returned to the community and are working and leading meaningful lives.

It was a long struggle for the Harris family. Years of discrimination and government interference and centuries of indifference toward neglected minority children had to be surmounted. They were triumphantly successful and today the Harris Home for Children is licensed by the Alabama State Department of Pensions and Security and is supported to some extent by the United Way of Huntsville.

It was the Harris Home for Children and other programs described in this chapter that gave me hope when the tides of despair came crashing in on my optimism. It was the discovery that there are not only successful alternatives to locking up children but also that there are hundreds of decent, dedicated human beings serving that end, that made it possible for me to tolerate my daily diet of child abuse and official corruption for thirty months.

Here, I must, however, caution the reader. In describing programs I consider to be excellent, I must emphasize and re-emphasize that I witnessed these operations between 1972 and 1974. They were, in my judgment, outstanding in both their dedication and achievement during that period of time. But I do not intend a blanket endorsement: They do not and should not have one. I have learned that large grants and even larger ambitions can turn good programs into nightmares. The potential for corruption is always present. Those who work and labor with children must always be held accountable. They should always be asked to defend and explain. Children are not abstractions—they are real flesh and blood—and the price that custodians of children must pay and should pay is eternal vigilance by us all.

These reputable programs share common characteristics: almost all have modest budgets; all save more children for fewer tax dollars (by and large, they require one third the annual financial subsidy of state training schools, and even less when compared with the fly-by-night private institutions that have sprung up upon newly available federal and state monies); recidivism rates are 100 to 500 percent better than their expensive counterparts. Emphasis is placed on making the child face his or her problem realistically, and an integral part of the overall program focuses on the biological link with the child's blood family, who are called upon whenever possible for discussions and counseling. Where the involvement of the actual family is impossible, a family-like structure is organized around the needs of the troubled child, so that he can know the pride and dignity of concerned human relationships.

Oftentimes lost or abandoned infants are taken to youth detention facilities. Since these babies cannot be carefully watched, they are placed in "iron mothers"—iron cribs covered with heavy netting. Nashville, Tennessee, has diverted this potential catastrophe for very young lives by means of a demonstration project funded by HEW's Office of Child Development. For the last three years comprehensive emergency services have been in operation so that if a child is lost or abandoned, concerted effort is made to find the rightful parents or a temporary home until a permanent arrangement can be made. As a result of this project, 322 children (200 were younger than six years of age) who normally would have been institutionalized were saved from that fate. Although 22 youngsters were incarcerated in the first two years of the program, during the last six months, proper community resources have been found for every child.

Untold numbers of children in the public schools across the nation are daily reminded of their failures and frustrations. While very little is being done on a large scale for the near dropout or the incarcerated child, I found certain exceptions in Vermont, Massachusetts and Colorado.

In Burlington, Vermont, Project Aspire is a school within the school system for volunteer students with high dropout potential. The structured classroom is gone. Teachers Evelyn Carter and Ken Hannington are extremely creative and dress very casually. Reading is taught on a one-to-one basis, a relationship that encourages counseling as well as learning. The program fosters the talents and interests of children who have known only failure.

Project Aspire has re-directed many potential failures over the last five years. Many students have improved their record of school attendance because school now has a purpose, for it helps them develop useful and needed skills and, most importantly, gives them a feeling of importance because the teachers care deeply about their personal and educational well-being.

Also employed by the Burlington school system is Bob Rivers, a unique guidance counselor at Edmunds Junior High School, who not only visits incarcerated students at the Vermont Weeks Training School but has started an After Care Release Program. Here the child coming from the training school can be eased back into the regular school structure in the most unobtrusive and beneficial way possible for both student, teachers and classmates. To my knowledge it is the only program of its kind in the country. It is the sort of program that is desperately needed and with the vast resources at the command of American Education, its absence is an indictment.

In the shadow of Harvard University in Massachusetts, children of working-class parents have dropped out of the Cambridge public schools and started their own Group School. Fifty percent of the students enrolled have been convicted of criminal offenses in juvenile or adult courts. Close to 60 percent are living in public housing. Group School offers courses that are relevant and meaningful. Their ethnic origins are emphasized and for the first time, many of these students have developed an identity and dignity that wasn't possible in the Cambridge public schools.

The results are impressive. The Group School dropout rate was only 7 percent compared with 25–35 percent in the public schools. Thirty-nine have graduated from their accredited Group High School and gone on to college and other training programs. During the 1972–73 school year students and staff of the Group School led workshops in alternative education at the Harvard Graduate School of Education, Southern Massachusetts University, Wellesley College and Rhode Island School of Design. The Group School curriculum materials are now being used by many public schools in the area.

When Ricardo Falcon was twenty-five, he was an alcoholic living on Skid Row in Denver, Colorado. Five years later, on August 30, 1972, he bled to death at a gas station in New Mexico. But in those last five years Ricardo Falcon had found himself and his roots. In Fort Lupton, Colorado, he organized young Chicanos into a local "Los Zapatistas" (followers of Emiliano Zapata, who fought with Mexican leaders for the liberation of Mexico). Because Falcon injected massive dosages of ethnic pride and history into those youngsters who were responsible for 80 percent of the crime rate at Fort Lupton, within a short period of time, the incidence of crime there was almost zero.

In 1974, I interviewed Falcon's young followers. Mike Hernandez and Ernie Sandoval took me to their youth center on Harrison Avenue in Fort Lupton, where pictures of Emiliano Zapata and Ricardo Falcon* hung. They explained the Group School programs to help the Chicano youth and aged. We then walked through the deserted migrant living quarters as the young men talked about teaching their people how to read and write and how to obtain legal aid, medical assistance and food for their brothers and sisters. A sad but proud historical past is now the

---

* Ricardo Falcon was shot and killed en route to a Chicago political convention in New Mexico with friends. They stopped at a gas station for water for an overheated car. Falcon was called "boy" and told he must pay for the water. An argument ensued and unarmed Falcon was shot. For fifteen minutes he lay between life and death, but help was refused and he bled to death. The gas station owner was accused of murder and manslaughter but at his trial, a number of white people from Fort Lupton testified that Ricardo Falcon was their local "troublemaker" and "hothead." The man was acquitted.

foundation upon which young Chicanos outside Denver can build a future. Federal and state social planners and professional experts can learn much from this program, which deals with juvenile and adult crime among all ethnic groups.

Father Malcolm McDowell, or "Mac," is the assistant pastor of St. James Episcopal Church in Glastonbury, Connecticut. Margo St. James is an ex-hooker of the Bay Area of San Francisco. Father Mac and Ms. St. James live a vast country apart and do not know each other, and it may seem that they could not have much in common. However, each of them has a mutual concern—the plight of the runaway child.

Father McDowell is a fisherman for troubled youth and operates a runaway program called the Net in a town of 23,000 called Glastonbury outside Hartford, Connecticut. The core of his successful program (which cost only $475 in 1974) is made up of some fifty families that have agreed to accept runaways in their homes for a few days to a few months, depending on the child and the nature of his problem. Not only has Father Mac mobilized families; he has stimulated professionals and institutions to a degree of responsiveness that is remarkable. A doctor as well as a lawyer and other professionals gives free assistance to Father Mac's kids. The local high school enrolls out-of-town runaways from California, Iowa, Michigan, Florida, New York and Vermont, as samples. Usually after a cooling-off period of seven to fourteen days, the child and his family are reunited and offered family counseling.

If necessary, Father McDowell will bend the law if he deems it best for the runaway. For instance, a girl ran from home because her father had been sexually molesting her. While she was preparing to lodge charges against the father, he located her and ordered Father Mac to return the girl to her "right home." The priest pretended ignorance, then quietly buried her "underground" at a Hartford Runaway Center, which in turn placed her with people willing also to bend the law so that the girl would not have to return to her father.

For young females in big cities, especially blacks who run away from home, organizations like the Net cannot always provide a solution. In some states such facilities don't even exist. Frequently, pimps take advantage of the state of mind and life-style of runaway children (many as young as thirteen and fourteen) and the streets soon become their livelihood.

In San Francisco, Margo St. James established COYOTE (Call Off Your Old Tired Ethics), the first national organization to provide legal and other assistance to these girls and to fight the system that locks up the prostitute and lets the man go free. Margo believes that, in lieu of incarcerating them, prostitutes should be given a mild citation and "token fines, to be channeled into a scholarship fund for women who wish to learn an alternative means of survival." Currently in San Francisco, each arrest of a lady of the evening costs the taxpayers $175.

Although aided by the contributions of a few interested persons, for the most part Margo St. James herself shoulders the financial burdens of COYOTE. Even with a small budget, she maintains a "hot line" over which she can offer courage and legal assistance to the arrested girls.

As discussed in Chapter 3, Sacramento County, California, has replaced its old-fashioned detention lockup system with "crisis intervention teams," which work directly with the child and his parents or guardians. It is very successful and far less expensive than the old way. In St. Louis, Missouri, a modified concept of crisis intervention, called Home Detention, is in operation. Here the child is permitted to go to his natural home or a temporary home under the close supervision of a youth leader from City Youth Center. If he doesn't cooperate or if the home life is destructive for him, he comes back to the detention center.

The usefulness of Home Detention can be measured by two very telling points: Of sixty-six children who were runaways, not one has run from the program. Secondly, the new at-home plan costs the city of St. Louis $4.85 per day as compared with $17.54 per day per child for the old security detention program.

One program that developed during a five-year research project within the juvenile detention facilities of New York City could have an invaluable effect upon the health of all children in need of medical attention. Developed by Dr. Iris F. Litt, Division of Adolescent Medicine, Montefiore Hospital, and assistant professor of pediatrics at Albert Einstein College of Medicine, the program took advantage of the time children were incarcerated and gave them extensive health care treatment. Prior to Dr. Litt's efforts, medical care at New York detention facilities was confined to the efforts of a salaried doctor who came in a few hours weekly to tend to serious medical problems.

Dr. Litt's five-year program provided 31,000 children with complete medical histories and physical examinations within twenty-four hours of their admission. Examinations were conducted by young pediatric interns and supervised by the hospital's medical director and attending physicians. They were assisted by seventeen registered nurses and medical students, along with dental personnel, an oral surgeon, a pharmacist, laboratory technicians and clerical personnel. They found that 50 percent of the children suffered from "physical illness, exclusive of dental or psychiatric problems." As many as 3,700 were suffering from hepatitis because of illegal drug use. Approximately 2,000 were admitted to the infirmary and 400 were transferred to the adolescent in-patient unit at Montefiore Hospital.

Dr. Litt's report stated: "A large number of girls were not aware they were pregnant... others suffered from congenital abnormalities, ranging in severity from heart disease, kidney and endocrine defects to hernias requiring surgery." The report concluded: "In some cases, the presence of these defects may have actually contributed to the youngsters' school difficulties with resultant truant behavior and may have, in fact, been a factor in their difficulty with the law.... Another, perhaps more subtle, bonus of an independent medical staff is the freedom to report suspected abuse of children by the custodial staff."

Not only did the medical students profit by the training, but for most of the children involved in Dr. Litt's program, this was the first time somebody showed an active concern for their health and well-being. This in itself is powerful medicine, for both the body and soul of a youth in crisis.

Children in detention find themselves with an abundance of time to contemplate their court appearance before the judge—usually a family court juvenile judge. As discussed earlier, the juvenile court system was established as a reform measure to help children and their families who are in trouble—hence the family court.

During my travels I met an outstanding judge whose every effort in his Richland County family court (Columbia, South Carolina) is aimed at helping and supporting the family unit. The Honorable J. McNary Spigner, a man of great warmth and imaginative judicature, symbolizes his court with a flower. The petals, representing the school, the family court, the police, mental health, the church, group homes, Alcoholics Anonymous, vocational rehabilitation, etc., surround the center—the family. This, the Judge believes, is the way the system should work—all community services touching and supporting the family when needed.

When a child becomes involved with Judge Spigner's court, so does his or her entire family, and the experience changes their life-style. First off, the Judge's staff checks the county jail every day in order to remove children who have been incarcerated with adults. At the intake section of the court, a social summary of the child and family is compiled and passed on to other members of the court.

Mrs. Telicious Kenly, a home economist, reads all these reports. She then visits the home of the troubled youth and assists the mother and father with any existing domestic problems—employment, budgeting, cooking, meal planning, housing, education, job training, marriage counseling. The youth is provided with legal assistance from the law school of the University of South Carolina. If adjudicated, he is turned over to the court's probation department, where caseworkers ensure placement in such constructive programs as vocational rehabilitation. To date they have aided well over 1,000 youths by providing job training and placement.

Judge Spigner has developed an impressive arsenal of support for the child. For years a pretrial intervention staff has provided immediate counseling services for children and their families for forty-five days or longer if necessary. The family court then has the option of offering successful enrollees a "dismissal of charges" so that the child will never be brought to trial and will never have a conviction record.

Neither is the Judge's outside volunteer program, which makes maximum use of community resources, left to chance. Volunteers have a say in their activities but must enroll in and complete the training program conducted by the advisory board for the volunteers for training to tailor, temper and properly channel their idealisms and enthusiasms. Even the "big brother" concept is utilized as volunteers called "partners" take children living in the court's group house to movies, bowling, sporting events, etc.

At intervals during the year, Judge Spigner will retire to the woods with his entire staff, including volunteers, law professors and student juvenile police officers, for sessions on how better to improve the Richland Family Court. The dividends from such a fine court and community investment are shown in the Columbia police records. Youth crime is down. In 1971, the number of children coming before the Judge dropped by 20 percent and recidivism dropped as much as 66 percent.

Most district attorneys can't be bothered with juvenile delinquency, but in Colorado Springs there is one DA who is coordinating youth rehabilitation services and saving children from hard-core crime in later years. Bob Russel is a tough law-and-order district attorney who tired of seeing juvenile delinquents graduate to serious adult crimes in El Paso and Teller counties, Colorado. He is convinced that the first-time nonviolent offender simply has to be removed from the court process within the juvenile justice system. His alternative is a Diversion Program patterned after one in Flint, Michigan, which has operated with great success since 1965.

If a child who has committed his first offense and his parents are willing to be placed under the guidance, supervision and counseling of the Youth Services Bureau, the DA will not prosecute immediately. After six months, if the child has benefited from the Diversion Program, all criminal and/or delinquent charges will be dismissed and the child will have avoided a delinquency record.

In the period from July 1, 1974, to January 1, 1975, the number of juvenile petitions was cut by 37 percent, the recidivism rate was less than 5 percent and the financial savings in prosecutorial and judicial time, witness and jury fees, and administrative costs were readily apparent to government leaders and taxpayers alike. Russel's office also assisted in starting a Shelter Care facility for children without parents and trained and mobilized the local police forces to help ensure the success of the Diversion Program.

Dr. Ruth Love, the granddaughter of slaves, is director of

a federal program that confronts another form of slavery—illiteracy. Her National Right to Read program has funded two very successful reading programs, one, in a federal prison for women and the other in a juvenile correctional facility in Bordentown, New Jersey. Through Dr. Love's efforts and creative concern, inmates are either reading for the first time or have improved the reading skills they had by as much as 50 percent. The program trains even poor readers to teach nonreaders; with this one-to-one relationship both improve—even more appreciably than when professionals are involved.

Dr. Love's program should be an intricate part of rehabilitation in every prison and youth jail throughout America. It is invaluable for the ex-offender trying to go straight, for one must know how to read if one is to obtain and maintain meaningful employment. The unskilled labor market has dropped from 17 percent to 5 percent in just seven years.

Following is a story told me by Dr. Love which exemplifies the growth and freedom that reading provides:

> Twenty-year-old Eddie had spent nine years in a state institution for the mentally retarded. He could not identify the letters of the alphabet, and lacked any job skills. He moved about the country unable to establish a satisfying base anywhere. Finally he was arrested on a drug charge. In the special court program in which he was placed, he could have a 90-day continuance as long as he made an effort to improve himself in some way. He chose to learn to read at the Education Warehouse in Cambridge, Mass. and began a program there in August, 1972. Today, a year later, Eddie can read any newspaper and has made such progress that he is now being trained to teach other persons to read as he furthers his own skills at the Education Warehouse.

In Miami, Criminal Court Judge Alfonso Sepe sentenced seventeen-year-old Margaret Fleming, who had pleaded guilty to marijuana possession, and nineteen-year-old Richard Wade, who had admitted to disorderly conduct, to three years. The sentence was not prison but rather to come back once a week and teach reading to illiterate delinquents in the Dade County Stockade. Judge Sepe believes that "many people who end up in trouble do so because they are victims of the educational handicaps of poor people such as being unable to get an education and the inability to communicate verbally."

Dr. Larry Dye of the School of Education, University of Massachusetts, agrees with Judge Sepe. Dr. Dye, former illiterate and the product of a broken family, has come a long way since 1955, when the Los Angeles police roped off a city street and moved in to take Dye and his associates for armed robbery. That arrest was his forty-fifth; his first run-in with the police occurred when he was twelve years old.

Three months before Larry was released from prison, he and seventeen other hard-core criminals were enrolled in a program called New Careers Development, offered by J. Douglas Grant. Sixteen of the criminals were rehabilitated and obtained good jobs. So successful was the endeavor that correctional personnel in California killed the program because ex-cons were getting better jobs and pay than they were.

Today, after earning his doctorate at the University of Massachusetts and creating many programs for juvenile delinquents, Dr. Dye has taken over his own prison. Berkshire County House of Corrections will never be the same: it is being converted into an institution for educational change. Remembering what happened to the California program, Dye opened the doors to correctional people, and both they and inmates are enrolled in educational endeavors accredited by the University of Massachusetts. Inmates are required to work in institutions such as schools for the retarded. Every Monday in his home in Amherst, Massachusetts, Larry Dye provides free beer and food for staff and students and conducts seminars on prison reform, juvenile justice and the real world of "changing the system." He hopes these experiences will make his "former colleagues" agents for social change as they, too, improve their own opportunities through educational skills and college accreditation.

By and large, reform within the institutional setting is patch work and oftentimes designed to create the impression of change. But slowly, ever so slowly, the huge, impersonal facilities on sprawling rural acreage are being phased out. In their place are being formed community-based alternative programs, some public, some private, but all with impressive records of success and considerable financial savings.

A project to help juvenile offenders in Schenectady, New York, has proved that if a vast array of community services and resources is made available to young people in trouble, the likelihood of future crime will be minimal. After its first eight months of existence, no new complaints were filed against 92.5 percent of the children involved in the program, and juvenile court cases were reduced by 52 percent. By preventing incarceration, a projected annual savings for the state and city totaled half a million dollars.

Rochester, Minnesota, initiated a program called P.O.R.T. (Probationed Offenders Rehabilitation and Training). Instead of being sent to training schools or being put on probation, first-time male offenders are sent to a community halfway house, where male college student volunteers stay with the boys, serving as residential counselors and, to a degree, big brothers. The program has concentrated heavily on peer pressure and peer decisions, along with individual and group counseling. A small operation, it has enjoyed moderate success in the four years it has been in existence. Thirty-seven youngsters have been rehabilitated and sent home. Nineteen failed and were sent to institutions. The expense, however, has been very low compared with that of training schools. P.O.R.T. costs $3,888 per year per boy. The same boy would cost the state of Minnesota $10,411 per year.

Vision Quest is another program that impressed me. Robert Burton, who worked for years with the youth correctional systems in Delaware and Nevada, designed his own program around the group-home concept, with heavy emphasis on confronting both the child and the parents and forcing them to face their problem together. The participants in Vision Quest are from the Pima County Juvenile County Court in Tucson, Arizona, and must earn their way into the program by taking part in an Arizona desert survival trip with a small group of peers and one or two staff personnel. Burton believes that if a child "can make it" on this survival trip, his toughness can be redirected into positive behavior.

The young men and women in Vision Quest live in group homes with professional staff people, who are on duty twenty-four hours a day. The students attend local schools during the day and benefit from counseling with peers, parents and staff in the evenings. Psychiatric help is available if needed. When Vision Quest feels that the juvenile is no longer a problem to himself and others, he is required to serve as a paraprofessional, working with staff and new candidates. This provides the program with a built-in evaluation by and input from those who "have been through it."

In Kentucky, two very significant programs have helped to replace the old training school system. Operation Bootstrap has trained unemployed coal miners in eastern Kentucky, who suffered from black lung or who had been laid off, to be foster parents. The program placed some 800 delinquent youths with foster parents during its first eighteen months in operation. Operation Bootstrap has provided income to hard-pressed families, as well as freedom from institutionalization for the children. It is a positive program with a significant degree of success and appreciable savings to the Kentucky taxpayer.

The other Kentucky program is special Foster Care for "hard-to-place children"—those whose total incarceration time has ranged from eight to ten years. Bill Ryan, believing that the wards of the state are "over (social) worked," recruited nonprofessional citizens. TV ads asked the public: "Are you crazy enough to take a delinquent into your home?" During its first two years of operation, 252 hard-to-place youths found homes, and the recidivism rate dropped to less than 26 percent, an impressive showing for high-risk children.

In St. Louis, I visited Providence, a rehabilitation program for boys with multiple, serious arrest records. Of 164 enrolled since September 5, 1972, only 11 boys have been institutionalized. The recidivism rate remains steady at around 25 percent, a great savings to the Missouri taxpayer. Rehabilitation and a creative educational program (resembling Vermont's Aspire techniques) cost $3,309 per child per year compared with a very poor program at the Missouri State Training School at Boonville for $11,000 per child per year. Had the preventive Aspire program been available in St. Louis public schools for those boys at Providence, 850 crimes might never have been committed. The juvenile court conducted a study that showed that 81 percent of the juveniles institutionalized by the courts between 1965 and 1969 were arrested as adults within three years of release.

These programs do work. Their humanistic ideals, which include saving all children in trouble—from abandoned infants to adolescents who are five-time felons—are logical and proved effective. They also are one third as costly and approximately 65 percent more successful than the traditional programs followed by state training schools or private, profit-making agencies.

However, two factors must be kept in mind. First, that the most humanistic concepts can be corrupted by those who are relied upon to actualize them when the lure of financial gain relegates the welfare of the children to secondary importance. This potential for corruption demands that these programs be monitored by persons who have no financial interests in them. And second, these programs are threatening to those who have jobs, professional power and money invested in the perpetuation of existing institutions (state training schools, city and county jails and private institutions). Changes will not come easily, but the battle, however long, can be won through dogged persistence, dedication and intelligent concern for these children.

A truly good book teaches me better than to read it. I must soon lay it down, and commence living on its hints.... What I began by reading, I must finish by acting.

—Henry Thoreau

18/Political Strategies and a Sculpture for Change

Over the years the American juvenile justice system has become a formidable fortress, built with the powerful forces of status quo and vested self-interest and reinforced by traditional thinking and political realities. Most of our citizenry have long believed that a jailed child is a convicted criminal. Predominantly rural state legislatures have consistently granted political favors to the owners and operators of state training schools, county jails and other youth facilities.

In addition to this basic weakness is the power of private entreprenuers and their influential attorneys with direct lines into the state houses, city halls and county courthouses across the land, the power of the nonprofit groups like the Roman Catholic and Protestant churches, along with fraternal organizations, all synchronizing their efforts to keep the state from interfering in the day-to-day operation of their private institutions for children; and finally, the growing power of professional organizations, especially the American Federation of State, County and Municipal Employees. Their support of chosen politicians is traditional and it doesn't come free.

This bulwark of power notwithstanding, I believe the time has come for change in juvenile justice. The existing power is vulnerable and if challenged properly by new forces, significant changes can be made. In the past few years a number of national organizations, including the General Federation of Women's Clubs, the National Council of Jewish Women, the Young Men's and Women's Christian Associations, the American Association of University Women and the League of Women Voters, have taken on the issue of children justice. Their local chapters have moved into the courts and even the jails to watch and observe. In the words of Philadelphia Judge Lois Fore, "They have become truly the eyes, ears, conscience and soul of each community."

I would also hope that the established labor unions who have consistently fought for a better life for their members will not forget the children of that membership. For it is the youngsters of the United Mine Workers, the auto workers, the textile workers and other blue-collar union members who are most vulnerable to incarceration. The vast labor membership in the United States must join forces with other national organizations to ensure the political clout necessary for important and long overdue reform in the juvenile justice system.

Collectively, these organizations would be a dynamic force to reckon with: their numbers, like an army on the march, could crack the old entrenched power fortifications of the training schools, political judges, private warehouses, etc. They, along with other interested groups and individuals, can and should merge as a coalition to work at all levels of government for the physical, psychological and civil well-being of children. For although legislation at the national and state levels is needed, it is not the final answer to the crisis of juvenile crime. And although new intergovernmental regulations for child care are desperately needed, neither will they alone bring juvenile justice into being.

Therefore, at community level, a national child advocacy coalition would propose to properly channel its influence to move and mold agencies whose jobs it is to provide assistance and guidance to troubled children. Reform, rather than imposed from above, must be planted like a seed within each town, city, county and state in the nation; then those of us who care deeply for the plight of youth, must fight tenaciously for its growth and acceptance.

First of all, goals must be set, guidelines for legislation spelled out and a strategy developed to make the first two a reality. Objectives, as I see them, are the following:

1. Abolish forever the use of county jails as facilities for detaining or housing children, under any circumstance.
2. Close all state training schools. Transfer dangerous and seriously ill youths to smaller units for intensive treatment and care, and noncriminal children to their homes and/or community-based programs.
3. Create community-based programs where they do not exist. Use successful programs from around the country as models.
4. Place children arrested for the first time in home detention and crisis intervention programs with family counseling. With the exception of very dangerous youths, none of them should be incarcerated.
5. Reconstruct local resources and governmental agencies to serve the needs of the entire family simultaneously, not just the delinquent youth.
6. End the practice of processing status offense children (truants, runaways, incorrigibles) through the judicial system.
7. Eliminate the partisan political process by which juvenile court judges are selected.
8. Halt the interstate commerce of children except where unusual or unique treatment or care is warranted.
9. Close those boarding schools operated solely by government officials who take Indian children away from their families and tribes to educate them.
10. Develop tighter, more comprehensive laws for state licensing of private child care facilities.
11. Enforce criminal laws against adults who physically or fraudulently abuse children.
12. Create publicly supported nongovernmental child advocacy programs.
13. Abolish IQ testing and protect children's school files from becoming potentially damaging and criminal records.

These goals are mere words unless political action at all levels of government transform them into viable laws. There is a crying need for federal legislation to protect the constitutional rights of children in several areas.

At the present time, it is impossible for the United States

Justice Department to investigate or bring charges against any facility—state training schools included—for the civil protection of children. In the Morales trial the U.S. Justice Department was invited as a "friend of the court" into the class action law suit already initiated by Legal Aid attorney Steve Bercu.

In 1972 some concerned young lawyers in the Justice Department wrote a bill for congressional consideration, giving them that power of intervention. The draft of the bill read:

> To authorize the Attorney General to seek civil relief against deprivations of constitutional rights occurring in state correctional facilities.

Section 2 read:

> When the Attorney General has reasonable cause to believe that there is a pattern of practice whereby persons in any correctional facility are being deprived of any rights, privileges, or immunities secured or protected by the Constitution or laws of the United States, the Attorney General is authorized to institute a civil action for or in the name of the United States in any appropriate district court of the United States against such parties and for such injunctive, or other relief as may be appropriate.

Top Nixon officials in the Justice Department, apparently concerned with Watergate and other pressing matters at the time, rejected the proposed legislation before Congress had even had a chance to study it. Surely incarcerated, troubled children deserve better than this. I propose introduction and passage of this legislation so that, when necessary, the full power of the Federal Government and the United States Justice Department could quickly move into legal action without delay.

I also propose that Congress give serious consideration to mandatory psychological testing and fingerprinting of all owners of and staff personnel working within child-care institutions. I realize that such legislation would be very controversial and should be studied in depth, with public hearings—but it nevertheless should, in my opinion, be made into law.

For civil libertarians who cry "foul" and talk of the rights of those being fingerprinted, I ask, What about the rights of children who not only have no say in where they are placed, but also have no defense against sick adults who sexually attack them while in custody? Whose rights are violated when a certain physician conducts vaginal examinations on very young females which take hours,* or puts them in straitjackets to enjoy hearing them cry? How can one compare the civil rights of that man to the civil and human rights of children too young or too ill to protect themselves? Who speaks for them? Who cares for them? It is common knowledge that certain perverted people are drawn to institutional work to prey upon hapless inmates.

In Louisiana a male probation officer was found guilty of forcing a thirteen-year-old boy into sexual relations. Criminal Court Judge Alfonso Sepe handed down a ten-year sentence to Joseph V. Hale, Jr., and said: "You not only inflicted your sickness upon the boy, but you used an agency that is designed to rehabilitate youngsters. You knew what lurked within yourself, yet you deliberately inflicted your sickness upon others."

Another area of concern which may or may not require congressional action is the practice of sending Indian children to the Department of Interior's Bureau of Indian Affairs boarding schools. These out-of-state boarding schools, which are accountable to no one, do great harm to the Indian family unit. As mentioned earlier, many youngsters have tried to run back home to parents and families and have suffered for it. Congress must act to construct schools operated by and for Indians on their lands so that a proud heritage may never be lost.

Federal action should also be taken in the Department of Health, Education and Welfare's social services program development to entice communities to rethink and possibly reform their agencies that handle separate but related problem areas facing the family unit. Until Senator Walter F. Mondale of Minnesota held hearings in September of 1973, Washington was basically unaware of the American Family Crisis. A problem juvenile is usually indicative of other problems in the home and it is hard to treat one without the other. Therefore, I propose restructuring all existing programs and diverting them to local communities under

---

* Told by two nurses in separate interviews, neither of whom would come forward with a public statement.

an integral counseling agency—a Family Crisis Intervention Service.

I further propose that the Congress create a National Child Health Care Enforcement Agency, which, as outlined, could help immeasurably in frightening away entrepreneurs. This agency would set up a Health Care Strike Force which would make unannounced visits to child care centers, group homes, private and public residential treatment centers, state training schools, etc. It would be composed of experts and professionals as follows:

1. Medical Doctor	Basically a general practitioner with training in possible drug assaults and abuses to children.
2. Psychiatrist	To evaluate psychiatric and psychological treatment and drug dosage and administration.
3. Psychologist	
4. Psychiatric Social Worker	To evaluate semiprofessional treatment and staff.
5. Registered Nurse	To evaluate the general nursing care and drug usage.
6. Lawyers (2)	One lawyer with experience in criminal prosecution, particularly in crimes of fraud and embezzlement. One lawyer with expertise in civil rights.
7. Certified Accountant	To examine financial records and books.
8. Dietitian	To evaluate the quality and quantity of food.
9. Public Health Officer	To examine basic health facilities.
10. Educator	To evaluate the educational programs.
11. Correctional Officer	Someone with experience in penal work who will know if an institution is really a "jail."
12. Investigative Reporter	To research and track down former patients, parents, staff, etc., and to expose abuses.

The ultimate value of such a strike force is the shock waves that would spread in that loose but interlocking network of communication which connects the owners of "human warehouses" and professionals who have become affluent at the expense of the countless children and taxpayers.

I also call upon Congress to create Regional Child Advocacy Centers. For purposes of accountability and creditability, I propose a radical departure from past funding methods. First of all, these child advocacy centers should be free of government control at any level but supported by tax dollars. Secondly, they should be placed under the structural jurisdiction of established national organizations that have expressed through their actions a genuine concern for children in trouble—eg., the YWCA, YMCA and the General Federation of Women's Clubs.

Child advocacy groups could provide invaluable protection to incarcerated youngsters in a number of ways, including: monitoring state licensing laws for private and public facilities (here the system is weakest and therefore most vulnerable); visiting and monitoring state facilities and alerting federal health enforcement teams and the Justice Department if action is necessary; keeping track of children attending out-of-state treatment centers, thereby preventing any large-scale exodus such as took place in Illinois, Louisiana and New Jersey.

I would urge Congress to make the National Right to Read Program out of the United States Office of Education a major priority in the office's budget. With an annual pittance of $13 million, Right to Read was delegated the reponsibility to end illiteracy in this country by 1980. Roughly one out of every four school children in the United States still have a reading problem. Unless we take drastic and bold steps to improve the quality of education at a basic level, children in increasing numbers will fill the youth jails and later the adult prisons.

Finally, as stated earlier, persons with suicidal tendencies, more than any other human beings, need a place to go, someone to talk with, a telephone call to save them from self-destruction. I urge Congress to pass a National Suicide Prevention Act for Incarcerated Youth, which would make it mandatory to keep all lines of communication open to the detained child and, by the very nature of the act, end the heinous practice of placing children in solitary confinement.

The proposed law should make punitive use of solitary a felon, with penalties including a stiff fine, maximum prison term and banishment from the child care profession. This may seem harsh, but surely solitary confinement is the harshest of treatments for the human spirit.

At the state level of government, I strongly urge child advocacy groups to promote legislation that would provide tough licensing laws, abolish county and city jails for juveniles and strike from state statutes those provisions that make status offenses criminal and subsequently lead to incarceration of children. State legislatures should also pass a three-year phase-out bill which would close training schools and county detention facilities and rechannel public funds into community group homes, runaway shelters for intensive care and counseling and small hospital units for the profoundly and severely retarded children.

Lastly, the practice of nominating juvenile court judges by partisan political parties should be abolished and replaced by the so-called Missouri Plan, a merit system of selection. Here a non-partisan nominating panel of seven persons (three appointed by the state bar association, three laymen appointed by the governor for staggered terms and a judge) submits three recommendations for juvenile court judge. The governor makes his choice from these three. When the judge's term is up, he runs not against another man or political party but rather his own record: during general election the voter is asked: "Shall Judge X of the juvenile court be retained in office?" If he is voted out, the above procedure is repeated for the new judge. Before the election a poll is taken among all state attorneys regarding the qualifications and records of judges now holding power. The results are given wide circulation.

At the same time that all this proposed state and federal legislation would provide immense relief to troubled children and overburdened taxpayers, it would spell doom for the vested interests of many now engaged in the child care industry. Opposition to change would be immediate and bitter. But with full knowledge of such imminent hostility, it is still possible to implement the politics of change.

First of all, political power comes from the people via their vote; therefore it is imperative to reach the voter on the issue of children's justice. Secondly, one must attempt to measure or gauge power in order to fight it with power. Over the years I have developed my own formula for that purpose and I utilize it daily. I pass it on to those who may find it useful in changing the system: *The amount of power one has is in direct proportion to another's three G's—Greed, Gripe and Gratitude.*

Four areas of strategy development include: (1) investigative fact-gathering; (2) political action—the holy alliance; (3) public information—the media campaign; and (4) legal offensive.

Francis Bacon once said that "knowledge is power." Before building the holy alliance with honest and concerned political leaders, you must have concrete evidence that there is indeed a problem facing incarcerated youths. The source of information must be impressive and accurate. And you should have answers to some good alternative programs. The National Institute of Law Enforcement and Criminal Justice and the National Mental Health Institute, both in Washington, D.C., can supply an invaluable wealth of information on effective program material at their computer fingertips.* Once you define your area of interest and make the proper request, a computer readout is yours for hours of reading. (The readout sheet alone makes one look like an expert!)

Although information on ineffective and abusive programs and facilities is more elusive than facts on positive programs, always remember: *There are people who will talk*, who either feel guilty or can no longer be "partner to the crime." Be alert and let them talk. Usually they will be joined by others. Check to see if there is any legal action against the institution they are concerned with. If so, talk with the attorney representing the plaintiff. Often an attorney will give you the opportunity to talk with his young client and his family. Children tell it all. They often point you in directions you might have missed.

In Texas, a group of professionals formed an organization called Free the Slow. Two thirds of the membership are active employees of the Texas Department of Mental Health and Mental Retardation (TDMHMR) who feed undercover information to ex-employees, who represent the other one-third membership. In their own words: "Our goals as professionals, para-professionals, parents and friends are to expose the consistent day-to-day abuse of the residents in public and private custodial institutions." They

---

* The computer doesn't, however, always produce if there has been little research in the area. I was shocked to learn, for example, that with all the millions of dollars poured into juvenile delinquency research in the areas of suicide and incarceration, the short- and long-range effect of solitary confinement on children and the relationship between solitary confinement and suicides, there has been very little research work. It is desperately needed.

provide the public with extremely well-documented copies of the goings on at the department, hold press conferences and attend legislative hearings. An example of their work follows:

> From the bureaucratic defensiveness we get a finely tuned stockpile of mechanism to deal with confrontations, the most common of these to quote Dr. Wade, Commissioner of MHMR, "We just don't have the money . . ."
>
> With a budget over $100 million, TDMHMR, with no accountability to anyone, squanders their money with an order of priorities that puts $250 chairs in central office and leaves the residents of the schools in plastic benches on cold cement floors. That spends $450,000 a year on data processing, yet many residents are half naked due to improper clothing.
>
> How can the system rationalize a $200,000 airplane with a $60,000 operating cost that in a review of at least 200 flight logs only flew three residents?

Free the Slow members, who constantly risk loss of their jobs, or even worse, a blackballed career, quote the following poem in their literature:

> don't look, or you'll see
> don't seek, or you'll find
> humanity
>   dying.
> it's not your fault;
> you didn't see

I hope that organizations like Free the Slow will grow because of the concern, experiences or humanity of us all, and especially of the professionals and nonprofessionals who suffer a 50 percent turnover rate in institutions because they can no longer abide with abuse of inmates.

If a state has a good Sunshine Law (public right to know), you can request audits, budgets, evaluations and board of health reports on private and public institutions from the Public Welfare Department or state licensing agent. If there is no Sunshine Law, team up with Common Cause (the citizens' lobbying group headed by John Gardner) and fight to pass one. This legislation is indispensable for individuals doing investigative research. And keep your eye on the money. Where does it go? Who gets what? (Now, thanks to the little-known Tax Reform Act passed by Congress in 1969, it is possible to request Form 990—the yearly return of income-tax-exempt organizations from the IRS (for $1 a Xerox page). By law, all non-profit organizations must list their receipts, expenses, assets and liabilities. It is an excellent way to check out how nonprofit monies find their way into blue chip stocks, real estate holdings and other choice revenue boosters.

As state training schools slowly and painfully close their doors, more and more private, profit-making residential care centers are appearing, with cost figures that are hard to pin down—that is, costs that reveal how much is actually being spent on the care of each child. Generally, the owners lie outright. One proprietor allegedly was using most of the Federal CHAMPUS money to illegally import antique furniture from Argentina before Juan Perón's takeover. Others use funds earmarked for treatment and other care to purchase real estate. Child Advocate Patrick A. Keenan of DePaul University gives his formula for a more accurate account of what is really spent on the children:

Keenan Formula

$————per diem (per day)
$————less profit
$————less capital expenditures
        (including mortgage payments)

$————actual cost of caring for children

If a facility is using its inmates as laborers of any type—this is most prevalent among the mentally retarded—ask to see its Low Wage Exempt Status Form, properly signed by the United States Labor Department. If the institution cannot produce it, they are in violation of the law and are probably exploiting the children, paying "Hong Kong" wages.

Always remember that if an institution is licensed, periodic evaluations are being made that are potentially interesting reading. As discussed earlier in the book, even though some facilities are judged poor and evaluators recommend revoking the license, many times the operation ultimately receives an O.K. This being the case, you can certainly raise a public objection and hunt down and expose the official and/or agency and their reason for ignoring health hazards and other abusive conditions in their approval of the institution.

Once the facts are known and copies are in hand, it is time for political action—the holy alliance. There are in this country some honest and dedicated politicians. Although often deemed guilty by association, honest, decent men are there, ready to respond effectively to their constituency.

I was privileged to work with such an honorable man in the very corrupt state of Texas. Representative Lane Denton of Waco and his administrative assistant Bill Aleshire are two of the best child advocates serving in any state legislature in the country. Denton, a giant of a man whose integrity is refreshing and gives one hope for our political institutions, grappled with the powerful Texas Democratic party on the issue of child care and refused to give in. It was Representative Denton who conducted hearings in Texas after the Artesia Hall scandal, even when the Speaker of the House and other committee chairmen told him to stop investigating. Denton endured "McCarthyism" and "political opportunist" charges when he pushed for a comprehensive statewide investigation of child abuse in both public and private institutions. But the people believed in Lane Denton and returned him to office in the fall of 1974 with 70 percent of the vote.

I tell this story because I believe there are Representative Dentons throughout the nation, and any juvenile facility in any state checked at any time will yield enough material to sufficiently provoke the interest of some public official into investigating and initiating hearings. Simultaneously, voters may be aroused by exposing material in a well-documented manner to the media mainstream. Obtain names of every radio and TV station and newspaper in your state. When you have a big story, write a press release, but more importantly, take it and your documentation in person to the press. Solicit their interest. Politicians, regardless of their power—real or unreal—will take on an issue only when it has greatly aroused their constituencies.

The fourth level of strategy is a well-planned, well-orchestrated legal offense. In the last few years, private facilities particularly have wheeled out their own legal arsenal—"the public relations libel suit."* It serves two purposes. It scares off the "do-gooders" who have no legal expertise or resources and it counters and/or neutralizes the class action suit brought against them. Remember, however, that private and public facilities both are extremely vulnerable to right-to-treatment suits because treatment simply does not exist in almost every case. Your chances of winning are excellent; the facility's dubious, at best. Furthermore, citizen groups must be willing to use their legal weapons not only to make restitution to those children who have been badly hurt by the experience of incarceration and abuse, but to discourage public relations libel suits by the institutions and to serve notice to other judges, correction professionals and facility owners.

Many organizations and lawyers stand ready to assist child advocacy groups with right-to-treatment cases. These include your local chapter of the American Civil Liberties Union, the newly created Children's Defense Fund operating out of Cambridge, Massachusetts, and Washington, D.C., the Legal Aid attorney in your community and hundreds of attorneys listed in the Juvenile Law Litigation Directory of the Juvenile Standards Project. The head of New Jersey's Crime Commission and outstanding malpractice attorney Joseph H. Rodriguez of Camden, New Jersey, has been training lawyers from around the country in the fine points of malpractice suits.

Child advocacy groups should hit hard legally in the areas of IQ testing and malpractice. IQ testing has been covered earlier in this book. Malpractice suits, for the first time, demand accountability of doctors whose names listed on stationery or brochures lend

---

* I have found that these institutions' lawyers have vested self-interests, serving on the board of directors and using legal and political contacts to peddle their influence in securing federal or state approval for their institutions. I found this kind of legal influence-peddling all too common during my research for this book.

Whenever possible, do your own investigating. Gather evidence as to who he is peddling his influence, and why. What is his role in the facility he represents? Does he have ownership—partial or total? Forward your information to the state and national ethics committee of their bar associations and keep them informed if there are pertinent developments. Leak it to the press if the ethic committees are unresponsive. Go after power with the power of information; neutralize it on the stage of professional ethics. Influence peddling is not the practice of law!

credence to private facilities but who actually do nothing toward child care or supervision of medical treatment or drug usage. In Florida, a federal district court ruled a patient was denied "due process"—did not receive proper treatment—and ordered two state employed psychiatrists to personally pay the patient $38,500* in punitive and compensatory damages. In Kentucky, a juvenile court judge was fined $5,000 for approving sterilization of a girl. I have witnessed the plight of hundreds of children who, if they had had the aid of an attorney, could have filed malpractice suits and won.

If the four-point strategy (investigative fact gathering, political action, public information and a legal offensive) is well executed and sensibly and methodically orchestrated, the politics of change will become a reality. It is the very plan I incorporated to expose the CHAMPUS scandal. It isn't new, however: There are others who have also successfully utilized the basic formula to bring about change for children in their own areas of expertise or interest:

One group of mothers, in Phoenix, Arizona, called the Better Child Care Bureau and, led by Mrs. Norma Jo Bifano, organized around the need to find decent child care facilities for their infants. Months later, after 132 unannounced visits to 105 centers, they released a report that shocked the entire state. They had found 52 percent of the centers in violation of the Arizona law regarding ratio of staff to children and 41 percent with no drinking water, except that served at meals, accessible inside or outside. Twenty-five percent failed to serve the menu they posted and 22 percent did not provide continuous adult supervision. The bureau discovered infants locked away in isolated rooms crying, unchanged and unattended or boxed in "rat-like cages." From what these mothers learned, they set up guidelines by which other parents in the future could realistically choose a child care center for their youngsters.†

* Upheld by the Supreme Court.
† Thieves broke into the Better Child Care Bureau office and removed all files dealing with child care centers in the state who were receiving federal funds, copies of the bureau's evaluations and other damaging information that had been collected. Mrs. Bifano was also dropped from the Arizona State University, where she was enrolled in a master's degree program, on the ground that she was too controversial.

In Montgomery County, Pennsylvania, when local politicians wanted to construct a new $6 million detention center with 144 beds, a group of women organized under the leadership of Barbara Fruchter and Constance Voynow and fought the juvenile detention system. With court injunctions and public information battles, they replaced the police at the detention facility with professionals—social workers, doctors, nurses—and pressured the county commissioners to cut the new facility down to 38 beds. The local juvenile judge calls them "the do-good menace." They have opened up the only Citizens' Juvenile Justice Center in Pennsylvania, and progressive legislators are calling on them to help draft new legislation for children's rights in the commonwealth.

When Dr. Jerome Miller came to Massachusetts in 1969, the state training schools were at best, custodial institutions. In three years the function of Miller's department changed from that of custodian to advocate as he emptied all major juvenile facilities. With imagination and guts, he took the children out of some of the most destructive institutions in America. He did it by obtaining information from the youths who trusted him, then sharing that information with the press. He also built powerful friendships with progressive members of the legislature and the governor. Moving with great speed, he utilized state resources like the University of Massachusetts: student advocates were found to care for more than 100 boys from the Lyman State school until proper placement could be arranged.

Recidivism rate in Massachusetts ranged from 68 to 92 percent before Miller arrived. Since then recidivism has averaged 48 percent. The rapid crime increase that people feared because juvenile offenders were no longer locked away in prisons never materialized.

Finally our country celebrates its two hundredth anniversary, it is time to extend our freedoms to our children. It is time for a Bill of Rights for Children, in the present and for all generations to come.

CHILDREN'S BILL OF RIGHTS

That all Children have the RIGHT TO FREEDOM, which excludes punishment for being a runaway, truant, mildly retarded or unwanted. That they enjoy the blessings of liberty, free from governmental tyranny to imprison without constitutional or just cause.

That all Children have the RIGHT TO A FAMILY AND A HOME and not banishment to distant states and communities. That they have a right to blood ties over child entrepreneurs, caseworkers, guards and part-time doctors. That when a family situation is impossible because of death, serious illness or unsolvable problems, a select substitute family and home arrangement be preferable to the cold corridors of institutions.

That all Children have the RIGHT TO AN EDUCATION regardless of station in life, and that, without exception, they be taught to read and write. That they be given the chance to learn and to develop whatever talents they possess. That their school records be open to their parents and not be the playthings of social planners and educators. That the right to an education be unending regardless of age and biased predictions of ability. That repressive IQ testing, computers and illegal dossiers be abolished forever, along with the social class tracts that have taken untold generations of children into oblivion.

That all Children have the RIGHT TO PROTECTION by laws of concern and not laws of fear. That they be protected from inhuman abuse, economic exploitation and human experimentation. That they be protected from malnutrition and the hunger of their heritage. That their rights be protected by the courts. That the courts order accountability in the schools and alternative programs to replace the education of failure. That children, for the first time, be protected from psychologically sick guardians whom institutions care not to screen. That they be protected from the ambitions of politicians, indifference of jobholders and greed of professional groups and labor unions. That they be protected by laws as specific as those governing the treatment of animals and criminal fraud. That those who are ill receive the best we are capable of providing. That they never again be subject to cruel and inhuman punishment, leading them to despair and suicide. That they be protected in the same humane manner an adult would demand. And lastly, that all children be protected so they can grow and blossom into the flower of their own potential.

Even with all I have witnessed, I am optimistic that such a Bill of Rights for Children can become law and, without question, will be upheld in the higher court of humanity. I have unwavering faith that our nation will respond favorably when informed of the vast injustices our incarcerated children endure. The human heart is good. We can, we must and we will bring about juvenile justice in the United States.

With that faith and acknowledging the long history of legalized child abuse, I make one last proposal. In keeping with the very principle of the 1976 Bicentennial—an expression of freedom and the birth of new liberty—I urge the American people to commission an artist to build an ongoing monument to be completed only when every youth jail in America has been excised from our national character. The monument would be sculptured from the steel and iron doors, the brass locks, the mesh windows, the bars, the barbed wire and Cyclone fencing of every institution that closes its last door with finality.

This welded, pounded, molded sculpture would entomb the echo of shouts, insults, obscenities, the resounding clang of steel doors and brass locks, the fear of no freedom, no fulfillment, no future, the unanswered hope for help, the muffled sobs of despair, the silence.

The sculpture would grow in size as progress is made to close each institution. A monument that would forever mirror the tear-stained, twisted faces; eyes hating but hoping for love, acceptance, recognition; hands reaching out from the loneliness of neglect, misunderstanding, prejudice and the cold empty cells of the past.

It will be completed when the last lock and key have been melted and molded. Then and only then will this country mark a significant advancement toward a higher form of civilization.

Major Sources of Information

I am grateful to those generous writers who shared their information with me. Curt Gentry and Vincent Bugliosi, who wrote *Helter-Skelter*, gave me unpublished material on Charles Manson while their own manuscript was still being typed. Pat Murphy, author of *Our Kindly Parent the State*, did likewise. The same was true of newspaper reporters Don Buchanan of the Baton Rouge *State Times*, Mimi Crossley of the *Houston Post*, Murry Engle of the *Honolulu Star-Bulletin*, Carol McMurrough of the *Denver Post*, Jerry Taylor of the *Boston Globe*, and Carolyn Toll of the *Chicago Sun-Times*. To those whom I have inadvertently failed to give credit I give my apologies, and trust they will forgive human error.

BOOKS

Ambrosino, Lillian. *Runaways*. Boston: Beacon Press, 1971.

Bugliosi, Vincent, and Gentry, Curt. *Helter-Skelter—The True Story of the Manson Murders*. New York: W. W. Norton & Company, Inc., 1974.

Child Welfare League of America, Inc. "Child Welfare League of America Standards" for Services of Child Welfare Institutions, 1963–1973.

Cole, Larry. *Our Children's Keepers*. New York: Grossman Publishers, 1972.

Danto, Bruce L., M.D. *Jail House Blues—Studies of Suicidal Behavior in Jail and Prison*. Epic Publications, Inc., 1973.

Hurley, Rodger. *Poverty and Mental Retardation—A Causal Relationship*. New York: Random House, Inc., 1969.

James, Howard. *Children in Trouble: A National Scandal*. New York: Pocket Books, 1971.

Konopka, Gisela. *The Adolescent Girl in Conflict.* Englewood Cliffs, N.J.: Prentice-Hall, Inc., 1966.

Menninger, Karl, M.D. *The Crime of Punishment.* New York: The Viking Press, Inc., 1966.

Murphy, Patrick T. *Our Kindly Parent the State: The Juvenile Justice System and How It Works.* New York: The Viking Press, Inc., 1974.

National Conference of Superintendents of Training Schools and Reformatories. *Institutional Rehabilitation of Delinquent Youth.* Delmar Publishers, Inc., 1962.

Polk, Kenneth, and Schafer, Walter E. *Schools and Delinquency.* Englewood Cliffs, N.J.: Prentice-Hall, Inc., 1972.

Rasmussen, John. *Man in Isolation and Confinement.* Chicago: Aldine Publishing Company, 1973.

Sussmann, Frederick B., and Baum, Frederic S. *Law of Juvenile Delinquency.* Dobbs Ferry, N.Y.: Oceana Publications, Inc., 1968.

CONGRESSIONAL HEARINGS, WASHINGTON, D.C.

Juvenile Delinquency. Committee on the Judiciary, U.S. Senate, March to October of 1970.

Juvenile Confinement Institutions and Correctional Systems. Committee on the Judiciary, U.S. Senate, May 1971.

Runaway Youth. Committee on the Judiciary, U.S. Senate, Jan. 13 and 14, 1972.

The Detention and Jailing of Juveniles. Committee on the Judiciary, U.S. Senate, Sept. 10, 11, and 17, 1973.

Quality of Health Care—Human Experimentation, 1973. Committee on Labor and Public Welfare, U.S. Senate, Feb. 21, 22, 23 and Mar. 6, 1973.

American Families: Trends and Pressures. Subcommittee on Children and Youth, U.S. Senate, Sept. 26, 1973.

Defense Department's CHAMPUS Program. Permanent Subcommittee on Investigations, U.S. Senate, July 24, 25, and 26, 1974.

LEGAL CASES:

Juvenile Justice Standards Project—Juvenile Law Litigation Directory. Institute of Judicial Administration, New York University School of Law, 1972.

Gray W. v. State of Louisiana—Louisiana.

People *ex rel.* James Hatter v. John T. Nelson—Illinois.

Maria Mercado *et al.* v. Nelson A. Rockefeller *et al.*—New York.

Alicia Morales *et al.* v. James Turman *et al.*—Texas.

National Indian Youth Council *et al.* v. Louis R. Bruce *et al.*—Utah.

National Indian Youth Council *et al.* v. Rogers Morton *et al.*—Oklahoma.

Eric Nelson *et al.* v. Robert P. Heyne *et al.*—Indiana.

Joe Pena *et al.* v. New York State Department of Social Services—New York.

Pennsylvania Association for Retarded Children, Nancy Beth Bowman *et al.* v. Commonwealth of Pennsylvania, David H. Kurtzman *et al.*—Pennsylvania.

Emmett Player *et al.* v. State of Alabama Department of Pensions and Security, Reuben King *et al.*—Alabama.

Pamela Wesley v. Glass—Illinois.

PROFESSIONAL PAPERS AND REPORTS

DeFeudis, F. V. "Biological Basis of 'Loneliness.'" 1973.

Friedman, C. Jack, and Sibinga, Maarten S. "Psychological and Behavioral Correlates of Early Physical Restraint."

Keenan, Patrick A. "An Illinois Tragedy: An Analysis of the Placement of Illinois Wards in the State of Texas." DePaul University, 1973.

League of Women Voters of Sacramento, Calif. "A Guide to the Juvenile Justice System." 1975.

National Council on Crime and Delinquency. "Where Have All the Children Gone?" 1973.

National Institute of Mental Health. "Suicide, Homicide, and Alcoholism among American Indians."

Rutherford, Andrew. "The Dissolution of the Training Schools in Massachusetts." 1974.

———. "Towards Advance Corrections." 1973.

Saleebey, George. "Hidden Closets." 1975.

NEWSPAPER AND MEDIA REPORTERS:

Len Ackland	Cervis Rocky Mountain Journal
Ben H. Bagdikian	Washington Post
Howard Blum	Village Voice
Larry Brown	Richmond Times Dispatch
Don Buchanan	State Times
Nicholas Chriss	Los Angeles Times
William Cockerham	Hartford Courant
Bill Collier	Houston Chronicle—Austin bureau
Mimi Crossley	Houston Post
April Daien	Arizona Republic
Murry Engle	Honolulu Star-Bulletin
Elizabeth Geimer	Fayetteville Observer
Peter Gorner	Chicago Tribune
Molly Ivins	Chicago Tribune
William Juneau	Houston Chronicle
George Kuempel	Texas Observer
Carol McMurrough	Denver Post
C. Diane Monk	Chicago Daily News
Edwin Newman and Martin Carr	"This Child Is Rated X," NBC News White Paper on Juvenile Justice
Lesley Oelsner	New York Times
Monica Reeves	Houston Post
Newton Renfro	Times Picayune
Gretchen Robinson	Greenville News
Jerry Taylor, Jean Caldwell, Bernadine Coburn, Michael Kenney, Mary Shara King, and Rachelle Patterson	Boston Globe
Carolyn Toll	Chicago Sun-Times
Chase Untermeyer	Houston Chronicle
Douglas Watson	Washington Post
Susan Watson	Detroit Free Press
Paul Williams	Sun Newspapers—Currently teaching Investigative Reporting at Ohio State University
Don Wright	Omaha Sun

Index

Weeping in the Playtime of O

America's Incarcerated Children

Kenneth Wooden

Where are America's children tonight? Over 50,000 of them between the ages of five and sixteen are locked away in prisons though they are innocent of any crime. These prisons are called detention centers, reform schools, and training schools—but there are no euphemisms for their brutality and their cruelty. They constitute a child-care system that perpetrates such conditions as:

- the Florida facility which punishes children by subjecting them to mock burials
- a Southern school for disturbed children which regularly employs bull whips and leg irons to restrain its charges
- a Texas facility that finds an electric "bull shocker" an effective disciplinary measure
- a psychotic child in an Arizona detention center who escaped solitary confinement the only way he knew: he killed himself by violently flipping his body over a bar and breaking his neck.

These are not isolated instances; they indicate a shocking pattern of child abuse and experimentation that has become a virtual business in this country.

This gripping exposé reveals for the first time on a national scale the grim truth of our juvenile jails and constitutes an indictment of an exploitive